The Absolute Beginner's Guide to Showing Your Dog

Cheryl S. Smith

THREE RIVERS PRESS • NEW YORK

Published by Three Rivers Press, New York, New York.
Member of the Crown Publishing Group, a division of Random House, Inc.
www.randomhouse.com

THREE RIVERS PRESS and the Tugboat design are registered trademarks of Random House, Inc.

Originally published by Prima Publishing, Roseville, California, in 2001.

All products mentioned are trademarks of their respective companies.

Illustrations by Judith L. Winthrop.
Photographs by Cheryl S. Smith unless otherwise noted.

Printed in the United States of America

Library of Congress Cataloging-in-Publication Data
Smith, Cheryl S.
    The absolute beginner's guide to showing your dog / Cheryl S. Smith
      p. cm.
    1. Dogs—Showing. 2. Dog shows. I. Title: Showing your dog. II. Title.
III. Series.
SF425.S55 2001
636.7'0811—dc21   00-068148

ISBN 0-7615-3359-1

10 9 8 7 6 5

First Edition

To Sundance, Bobby, Spirit, Serling, Starsky, Harry, Diamond, and Nestle, and all the wandering dogs I met before I finally had a dog of my own—you've all taught me something about being a dog.

CONTENTS_____

ACKNOWLEDGMENTS _____

An awful lot goes into trying to explain the quirky world of dog showing, and I had a lot of help along the way. Darlene Arden introduced me to scads of judges, breeders, and exhibitors and allowed me to quote from her book a time or two. Amy Shojai provided some of her photos from Westminster, and lots of cheerleading. Ranny Green was always ready with a kind suggestion and an intro to some of the powers that be in the AKC. David Frei answered last-minute questions on his car phone before buzzing off to do TV duty for the World Show. Thomas Bradley extended full press credentials to me for Westminster, from which both interviews and photos resulted. Bernd Guenter, of Germany, provided some of his fabulous photographs as well as helping to get my questions about showing under the FCI answered. Arlene Czech talked a first-time spectator through Westminster and then told me about it so I would remember just how much people don't know when they first take a look at the ring.

Of course, all those who graciously provided the "Tips from the Pros" contributed enormously to the book. For their well-considered advice, my sincere thanks to Lilian S. Barber, Sharon Irons Strempski, Tom Glassford, Bill McFadden, Corky Vroom, Chris Walkowicz, Taffe McFadden, Violet K. Denny, Karen A. Brancheau, Linda Ward, and Pamela Kernan.

And finally, thanks to Lorna Eby and Prima Publishing for seeing the need for this book after its original supposed publisher was bought and the contract was canceled, to agent Meredith Bernstein for making the contract workable for all of us, and to project editor Tara Mead for seeing the book through production.

INTRODUCTION _____

Welcome to *The Absolute Beginner's Guide to Showing Your Dog*. I wanted to write this book because I remember well how confusing this sport of dog showing is to the newcomer. It has a language all its own, and sometimes it really does seem like you'd have to be a rocket scientist to understand it all. But really—it's not that hard.

I think I realized that I wanted to be a writer and I just had to have a dog at about the same time, around age 6. I had to wait a while for both, but at age 20 I made my first money as a published writer and bought my first dog, a delightful Keeshond.

I didn't know anybody "in" dogs when I bought that first purebred. I just started going to different events because I was interested. And while obedience required more training, conformation required more help! I was lucky enough to form friendships with some of those more experienced than myself and was talked through those beginning nervous ventures into the ring. Gradually, I learned to make a living writing about dogs, and I acquired more dogs of my own along the way.

I hope this book will provide some of that sort of early help to you—though it never hurts to have some dog show friends around you. For those more experienced in the ring, this book covers not just the AKC but several other dog showing options as well. You might never have considered the UKC, or a Canadian or International title.

Now my vocation and my avocation revolve around dogs. I've competed in conformation, obedience, agility, field trials, water rescue, carting, scent hurdles, and talent shows. One of my dogs appeared in a movie, and the newest of the bunch is taking me into herding. You might concentrate on conformation alone, or you might choose to branch out. Either way, you're bound to have a good time.

You're probably as proud of your dog as I am of mine. My office walls are covered in ribbons and show shots and trophies. I try not to brag, but if anyone asks, I'll tell them the story behind each piece. You'll be collecting ribbons and trophies of your own. They make nice décor and memories.

So read the book, when you aren't busy playing with the dog. There's much to be admired and enjoyed in the sport of conformation. Any activity that celebrates the wonderfulness of dogs has to be a pretty good one. Don't get caught up in the gossip and back-biting and remember that your dog is a great friend whether or not the judge gives you a ribbon and you'll do fine.

HOW TO USE THIS BOOK

As you read *The Absolute Beginner's Guide to Showing Your Dog*, you may feel a little overwhelmed. There is a lot involved in conformation. But the good news is you don't have to know it all right now. You can just read whatever information you're most in need of at the moment. When you're ready, you can tackle more.

Although the information in these pages is all related, you can certainly start out without knowing the anatomy of your dog, how championship points are calculated, and what to do after you've earned a championship. I tried to put chapters in an order that would make sense to a novice, but feel free to skip around.

The book is divided into five parts, plus some really valuable appendixes.

Part I: Is Showing Right for You? This is the history and reality of the world of dog showing. There's good, but there's also bad, and you and your dog must both be suitable for the ring if it's to be a pleasurable experience. While you're getting ready to show, be sure to read the chapter on "Conformation as a Spectator Sport" and go and watch a show or two.

Part II: Basic Training. The first two chapters here, on setting your goals and ensuring the good health, good identification, and good manners of your dog, are essential. Read the others as they interest you.

Part III: Mechanical Skills. Now we come to the meat of actually being in the ring—grooming, stacking, gaiting, and baiting. You'll need all of this.

Part IV: Paperwork and Paraphernalia. If you're showing with the AKC, be sure to read chapter 19 for help in deciphering the entry form. Lots of novices make mistakes. You'll also want to know about choosing show clothes and equipment.

Part V: Show Time! Here there's information about setting yourself up on the show grounds and maximizing your ring time, as well as more advanced information on high-powered showing and breeding.

Appendixes. There are useful addresses, a look at a few of the bigger shows, other books and magazines you may find of interest, and a long alphabetical list of hundreds of dog breeds and the registries that accept them.

BOXES USED IN THIS BOOK

As you read this book, you will find different little boxes in the text. These boxes highlight or help you find special types of information throughout the book. Here's a rundown of what each box holds:

Fancy That! boxes contain fascinating facts about dog showing, a few personal observations, and sometimes just bits and pieces that didn't fit anywhere else.

Talking Dog serves as a read-as-you-go glossary, explaining some of the language of the sport of conformation. There's a regular Glossary at the back of the book, but lots of people have to know what a word means right now.

Watch Your Step! should be a clear warning in any situation. Take heed of the cautions in these boxes.

Tips from the Pros is your in-print mentor. You can learn so much by reading these helpful pieces of advice from experienced exhibitors, judges, and professional handlers!

Remember, at the ends of chapters, contains the essential information boiled down to a few short sentences. Read them again—this is stuff you need to know.

SOME FINAL WORDS

You can see some of my dogs, and even ask questions about dog care, training, and exhibiting at my Web site (www.writedog.com). There is information on my other books there as well. For those of you not yet online (and I'm only a recent convert myself), you can write to me care of the publisher at:

Three Rivers Press
1745 Broadway, 13-3
New York, NY 10019

Any comments or questions will be forwarded to me.

Part I

Is Showing Right for You?

Photo courtesy of Dr. Bernd Guenter

If the only dog show you've ever seen is the TV coverage of Westminster, you need a bit more information before deciding to plunge into this sport. Locate a local dog show, take this book along (open to chapter 3, "Conformation as a Spectator Sport"), and observe. Watch both the winners and nonwinners coming out of the ring. How would you feel in their places?

Did just being around all those dogs get you excited? Do you hunger to hold one of those pretty ribbons in your hands and hang it on your wall? If so, you've already succumbed to the show bug. Take the time to learn more about the history and goals of this sport.

The reality of conformation is like any other organized sport—you will win and lose, make friends and foes, and have good experiences and bad. Be prepared for it all, ease into it slowly, and remember to have fun.

Fancy That!

When people talk about a "dog show," they mean the sport of conformation. You might also hear it called the "breed ring" or "the fancy." Whatever you call it, it's the biggest event in dogdom. Thousands of shows take place in the United States alone every year, usually with hundreds or even thousands of dogs at a single show. Only a few countries aren't involved in the sport, so the worldwide numbers of dogs and owners traveling to a show on any given weekend must be astronomical!

What attracts all these people/dog teams out of their snug and warm homes to shows that might be held in rain, sleet, or snow? If you're reading this book, you already have some idea that it's more than a little piece of colored silk or even a silver trophy. It's the breathtaking beauty of all those dogs, the teeth-chattering adrenaline surge of stepping into the ring, the chance to prove that your

Talking Dog

Let's get this out of the way at the beginning . . . confOrmation, the sport of dog showing, is spelled with an "oh." It's a test of how well dogs confOrm to the written breed standard. After you send in an entry, you will receive a confIrmation, to confIrm your place in the show. Mind your "ohs" and "eyes."

dog is the very best dog. It's a highly contagious benign malady called the "show bug."

A SHORT HISTORY OF CONFORMATION

The earliest existing record of an official dog show belongs to Newcastle-on-Tyne, England, and dates to June of 1859. Only Pointers and Setters were shown, and 60 dogs represented these two breeds. From this small start, the British Kennel Club (now known simply as The Kennel Club, or TKC) was founded in 1873. Dog showing proved so popular that another gun-dogs-only show was held a few months later. In its second year, this show added Non-Sporting dogs. An 1863 show topped 1,000 entries, and by 1892 more than 200 shows a year were taking place in Britain.

In the United States, the earliest records are for a dog show held in conjunction with a field trial in Chicago on June 4, 1874. The venerable Westminster Kennel Club held its first show three years later. Though records are incomplete, more than 35 breeds were represented. The annual competition—accorded the pop star honor of being known by a single name—Westminster, is the second oldest continuously held sporting event in the country, beaten only by the Kentucky Derby (and only by a few years, at that).

The American Kennel Club (AKC) followed soon after, established in 1884 to maintain the breeding records of purebred dogs in the United States. Once again, we have a second place—the AKC is second only to the U.S. Lawn Tennis Association as the oldest governing body of amateur sport still in existence.

The United Kennel Club (UKC), a family-owned kennel club, followed close on the heels of the AKC, beginning in 1898. Its founders worried that the original functions of dog breeds were being lost, so they focused on performance events (such as obedience and gun dog competitions), but also included the popular dog show. The UKC held only single-breed shows until the 1980s, when they started holding multibreed shows.

The first dog shows in Canada were held under AKC rules, with Canadian dogs registered with the AKC. This situation was quickly unsatisfactory, and the Canadian Kennel Club (CKC) sprang to life in 1888. Though its beginnings were rocky—financial problems returned control to the AKC for several early years—the Canadians persevered and by 1896 were fully in business on their own.

Internationally, it wasn't until 1911 that the Federation Cynologique Internationale (FCI) came into existence. Based in Belgium, the FCI recognizes a national kennel club in each of its 75 member countries and licenses international shows in those countries. The World Show, probably the world's largest dog show, is held in a different member country each year.

The Goals of the Sport

Dog showing began as a competition among friends interested in breeding dogs. Right from the start, the sport produced an odd blend of camaraderie and competition. Fanciers gathered to celebrate the distinctive features of their breeds and to see which of them was breeding truest to those features. Of course, judges have been maligned from the very beginning. Attempting to match a living, breathing dog to a written standard is subjective at best, and the judge's sight, honor, mental capacity, parentage, and more is frequently called into doubt by disgruntled exhibitors whose dogs didn't make the cut.

Fancy That!

The AKC and UKC are not the only registries active in the United States. The States Kennel Club has been in existence for about 20 years, though it has not become a major power. The American Rare Breed Association (ARBA) still puts on shows for breeds known in countries outside the United States. And there are others that spring up and disappear. These often try to appear more prestigious than they are through intentional efforts to confuse themselves with the larger registries—for example, a group called the FIC, hoping people will think it the FCI, and another called the CKC but definitely not the Canadian Kennel Club.

While kennel clubs and exhibitors will be quick to tell you that dog showing is for the betterment of the purebred dog, to choose those individuals worthy of carrying on the bloodlines, reality can be something else. Purebred dogs are big business, with more than a million a year registered by the AKC alone. "Papers" certify a dog as a purebred and increase its value. Champion parents up the ante even more. With so much money involved, conformation is no more a squeaky clean sport than is horse racing or professional wrestling. In fact, these days, the object of the whole thing often seems to be simply to produce dogs that will win in the ring.

But the original goal does still shine through, at least in places. Many dedicated breeders care only that their chosen breed continue in good health, both physical and mental. They work to eliminate genetic disorders and improve temperament while ensuring that the dogs physically match the standard as closely as possible. The section on mentoring in chapter 2 suggests ways to find and learn from these people.

WHO CAN PLAY

To compete in conformation, your dog must be a purebred registered with a kennel club. Purebred dogs adopted from shelters or rescue groups can get a special listing that allows them to compete in performance events, but not in conformation. Unless registration papers come with the dog, it can't take part in a dog show. (Other events are more open, and the UKC welcomes even mixed-breed dogs to compete in performance competitions.)

Watch Your Step

You will find the world of the fancy complex—both exciting and exasperating. Some fanciers will snub newcomers, heap insults on others' dogs, even resort to dirty tricks in the ring. But there are also kind and sharing exhibitors who love to share their enthusiasm for their breed and the sport. One or more of these paragons is likely to become a close friend and mentor.

Talking Dog

"Papers" means registration certificate, the form that shows the dog is listed in the kennel club books as a purebred. To register, the dog requires a pedigree showing the dog's parentage for a number of generations. The pedigree will also include any kennel club–recognized titles earned by the dog's ancestors. The conformation title is Champion, or CH.

There's another requirement. Unfortunately, dogs must be intact (that is, not spayed or neutered) to compete in much of conformation. This requirement is based on the belief that such dogs will be used for breeding. Certainly, a lot of people who start out showing a purchased dog do go on to breed their own, and we'll talk about that much later. But not everyone takes that step. Because there are definite health risks associated with intact dogs, owners must decide whether the risk is worth the enjoyment of showing a dog. The Canadian Kennel Club has recently begun a class for spayed and neutered dogs to show in conformation, the Australian Shepherd Club of America is also trying out the idea, and the UKC has plans to begin allowing spayed/neutered dogs to show in conformation in late 2001 or 2002. This shouldn't be surprising, as cat shows have had a class for spayed and neutered cats for years.

You don't have to own the dog to show it. You can show someone else's dog—professionals do it for a living. Before running out to buy yourself a "show-quality" puppy, you might want to try out the sport with a dog you know through friends or relatives. Some people find the experience of being in the ring totally unnerving, and they never return. Dog showing certainly isn't necessary to have a loving relationship with a dog, but breeders sometimes require that you show the puppy they are selling you. Before signing a contract, it's best to determine if this is a sport in which you want to participate.

TYPES OF EVENTS

The sport of dogs even provides you with places to practice. Matches are specifically for practice. The judges do not have to be licensed (approved) by any kennel club. Your dog will not earn any points toward a championship,

Tips from the Pros

The fellowship at shows and the lasting friendships you make are the good part of showing. Showing is fun if you are a good sport.
—Shirley Stroud, UKC exhibitor

even if you win. This is the place for you, your dog, and often even the judge to get some experience. You can learn how it feels to be in that ring under the eyes of a judge and the spectators. By all means, take advantage of matches.

Shows are the real thing, the place where you will compete for those coveted championship points. Do not bother entering until you and your dog are ready for some stiff competition—you will only be wasting your entry fees (which can be substantial) and possibly labeling yourself as someone not to take seriously.

Both matches and shows are further subdivided (see figure 1.1). With matches, the most informal is the workshop. A sponsoring club usually puts on a combined conformation/obedience workshop as a fund-raising event. At a workshop, dogs may be brought into the ring as they are available, rather than by breed or group (see "Breeds and Groups" later in this chapter). The judge probably won't place the dogs, but will often provide pointers on ways to improve your performance. The whole exercise offers valuable ring experience to both handler and dog and can be an excellent learning tool.

MATCHES (no championship points)			**SHOWS** (points to be won)		
Workshop informal, dogs judged at random, not by group or breed	**Fun Match** dogs judged by breed, usually with ribbons awarded	**Sanctioned Match** most formal unofficial show— excellent practice	**Specialty** single-breed show	**Multibreed** show with multiple breeds but not all those registered with a kennel club	**All-Breed** show with all the breeds registered by a kennel club

Figure 1.1. Types of conformation events

The fun match is slightly more structured. Again, clubs use this as a fund-raiser and will usually offer obedience along with conformation. There still aren't any championship points to be had, but dogs are judged according to breed, and placements are made. This could be where you win your first ribbon and possibly even a trophy.

The sanctioned match is just one step away from an actual show. Clubs seeking kennel club approval to hold licensed shows must put on sanctioned matches as part of the approval process. Here you will find a higher level of organization and competition. Judges can be fully licensed or in their apprenticeship. If you and your dog can keep your wits about you and show to your best advantage here, you're ready to move on to the real thing.

There are three types of sanctioned shows: the all-breed, the multibreed, and the specialty. All offer championship points to the winners. All may be held indoors or outdoors and be benched or unbenched.

The all-breed show is just that—a show for all the breeds recognized by the registry sanctioning the show. These shows are often quite large and may be multiday affairs. Some clubs offer multibreed shows, covering more than a single breed but less than all the breeds. The specialty is open to only one breed of dog. The size of these specialty events can vary widely, depending on the popularity of the breed. A Labrador Retriever specialty may be an all-day affair with hundreds of dogs, whereas a Keeshond specialty could be over in a couple of hours. Often the breed groups with smaller numbers of dogs get together and hold their specialties on the same date and at the same location. If your interests lie in a particular breed or two, a specialty offers an opportunity to see a great number of individual dogs in your chosen breed.

Talking Dog

At a benched show, all dogs entered for competition must remain on the show grounds in their assigned space whenever they are not actually in the ring or being exercised or groomed. This gives spectators an unequaled chance to see breeds and talk to their owners, breeders, and handlers. There are only a few benched shows remaining, Westminster on the East Coast and Golden Gate on the West Coast among them.

BREEDS AND GROUPS

You almost certainly know what a breed is: Dachshunds, Collies, Rottweilers, Bichon Frise, and Soft-Coated Wheaten Terriers are all breeds. The AKC defines a breed as "a relatively homogeneous group of animals within a species, developed and maintained by man." People created each breed by choosing dogs with the desired qualities and breeding them to each other. We thus designed some dogs to hunt, others to herd, some to guard, and some for companions. No other animal seems quite so malleable, adjusting size, coat type, color, and temperament at our whim. (See figure 1.2.)

Each registry arranges breeds into groups, though each does it slightly differently. The AKC uses seven groups: Most are classified by the function and purpose for which the breeds were developed (Sporting, Working, Herding, Hounds, Terriers), one is determined by size (Toys), and one is an odd catchall of breeds that don't fit any of the other groups (Non-Sporting). In addition to these seven groups, the AKC lumps breeds that are in the process of being recognized in the Miscellaneous Class. These breeds may only be shown when Miscellaneous Class is specifically included in a show.

Figure 1.2. This ring holds a class for the breed of Bichon Frise.

Fancy That!

The groups do not make the perfect sense that the AKC would like us to believe. The Norwegian Elkhound is certainly not a hound, although that is its group. Why are the Siberian Husky, Keeshond, Pomeranian, and Norwegian Elkhound scattered across four groups, though clearly related? The FCI collects these and others in the group they call "Spitz and Primitive Types," while the UKC collects them in its "Northern Breeds" group.

AKC will be eliminating the Miscellaneous Class some time in the future, instead bringing newly recognized breeds directly into the appropriate group.

The UKC does it slightly differently, using eight groups and basing each one on a purpose. UKC's groups are Gun Dogs, Scenthounds, Herding Group, Guarding Dogs, Sighthounds, Terriers, Companion Dogs, and Northern Breeds.

The Canadian Kennel Club (CKC) and the States Kennel Club (SKC—a newcomer with limited geographic distribution in the United States) use the same group breakdown as the AKC. Instead of Non-Sporting and Toy, ARBA (American Rare Breed Association) uses Spitz and Companion. The FCI uses ten groups, with further breakdowns by country of origin of the breed.

Remember

- ○ Conformation is the sport of showing dogs to determine which most closely match the standard.
- ○ Only purebred dogs registered with a kennel club can take part in conformation.
- ○ There are a variety of kennel clubs, both within the United States and internationally.
- ○ All forms of matches (workshops, fun matches, sanctioned matches) are for practice only. Championship points can be won only at sanctioned shows—all-breed, multibreed, or specialty.
- ○ Each kennel club arranges the dogs into groups, based loosely on function.

2

The Good, the Bad, and the Ugly

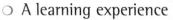

In This Chapter

- ○ A learning experience
- ○ Camaraderie and mentoring
- ○ The other side of the coin
- ○ Fakery and sabotage

Please don't let the unpleasant realities included in this chapter scare you away from dog showing. We would be remiss if we didn't point out some of the darker aspects of the sport, but conformation has a lot of good qualities to offer dogs and their people. After all, just because people get lost in the forest and die of exposure doesn't mean you can't go hiking and have a totally wonderful time. It just helps to know the pitfalls and how to avoid them.

Keep in mind that this is a sport, supposed to be fun and rewarding for you and your dog. Don't forget to have a good time. Your dog will still be your loving wonderful companion whether you walk out of the ring with a gaudy rosette or don't even make the cut. And isn't that why you got a dog in the first place?

A LEARNING EXPERIENCE

One of the delightful benefits of conformation is an enhanced appreciation for the sheer beauty of dogs. Even if you only own one dog yourself, at a show you will have the opportunity to see dozens or hundreds of dogs. Most will be in prime health and immaculately groomed. Some may be the very best of their breed. By watching as much as possible, and asking questions when the opportunity arises, you can begin to see some of the differences you may not have noticed at first. Pay close attention to those times when the judge repositions a dog during his or her examination. Most judges want to give every worthwhile dog a fair chance, and they may help out the inexperienced handler by restacking a dog or asking the handler to move the dog again, slower (or faster) than the first time. These moments of intervention can be instructive for both the handler in the ring and those watching from outside.

You may be surprised at how much you find out about your breed and maybe even your own dog. Many breeders devote themselves lifelong to one or two breeds and are veritable walking encyclopedias. The ancestors on your dog's pedigree—nothing more than names to you—could be living, breathing dogs to a long-time aficionado. They might tell of big wins, endearing quirks, or exactly which grandparent provided your dog's set of ears or tail.

But it's not all canine observation and history. Dog showing will also teach you some facts about yourself. Maybe you thought you'd be a nervous wreck in front of all those people, but you find yourself so proud of your dog's self-possession and poise that you share in some of those qualities. Or it could be you thought yourself assured and unflappable—until someone made a disparaging remark about your beloved canine just before

Talking Dog

Reading a pedigree can be well-nigh impossible for a newcomer to dogs. Some of the abbreviations you might see include CH for Champion, CD or CDX (obedience titles), TD or TDX (tracking titles), MH (for Master Hunter), HC (one of the many herding titles), and many, many more.

Figure 2.1. No, the circus isn't in town—it's a dog show! All these people represent possible future friends to a novice.

you stepped into the ring to be judged. If you have not competed in organized sports before, you may be surprised at how ferocious your desire to win can be—and may need to learn to rein it in.

Showing a dog will offer you plenty of practice in being a "good loser" (though we hope you realize that your dog is not and never could be a loser, no matter what happens inside a ring enclosure) and, we hope, an equal opportunity to show yourself a gracious winner.

CAMARADERIE AND MENTORING

As in many competitive sports, dog showing presents an odd blend of friendship and flat-out selflessness versus mean-spiritedness and sour grapes. Resolve before you begin that you will walk on the sunnier side of the street. Dog shows are a terrific place to make friendships that can last a lifetime.

Think about it—what brought you to a dog show in the first place? Probably admiration of the breed and love for your own individual representative of it. The same feelings brought many of your competitors into the ring, and you start by having much in common.

There is also a lot of time spent waiting at a show. Rather than sitting around and working yourself into a frenzy in solitude, make friends. Talk to the person set up next to you or at the next grooming table. Try to strike up a genuine conversation, not just blather on about yourself, your dog, and your experiences in the ring. Compliment the other person's dog—that shouldn't be difficult. Ask questions.

Over the weeks, you will start to run into the same people. These are potential lifelong friends. Of course, you will not be compatible with every other person who is showing the same breed as you. By being outgoing and pleasant yourself, you will find which of your competitors reciprocate. Some of these could easily become close friends.

No matter how hard you try to stay levelheaded about your wins and losses, it will help to have a friend to commiserate or celebrate with. To this end, make it your habit to *always* congratulate the winner of your class. It doesn't matter if you think the dog has a patchy coat and walks like a crab—your opinion isn't the one that mattered. Others may be thinking the same or worse of *your* dog when you score a win. How hard is it to smile and say "congratulations"?

By making friends, you actually increase your chances of having a win of sorts. No, I don't mean that you can somehow influence the judge through your friendships. But if you have friends in the breed and one of their dogs wins over yours, you can celebrate their achievement instead of mourning your loss. You will find that dog shows are a lot more fun if you have a circle of friends around you.

If you are truly fortunate and truly want to learn, you will find a mentor. Showing real interest in your breed and a sincere desire to learn all you can about showing to your best and improving the breed (should you venture into breeding yourself) may endear you to one of the "old-timers" (who could conceivably be younger than you, but vastly more experienced). You

Tips from the Pros

The people I met showing my breed were so helpful and welcoming that they became my entire social circle and showing dogs became as much my social outlet as anything else. There I met a group of people who were as "dog crazy" as I am. They became more family than merely friends and acquaintances. These people shared years of experience with a novice and I will ever be grateful and give them full credit for any success my dogs have enjoyed.

—Violet W. Denny, UKC exhibitor, Toy Fox Terriers

Tips from the Pros

A compatible and knowledgeable mentor is probably the most important step in getting into showing dogs successfully. If everything in the world were fair, this would be the breeder from whom you acquire your first dog, but often that's not possible. You may have to seek out a mentor by haunting your breed ring at dog shows and talking to people until you find the right person. Be sure not to bother a possibly already nervous exhibitor just before ring time. Ask if you might talk to him or her after the judging. You can read tons of books and read things on the Internet, but nothing takes the place of one-on-one personal guidance.

—Lilian S. Barber, AKC exhibitor and breeder, author of *The New Complete Italian Greyhound*

can even consciously choose someone you feel is an excellent ambassador for your breed and present your case as a novice who wants to learn.

Although there are snobs and self-centered people involved in dog showing (just as there are in any group of people), many long-time handlers remain down to earth and eager to involve others in the sport they have loved for many years. A knowledgeable someone who could sit at ringside with you and point out excellence or faults in the dogs being shown, good and bad handling, and how the judge works the ring can greatly accelerate your education. Or you may run across a grooming specialist who can teach you the finer points of preparing your breed for the ring.

Accept all such assistance graciously. Don't be so grateful as to be fawning. But be sincere. Try to practice what you are taught, and if given the opportunity, acknowledge the help you've received along the way.

If you aren't lucky enough to find a mentor and would really like someone to fill that position, see chapter 12, the section on Junior Showmanship and its section on apprenticing. Perhaps in exchange for some "scut work," a professional or simply more experienced handler will provide some instruction.

THE OTHER SIDE OF THE COIN

Unfortunately, the show experience is not all sweetness and light. There is backbiting and backstabbing aplenty, and there will be times when you will be sorely tempted to join in. Resist.

Tips from the Pros

The best mentor is your dog's breeder. The breeder should be willing to help you along. If not, maybe you've selected the wrong breeder. The breeder may put you in touch with other people in the breed. Try to become active in the national breed club.

—Sharon Irons Strempski, AKC exhibitor
and breeder of Affenpinschers

There's no harm in joining the often-humorous, seldom-serious jawing sessions that sometimes spring up after a breed is judged. People cast aspersions on each other, the judge, the weather, and everything down to the coffee cart vendor, but it's all done with a jovial air, and everyone takes it as well as dishes it out. This blowing off steam harms no one as long as it retains its good nature and focuses on no one in particular. Feel free to offer your own witty observations.

But don't venture over to the dark side. There are some who say things about judges and other exhibitors that they wouldn't venture to say about double murderers. And they say them not in jest, but in all seriousness. Such behavior benefits no one, not those maligned, and not those doing the maligning, as they quickly lose what friends they have and are left to gripe alone.

If you are truly unhappy with your show experiences, examine your reasons for being there. Why is it important to finish your championship this month or this year? What's your hurry? Are you in this to learn, or to glorify yourself through your dog's victories in the ring? Stop to think about this for a second—how does having a dog win in the ring glorify you? It doesn't. The judge awarded a ribbon to your dog, not you. Sure, you should

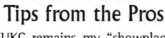

Tips from the Pros

UKC remains my "showplace." The shows are more relaxed and "family oriented." The other exhibitors are normally quick to congratulate the winner with real sincerity and take an interest in helping one another.

—Violet W. Denny, UKC exhibitor, Toy Fox Terriers

be proud, but don't let it go to your head. There are enough snobs in the sport already.

Do not indulge in spreading rumors. Excuse yourself if a conversation starts to turn that way—a potty break for your dog is always a convenient excuse.

Seek out those who could be true friends and avoid the others. And remember, when you have gained some experience, to be a friend to those less experienced.

FAKERY AND SABOTAGE

What a sad subject to have to include, but it happens, and one day it could happen to you.

Fakery should not concern you overly much. It may cost you a win along the way if a judge isn't perceptive enough to recognize a chalked coat, a nose blacked with felt-tip pen, or even a surgical alteration, but there's no real lasting effect on you or your dog. You probably won't even know it happened. But sabotage is another matter entirely.

As a novice, you must be aware of mistakes to be avoided at all costs, or your inexperience could be construed as sabotage. Knowing these tricks will also help you avoid being the victim of them.

Some handlers use a lot of bait in the ring (except in UKC shows). Sometimes a handler throws a chunk of liver to get expression from his dog, then neglects to pick it up. If you've watched Westminster on television, you've probably seen at least a couple of dogs breaking their trot to lunge for a piece of liver on the floor. When it's a close call between a couple of dogs, this sudden break of gait disrupts the smooth presentation of the dog and can count against you. Knowing this, some handlers have been known to drop liver purposely while the whole class is gaiting to distract the dogs behind them. You can hope that this never happens to you or that the judge can ignore it if it does, or you can train your dog never to pick up food

Fancy That!

Training your dog for house manners or even for other sports will not spoil the dog for the show ring, as some claim. Dogs are very good at associating activities with their surroundings, and they will easily recognize the show ring and know what it means.

Watch Your Step

Dogs are very sensitive to their owners' feelings, and if you are upset, your dog will be. Several negative experiences in the ring, and the dog won't want to be in there any more. He'll just want out of this thing that makes Mom unhappy.

—Karen A. Brancheau, UKC exhibitor and breeder

from the ground—a good idea, anyway, to keep your dog from possible hazards.

A trick particularly hard to avoid, and easy to inflict on others unintentionally, is running up on the dog in front of you. Judges often arrange dogs, particularly in the groups, in an order meant to put the faster movers up front. But some dogs just move faster than others, and some handlers prefer a faster pace. Handlers should see to it that they do not interfere with other handlers and their dogs. This can be difficult. Moving inside to pass another dog can earn you the wrath of the dog's handler for blocking the judge's view. Yet passing outside will block the judge's view of *your* dog. About your only option is to slow down momentarily to let the dog in front of you pull away. Do not slam on the brakes, or the person behind you may think you're trying to make it appear that he or she is running up on you!

Some handlers are quite adroit at "accidentally" stepping on another dog's foot. Keeping distance around you can help avoid this and many similar problems, including the handler in front backing the dog into your dog when he or she is setting up, the handler in back setting up so close that his or her dog is breathing down your dog's tail, or the handler brushing against your dog while moving to stand in front of the dog.

Anything done to frighten another dog in the ring is of course not kosher. This includes making noise to distract a skittish dog.

Even outside the ring, hazards lurk. Drinks have been spilled on dogs about to enter the ring, ruining hours of coat preparation. Bitches in season may be paraded through a male class waiting to go in, causing at least half the dogs to totally lose their focus. A loud remark about some defect in your dog, real or imagined, may be enough to shake your confidence and ruin a performance.

Obviously some of these traps are extremely difficult to avoid. Do your best, don't be guilty of any of them yourself, and remember there's always another show. Losing isn't the end of the world.

Remember

○ You can make many fine lifelong friends at dog shows.
○ Seek out those willing to share their experience, and remember to do the same when you become the experienced one.
○ Always congratulate the winner. If it's you, accept the congratulations of others with grace and sincerity.
○ Do not indulge in rumor and backbiting.
○ Do your best to avoid sabotage by other handlers, and don't be guilty, even if unintentionally, of impeding the efforts of others.

3

Conformation as a Spectator Sport

In This Chapter

○ The basics
○ The players and how to find them
○ What the judge and handler are doing
  and why

Your first experiences with conformation should be as a spectator. You wouldn't expect to run onto a football field, drive onto a racetrack, or ski down a black diamond hill without first putting in some study and practice. Although dog showing without training may be less hazardous to your health than these examples, it probably won't be much more successful.

So leave the dog behind for the day—he or she is going to be getting plenty of attention and exercise once you get into the sport—and go to the show! Be sure to bring your wallet. There's probably an entry/parking fee, and you're likely to see things you'll want to buy. In fact, your first purchase should be a show catalog. Clubs often run out of these early in the day, and you don't want to miss out—you can't tell the players without a scorecard, and at a dog show, the catalog is the scorecard. So ignore all those pretty pooches—for now—and find your way to the superintendent's table to buy a catalog.

Tips from the Pros

Try to find out in advance what time the various breeds will be shown. If you are unable to do this, go early or you're liable to miss the breed in which you have special interest.

—Chris Walkowicz, author and AKC judge

THE BASICS

If all the dogs around the grounds are the same breed, you're at a *specialty*. Hope you like the breed, because it's the only one you'll be seeing. Many clubs hold local specialties, and generally the national breed club will hold a national specialty once a year. Many national specialties include performance events as well as conformation. So you might see sighthounds lure coursing, terriers going down holes after rodents, or a variety of field events for sporting dogs.

If there are different breeds on the show grounds, but not so many as to make you dizzy, you're probably at a *multibreed show*. Local breed clubs with smaller memberships often get together to hold a show, thus spreading the costs and the workload. Or multiple specialties may be taking place at the same location, a common occurrence. Each breed is actually taking part in a separate show, and there is no competition beyond Best of Breed. Then there are *group shows,* where all the breeds in an AKC group are shown. This is most often done with the Terriers and the Toys.

And finally, if you seem to be surrounded by dogs of every imaginable size, shape, coat, and color, you're probably at an *all-breed show.* Every breed registered by the kennel club can be shown. Any of the renowned dog shows you may have heard of—Westminster, Golden Gate, Crufts, The World Show—are all-breed shows. Some of the larger shows take place

Tips from the Pros

Go to a show without your dog, and watch other people and how they show their dogs. You can learn a lot this way. Watch and listen.

—Karen A. Brancheau, UKC exhibitor and breeder

Talking Dog

You may hear people say a dog has been put down for the ring. To the average dog owner, "put down" is a fearsome phrase meaning that a beloved canine has been humanely euthanized for health reasons. In the fancy, however, "put down" for the ring means groomed appropriately for the breed and ready to show. Knowing this can keep you from gasping the first time you hear someone say it.

over two days. Roughly half the breeds are shown the first day and the other half the second day. If there are specific breeds you hope to see, you'll need to know which day they're being shown.

Whatever variety of show you may be attending, this is *not* a beauty contest. It is called *conformation* because all judging is meant to be based on how well each dog *conforms* to its written breed standard. Who in their right mind would try to judge one dog's beauty against another's?

For your purposes as a spectator, it really isn't important to know all the ins and outs of the classes, but if you have to completely understand what's happening in front of you, see "The Progression of the Classes" in chapter 10.

Find a seat at ringside—you did bring a chair, didn't you?—and settle in with your eyes, ears, and show catalog open.

THE PLAYERS AND HOW TO FIND THEM

All right, you're sitting down with a ringful of dogs in front of you. Choose one. It doesn't matter why—you like the color or the way the dog moves or the handler's grace. Just choose one.

Look up the breed in your show catalog. If you're at an all-breed show, breeds are listed in their groups, then alphabetically. Remember that the AKC reverses the names of some breeds, such as Setter (Irish). Once you've found the breed, look up the number the handler is wearing on his or her armband. You'll find a listing something like figure 3.1.

The first entry is from my local dog show organization, the Hurricane Ridge Kennel Club, the second from the Westminster Kennel Club. They have slight differences, but end up providing the same information.

The armband number leads you first to the dog's registered name. If there is a *handler*—or *agent,* generally in effect a handler—that comes next. The handler mentioned in figure 3.1 belongs to the professional groups DHG (Dog Handlers Guild) and PHA (Professional Handlers Association). Next is the dog's registration number. This is the number used to credit points to the winning dog.

The next number is the dog's date of birth. Following that is the *breeder's* name. You will eventually want to buy a dog for showing, and may choose a breeder based on what you see in the show ring. The catalog lets you know who bred the dogs you most admire. If you keep notes on your favorites, you may well find yourself attracted repeatedly to the dogs emerging from one kennel. Many breeders develop a recognizable "type."

Next are the parents of the dog in the ring, sire first, followed by dam. You could also find that you like the offspring of a particular sire. Some dogs put a very definite stamp on their progeny, and you might eventually want to try to purchase one of that sire's puppies.

ALASKAN MALAMUTES Open Bitch

8   Showlion's Sierra Noel. WP588401/01. 10-23-94. Brdr. J. Greenside & J. Watkins. CH R Mol Snowlion Mystik Zzambe – CH Snowlion's Kali Pevi. OWNER: J. Greenside & J. C. Watkins & J. C. Barker, PO Box 000, City, State

---

IRISH WOLFHOUNDS Best of Breed Competition

6   CH TenderLand's Rebel Rowser (Handler: Guy H. Fisher, DHG/PHA). HM55958401. 02-03-95. Breeder: Sue Engel-Elliott. By Singing Swords Solomon – Singing Swords Hattie. Dog. OWNER: Donna Robinson.

Figure 3.1. Sample catalog pages

Talking Dog

A *handler* is the person in the ring with the dog, doing the showing. It could be the owner, the breeder, or a professional handler. An *agent* is usually a professional handler, taking charge of the dog on the owner's behalf. A *breeder* is the person who owns the bitch that whelped the dog in question. It's easy to be a breeder. It's very hard and time consuming to be a good breeder, working for the benefit of the breed.

The Westminster catalog next has the notation "Dog." Because this is a Best of Breed class, with both sexes present, the sex is specified. In the Hurricane Ridge catalog, the entry you are examining comes from the Open Bitch class, so all the dogs in the ring are obviously bitches.

Finally, the name of the dog's *owner* is given. In the Hurricane Ridge catalog, the address is also in the listing. In the Westminster catalog, the addresses for owners and handlers are listed alphabetically at the back. An owner is the person listed on the registration form as owning the dog. Often there are co-owners on top show dogs.

Figure 3.2. In Europe, a number pinned to the handler's chest is often used in place of an armband. (Photo courtesy of Dr. Bernd Guenter)

If you see a listing where the breeder and owner names are the same and no handler is listed, you have found a breeder/owner/handler, someone intimately involved with the breed. This could be a good person to contact about your interest in the breed.

One final note about armbands: You may see dozens of handlers wearing the number 8, for example, but each handler will be showing a different breed. Repeating numbers within a breed would defeat the identification purposes of the number.

WHAT THE JUDGE AND HANDLER ARE DOING AND WHY

Now that you know who the people and dogs in the ring are—you'll also find the judge's name in the catalog, by the way, following the breed—you'd probably like to know what the heck they're doing.

The average adult watching his or her first dog show immediately becomes an inquisitive 2-year-old: Why are those people throwing pieces of food around? Why are they running around in a circle? Why are they holding the leash so tight? Why are there three dachshunds and one of everything else? Why is that dog up on a table? Why is the judge grabbing the dog *there?* Why?

The answers to all your questions are, we hope, included in the pages of this book. We will collect the most basic answers here to help you get started in your education as a spectator and future handler.

Fancy That!

Each of the various registries has certain breeds that are shown in several varieties. In the AKC, dachshunds are separated by coat, shown as Smooth, Rough, and Wire coated. This gives them three entries in their group and a seemingly unfair advantage. AKC Cocker Spaniels are divided into three colors. It does not make a lot of sense, but that's how it is. (All the varieties and class divisions are listed in appendix B.)

Standing Still

Now for that little procedure that newcomers to the sport find mortifying—checking that the dog (meaning male in this case) is suitably equipped. While going over the dog, the judge reaches un-

Talking Dog

Bite does not mean the painful application of canine teeth to human flesh. It means how the dog's teeth come together in the mouth. Different breeds specify different bites. A *level bite* means the upper and lower front teeth meet point to point when the mouth is closed. A *scissors bite* means that the upper front teeth slide just in front of the lower front teeth when the mouth is closed, just as the two blades of a scissors slide past each other. There are other bites, but these two are the most common.

derneath to feel that the dog has two testicles. Anything less is cause for disqualification.

At the other end of the dog, the judge looks in the mouth to check for the correct number of teeth (missing teeth is a disqualification in some breeds) and the *bite.*

The judge also feels various parts of the dog, searching out the angles of the shoulders and hips, the planes of the head, the spring of the ribs. Especially with heavily coated breeds, this hands-on exam tells much more than simply looking at a standing dog ever could. In fact, if you hope to hear worthwhile comments at ringside, listen for the disclaimer, "Well, of course I haven't had my hands on the dog." The person making this statement is wisely admitting that the judge may be finding good or bad points the spectator simply can't see.

Some of the smaller breeds are examined on a raised table. This is done by custom simply to save the backs of judges and exhibitors. You may see some handlers lift the dogs from the table to the ground with one hand under the chin and the other hand using the tail as a convenient handle. They do this to avoid mussing the dog's coat. It seems like it would be uncomfortable, but the dogs don't seem to mind.

With some breeds, you might see the handler hold the dog's ears over the face while the judge is examining the front end. This is not so the dog can't watch. It's done to better show off the length and arch of the dog's neck and to demonstrate that the ears are the correct length (some standards specify how far along the muzzle the ears should reach).

While the judge examines the rear portion of the dog, you might see the handler holding a fist in front of the dog, which the dog appears to be

Talking Dog

Bait is any food or toy treat used to gain the dog's attention in the ring. *Gaiting* is movement of the dogs around the ring at a trot to demonstrate how the parts work together. Some standards call for specific gaits, such as the hackney action of the Miniature Pinscher.

chewing. The handler has a fistful of *bait*—dried liver, steak, Rollover, or other food treat—and is letting the dog chew off small pieces. This occupies the dog.

You will also probably see handlers flinging pieces of bait out in front of the dog during the hands-on exam or at the end of a gaiting pattern (more about this in a second), or maybe just tossing and catching it. All this is meant to catch the dog's attention and get a little extra expression or spark.

On the Move

Although the hands-on exam tells the judge a lot about the dog, seeing it move tells even more, and that's what *gaiting* is all about. How the dogs move around the ring—all together or one at a time, up and down or around and around—is completely up to the judge. You'll see a lot of variations. But however the judge moves the dogs, he or she wants to see them from the rear, from the front, and from the side. Different views reveal different things to the experienced eye.

In the AKC and UKC rings, all dogs are shown at a trot. It is slow enough to fit the confines of the ring and to allow the judge to observe how the dog's parts are moving. (In England and some other countries, dogs are often walked around the ring.) There are all sorts of handler "styles" when gaiting a dog. You will eventually find your own. Try not to emulate the rigid-leash, dog-walking-on-a-tightrope style you will often see. The handler may be trying to hide some movement fault or may just have fallen into this bad habit. Watch the dogs that are given some slack in the leash, that surge out ahead of the handler and really show.

After examining and moving all the dogs, the judge might simply point to the winners, place the winning dogs at the front of the line and have

Watch Your Step

Some judges give no hint of their placements until suddenly pointing to the winner. This is not very instructive for handlers or spectators. Judges who make a cut and then start putting the dogs in order of preference allow everyone to consider how placements are being made.

them all go around the ring one more time before pointing to the winners, or, in a large class, *make a cut*. In this last case, the judge pulls out the dogs still in the running for placements. Usually the judge will have them gait again and may even do a little more hands-on examination before putting them in order and pointing to the winners.

Why Are There Different Dogs in There?

There are times when you will see a variety of breeds in one ring, and you should understand why and what is happening.

The first possibility is Junior Showmanship. Here all the handlers will be young—no more than 17—and the judging is based on their handling skills, not the dogs, so any breed could be there.

The second occasion for multiple breeds in one ring is group judging. At all-breed shows, the Best of Breed dogs for a *group* are brought into the ring to show again, and the judge selects the four top dogs. As always, the dogs are judged on how well they conform to the breed standard. In the AKC, the groups are always listed in the same order in the catalog:

Working
Terrier
Toy
Non-Sporting
Sporting
Hound
Herding

The placements are called Group First, Group Second, and so forth. After all the groups have been judged (sometimes over two days at large

Talking Dog

In a large group or large class, the judge may *make a cut*, pulling out those dogs he or she is still considering for placements. The other dogs may be asked to leave the ring, or may stand in the ring but around the periphery. In this case, being cut is a very good thing.

shows), the seven Group Firsts are brought back one more time to compete for Best in Show.

Novices often ask how in heaven's name the judge can pick out one dog from among so many gorgeous specimens. It's a good question. The judge considers how closely each dog comes to its own breed standard. But deciding which is closest is certainly a tough call. Asked about their picks, judges often say things like, "The dog just asked for it" (meaning that the dog showed to its utmost, radiating confidence) or "He was just so typey" (meaning that he was the essence of what the breed should be). It's a difficult process to explain. One thing that generally has no effect on the judge is the applause of spectators rooting for their favorites—though it can excite the dogs!

Dog breeds are divided into *groups* by each of the registries. Most of the groups are based on the dog's working heritage (such as Sporting or Herding) or area of origin (Spitz types).

That's it. You've watched the basics of a dog show. Learned a little of the lingo. Maybe even made your first ringside acquaintance or bought that first piece of dog show equipment. Take a deep breath—you've taken your first small step into the fancy.

Remember

- ○ Begin as a spectator. Leave the dog at home for now.
- ○ Purchase a catalog. Learn how to use it.
- ○ Go early and plan to stay for at least a few hours.
- ○ Make notes about dogs you find attractive, handlers whose style you like. It's never too early to start charting your preferences.
- ○ Study how things work in the ring. The more you understand what happens there, the less nervous you will be when you are there yourself.

4

The Life of the Party

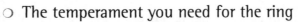

In This Chapter

○ The temperament you need for the ring
○ The temperament your dog needs for the ring
○ Travel time and money
○ Choosing a show dog

If you've read the first few chapters and gone to a dog show or two as a spectator, you're probably eager to get started. And who are we to hold you back? If you already own a registered purebred dog, or know someone who will loan you one to show, by all means go ahead and get started. But keep reading. There's much more you need to know.

Consider your first few shows as an exploration of new activities. Concentrate more on how you feel about this sport, both its good and bad aspects, than on hoping to win. If you are showing your own household dog, you may not be handling a dog that can expect to win in the show ring. Remember, this does not make your dog any less a wonderful companion. You are simply dabbling in a new sport to decide if you want to take the plunge. And if you do find yourself bitten by the show bug, and you go out to find a dog for the ring, don't forget your house dog. Maybe you are living with the world's

Tips from the Pros

The best part about dog shows is doing something with your dog. You both get to go out and have a good time together. The worst part is getting up early enough to get to the show on time!
—Karen A. Brancheau, UKC exhibitor and judge

best obedience or agility competitor and just don't know it. Plenty of shows include more than conformation. You're going anyway. Find what the dog you already have is good at and include that in your show plans.

THE TEMPERAMENT YOU NEED FOR THE RING

Dog showing is competition every bit as much as Wimbledon, show jumping, or the Super Bowl. As with any competition, there are winners and losers. As a newcomer to the sport, you will inevitably do more losing than winning—as you would in any other sport. Understand this going in. View your first year of showing as training and scrimmages. If any wins should happen to come your way, it's a lovely bonus.

Fancy That!

Discussions with professional handlers reveal that many of them began showing as teens in Junior Showmanship. So they have years and years of experience behind them. An amateur with a great dog can certainly beat a professional, but it will help to know what you are doing.

You must be mentally prepared to lose week after week. This is very difficult for some people. If you react badly to losing, it can be even more difficult for your dog, who doesn't know what he or she has done to disappoint you. So your first mandate is to expect to lose and to smile when you do. You are studying and learning, and if you stay with it, the wins will come.

Your show career will progress more quickly if you are outgoing and engaging—or if you can pretend that you are, at least for the duration of a dog show. You won't learn much if you sit off at the edge of a show's hubbub all morning, go into the ring when your number is called, then pack up and go home after your few minutes in the ring. Set up in the middle of the show

Figure 4.1. These young Shetland Sheepdogs may or may not grow up to be champions, but they'll be used to the show environment.

encampment, amid others with your breed if possible. Approach people and explain that you're new to this game. Often that's all you'll need to do. More seasoned exhibitors are mysteriously eager to recruit newcomers. Whether they see you as an easy mark to defeat—and one more dog to count toward a *major*—or as someone with whom to share their passion, many exhibitors will be eager to give you advice, point you toward future shows, or critique your performance.

Of course, some advice will be good and some not so good. Keep reading this and other books, going to your handling class, and listening to everything. As you gain some experience, you will be better able to sort out the valuable tips from the sour grapes. You require, at this point, equanimity.

THE TEMPERAMENT YOUR DOG NEEDS FOR THE RING

If you do plan to start showing with the dog you just happen to own at the moment, consider first how this fits with your dog's personality. For a dog who has been a house companion, not getting out into the world much more than for a walk around the neighborhood, the hubbub of a dog show can be quite a shock. For a shy, sensitive dog, it can be downright torture. This might not be a good way to go.

Dogs chosen as puppies to be show prospects receive all sorts of early training and socialization. Some still do not have the temperament to really go far in the ring. Your own personal dog may have the outgoing showmanship that makes a dog sparkle in the ring. If so, you're lucky. If not, you need to examine just how your dog feels about this new sport you've chosen. Show dogs, even ones just for learning the ropes, must at least tolerate travel and crowds of other people and dogs. It wouldn't be fair to subject a really shy dog to such conditions week after week.

Different shows may get different reactions from your dog. Some dogs definitely prefer outdoor shows and get nervous indoors, while others have just the reverse reaction. Some can tolerate smaller shows, but not the large extravaganzas. It could be worthwhile to try a few different venues before giving up on your dog.

Take your dog to a small local show or fun match. Watch for signs of stress. Panting, repeated yawning and stretching, a glazed look, cringing away from people all indicate that the show scene makes your dog uptight. You will have to look for another way to go. Perhaps a friend or coworker is in the fancy, and you can tag along and show a veteran or puppy that might not otherwise be shown. This has the added advantage of providing you

Tips from the Pros

This breed [Affenpinscher] is chary of strangers. Try to get the dog out to match shows, parks, and shopping centers to prepare the dog for the ring. Make each trip a positive experience and reward the dog for good behavior.

—Sharon Irons Strempski, AKC exhibitor and breeder of Affenpinschers

Figure 4.2. The benches at Westminster, before the doors open to the public. Later in the day, the aisles will be packed solid and nearly impassable.

with an interested instructor. Or if you don't know anyone in the fancy, talk to people at a show. Explain your predicament—you don't want to purchase a show prospect until you're sure this is a sport you're going to stick with. Someone should admire your level-headedness, and perhaps you will find a dog you can show.

If you just know this is the sport for you and want to buy your first show prospect now, see the last section of the chapter for some tips.

TRAVEL TIME AND MONEY

Before you plunge too deeply into this sport—certainly before you buy a show dog—understand the time and money that will be required of you. Dog showing isn't just driving down to the local park Saturday morning and waiting your turn!

First the costs. We'll assume for a moment that you have a dog you're going to be showing, and that you would be feeding and providing veterinary care to whether you showed or not. So we won't take those expenses into account. However, there is your major show equipment—a crate, exercise pen, grooming table, dolly cart, dryer, clippers. A quick look through one of the many dog supply catalogs reveals these prices:

Airline crate	$40–$90
Wire crate	$40–$130
Exercise pen	$40–$70
Grooming table	$100
Dolly cart	$60–$70
"Duck" dryer	$50
Clippers	$100

Items depend to some extent on the size of your dog—smaller crates and shorter *ex-pens* (exercise pens) cost less. You might not want both crate types and an ex-pen, but you'll probably want at least two of the three. Airline crates offer better protection in cold or wet weather, whereas a wire crate or the newer soft-sided fabric crate or an ex-pen provides better ventilation in hot weather. Then of course there are mats and covers and crate cups—none are that expensive on their own, but all add up—and all the combs, brushes, etc., for grooming.

But these are all at least one-time or long-term purchases. You will also have entry fees and travel costs associated with pretty much every show you attend. AKC entry fees currently average $20. So taking one dog to a two-day show weekend will cost you $40 in entries. If you live in a relatively metropolitan area, there will likely be shows somewhere in your vicinity nearly every weekend. So your travel expenses will amount to some gasoline for the family vehicle. But if your area is more rural, you may have to travel farther afield to find the shows you need, increasing your gas money and adding motel costs.

Talking Dog

A duck dryer is a small portable dryer that happens to resemble a duck when sitting upright in its stand. It is smaller, and hence easier to bring to a show, than the larger forced-air dryers.

Tips from the Pros

We usually tried to involve the family in our trips. The older ones did Junior Showmanship. We often planned a picnic or some tailgating at a show. Many times we'd visit an amusement park or other local attraction when traveling out of our area.

—Chris Walkowicz, author and AKC judge

So, say you're facing roughly $500 in startup costs, plus $50–$100 per weekend of showing. Is this something you can afford? Be honest. The average serious show hobbyists may spend twenty weekends a year at dog shows. That's $1,000–$2,000.

There's also the factor of time. If the rest of your family doesn't share your enthusiasm for the fancy, the time you spend with dogs can lead to serious dissension in the ranks. You need to confront this head on. If travel is involved, perhaps the other family members can visit local sites or take advantage of local sporting opportunities such as fishing or golf. That way travel time is spent together, but all family members get to do things that suit their interests.

Of course, this inevitably takes time away from your home. You will have to decide the appropriate balance of home duties and dog shows.

CHOOSING A SHOW DOG

If you don't already have a dog you can show, you'll be looking for one. Although you are probably excited about getting started in this new sport, this isn't a process that should be rushed. You can go on fact-finding missions to shows, meet breeders and handlers, maybe even find a future mentor without a dog at your side.

If you don't yet have a dog, you may not yet have chosen a breed. Or you may find yourself, like many others before you, inexplicably attracted to a breed that might seem wildly inappropriate. You live in an apartment but are drawn to Alaskan Malamutes, or you have several high-energy children but want a Pomeranian. Although you should try to make a choice that suits your living conditions at least moderately well, sometimes it's impossible to fight a really strong attraction. If you find your breath taken away by every Bearded Collie that you see, you're probably not going to be satisfied with a Beagle.

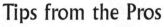

Tips from the Pros

Take your time—it should take you almost a year to find what you want to buy. Study the breed. Study more than one breed and compare them. And then study your standard. Go to every dog show you can find, talk to every breeder you can find, ask every question.

—Linda Ward, owner/breeder/handler of AKC Japanese Chins

Choosing a Breed

But if you have a choice, here are a few things to consider. A smooth-coated breed with a happy outgoing disposition will be easier to groom and show. Why make it hard on yourself if you don't have to? Size should suit both your living conditions and your own abilities. If you are a petite person, a large, active Sporting breed may prove to be more than you can handle. Large dogs also tend to cost more in upkeep. Although they are not necessarily the chowhounds they are often made out to be, they require larger (hence more expensive) crates and larger sizes of medication, such as heartworm preventives, which often cost more.

If you truly are attracted to all dogs in general, no breed in particular, find yourself a listing of breeds by popularity. The AKC often puts out such a thing. See if any breeds toward the middle of the list appeal to you. The unfortunate truth is that breeds with high popularity fall victim to puppy mills and backyard breeders out to make a buck. Although you will stay away from such people, high-popularity breeds tend to have a higher incidence of genetic problems such as hip dysplasia, epilepsy, heart disorders, eye disorders, and on and on.

Watch Your Step

Many breeders have been devoted to the betterment of their chosen breed for decades. Unfortunately, some choose to breed before knowing what pitfalls to avoid and what goals to pursue.

You don't want to go to the very bottom of the popularity list, or you will find that you have little chance of acquiring one of these dogs—in some breeds, less than a half dozen litters a year are registered in the entire country. Also, you may find it impossible to have enough competition in the ring to provide you with any majors, and you will not find many other exhibitors in your breed from whom to learn. These rare breeds can also suffer from genetic diseases because their gene pool is so small.

So look at the breeds near the middle of the popularity list. You'll find breeds such as Brittanys, Weimaraners, Rhodesian Ridgebacks, St. Bernards, West Highland White Terriers, Scottish Terriers, Pekingese, Bichon Frises, Lhasa Apsos, and Pembroke Welsh Corgis. Quite a selection to choose from.

Just remember—the most important consideration at this point is to choose a breed that you will enjoy living with. A dog is a long-term commitment, and the time spent in the ring is a drop in the bucket compared to the time spent in the home. So choose something you love, even if it isn't the most practical of choices.

Once you've narrowed your choices to two or three breeds, research those breeds intensively. Be sure to explore their good *and* bad points. Read the breed standard and breed books. Meet representatives of the breed. Talk to the breeders. Ask veterinarians about problems they see in the breed. Ask trainers what experiences they've had with the breed. Get the address and phone number of the parent breed club from the AKC (or

Tips from the Pros

Toys have been around for a very long time. . . . Unfortunately, in our century Toy dogs have earned an unfair reputation. There's no reason for them to become the neurotic little wimps or miniature terrorists they're reputed to be. A Toy dog can be a character without becoming a caricature. . . . The Toy should be a happy, fun companion. However, he also occasionally needs protection from the larger breeds, and will need to be obedience trained just like any other dog. Every dog is happier and better adjusted when he knows what is expected and what his place is within the family.

—From Darlene Arden, *The Irrepressible Toy Dog*
(Howell Book House, 1998). Used with permission.

UKC, etc.). Contact them for any written information they may have about the breed and for a list of breeders in your area. Phone each of the breeders and explain exactly what you are doing. Most should respect your serious interest and be willing to answer your questions. When you do decide on your breed, you will already have made contact with some breeders and potential suppliers of your show dog.

Finding Your Dog

Actually purchasing your first show dog is not a simple matter. Most breeders will be extremely reluctant to sell a good show prospect to a novice in the fancy. Too often they have sold a promising puppy to someone excited about beginning a show career, only to see the pup develop into a lovely adult while the person loses interest in the sport and never shows the dog. Good breeders put too much into developing their line to let their dogs disappear into oblivion. The most you may be offered by some breeders is a co-ownership. This can serve to protect the breeder's interests while allowing you to get started with a good dog, or it can provide all the power and advantages to the breeder. Such agreements can be difficult to negotiate and put in writing, and often result in hard feelings on both sides.

Perhaps a breeder will sell you a dog (male). Dogs are often flashier and more outgoing in the ring, and thus easier to show, and don't face the problem of turning "bitchy" and *blowing coat* twice a year due to coming in season. They also may not figure so intimately in the breeder's program.

Or you might possibly be able to buy an older bitch, especially if the breeder is *overdogged.* You will have to make a good impression on the breeder to be entrusted with such a girl, but if you are, you will have the opportunity to breed your own litter and have your pick of the offspring. You should only attempt this route if you have the breeder's advice on a stud to use, help with the care of the bitch and her puppies when they

Tips from the Pros

Start with a male. No one will sell you a good female until you've proven yourself with a male.

—Tracy Lucchina, owner/breeder/handler of AKC Japanese Chins come, and have advice on which are the best show prospects. You will need good advice on placing the puppies you choose not to keep and the wherewithal to keep the entire litter, if it should come to that. Breeding is not a step to be taken lightly (see chapter 27).

Decide on a breeder that you like and feel you can trust, whose kennel regularly produces champions. If the kennel is within driving distance of your home, you may be able to get hands-on advice on grooming and showing, but you may also be seen as a potential competitor. Some breeders may even be eager to start newcomers out with less-than-worthy dogs, thus providing themselves with an easy dog to beat and another count toward a major. A breeder farther away probably won't worry about you as a competitor, and may even be eager to publicize their kennel in your area by having you out there winning. But you won't have the person-to-person mentorship advantages.

Prepare to answer questions from the breeder, perhaps more than you are asking. Run from any breeder that does not show a great deal of interest in the home they will be sending their pup to. Answer truthfully. Don't profess to have more experience than you do, and don't promise to show more than you will.

Remember

○ You must be prepared to lose with equanimity.
○ The dog you start off showing must at least tolerate the travel and crowds of the fancy.
○ Showing costs money and time, and you must be able to afford both.
○ Finding and buying a show dog is a time-consuming process—don't rush it.
○ Choose a breed you will be happy to live with, no matter what happens in the show ring.

5

Leaving It to the Pros

This seems early to be talking about professional handlers. You've hardly even gotten your feet wet in the ring! But it also seems to be one of the first subjects novices ask about, at least insofar as wondering how an amateur can beat someone who does this for a living. So we'll take a look at the topic here. You can always come back and read it again if you achieve a championship and feel you have a dog that deserves to be taken out as a *Special*. (If you don't know what that means, it's all explained in chapter 26.)

Let us first make the important point that there are no professional handlers if you are showing with the UKC. The rules prohibit it. So this is one detail you do not have to worry about. Under the auspices of the FCI, rules about professional handlers are left to each member country to decide. You may hear that professional handlers are not used in European shows, but that's not true.

Tips from the Pros

Most people in UKC look at showing dogs as a family sport. There are no professional handlers allowed. The atmosphere at UKC shows is usually relaxed and enjoyable.

—Karen A. Brancheau, UKC exhibitor and breeder

Although there may be fewer of them than in the United States, they are definitely there. The AKC and, to a lesser degree, CKC both use professional handlers.

THE PROS AND CONS OF PROFESSIONAL HANDLERS

The first reason to think of using a professional handler is if you find yourself temperamentally unsuited for the ring. Some people get so nervous that they miss hearing the judge's instructions, trip over their own feet, and communicate their nervousness to their dog. This is certainly not good. Some people get over this with practice, and some never do. If you are just as nervous the fifteenth time you enter a ring as you were the first, and it's having a negative effect on the performance of your dog, you may be a candidate for a professional handler. Or you may want to take a look at different dog sports to see if another one suits you better. Some people find having their dog do the work for which it was intended so breathtaking that they forget to be nervous.

The second reason to consider a professional handler is lack of time. If you find yourself unable to go to shows where your dog would have an excellent chance because of the obligations of work or family or whatever, then having someone take the dog for you might be the way to go.

The third reason could be that you are simply not up to the task physically. Dog showing is hard on the knees and the back, and weakness in those areas could make the ring an uncomfortable place for you to be. Also, if you are showing a large, vigorously moving breed, you might not be able to keep up.

The fourth reason could be that your dog seems to dislike the show ring. It's possible that you just don't realize that your own attitude is affecting your dog. See if you can find a handler who will take the dog into the ring for you for a few weekends and see if the dog's attitude changes. If it does, you can decide if you want to continue with the professional or learn what he or she is doing to make the dog happy. If the dog's attitude doesn't change, then perhaps it's time to look for another activity for this dog and, if you want to continue in conformation, get another dog for that.

The fifth reason arises a little later in your dog's career—you find that you have a dog that deserves to be *campaigned.* This is expensive, involving far-flung shows, professional handlers, and magazine advertising. You shouldn't get into it if you can't afford it. But truly superior specimens of a breed should be known nationwide if possible.

It's not all sunshine and roses with professional handlers. There is a downside as well.

How much do you know about this person to whom you are going to entrust your precious dog? At one time the AKC licensed professional handlers, and as this is being written, the program is in the process of being revived. In the interim, anyone with a comb and a show lead could declare themselves a professional handler. Two organizations for professional handlers—the Professional Handlers Association (PHA) and the Dog Handlers Guild (DHG)—have continued through the shifting status of the AKC licensing program. The PHA requires a handler to have an established kennel facility, to have been a handler for ten years, at least five of those as a professional, and to supply rate cards and contracts to their clients. The DHG operates only by a code of ethics. Both organizations can expel members for cause, but neither can provide much of a guarantee

Talking Dog

Campaigning or *specialing* is done after a dog has become a champion and shown him- or herself to be of exceptional merit. A strategy is mapped out to win Group Firsts and Best in Shows at the most prestigious possible shows. The showing schedule may gear up to move the dog up the various ratings systems to achieve "Number One Sporting (or Working or Toy, etc.) Dog all systems." Magazine ads noting wins are taken out to spread the dog's name. It is expensive and time consuming, and the dog will rarely be home with the family. It's not a step to be taken lightly.

Figure 5.1. Andy Linton is a professional handler at AKC shows, well respected by his peers.

toward quality care and good ethics. The new AKC licensing program could be a good indicator but will have to be watched as it develops anew. We'll tell you what to look for in a professional handler a little later in this chapter, but the final decision will be up to you.

How much time will your dog be away from home? You did presumably get into this because you like being in the company of dogs. Sending your dog off to live with someone else because the show clusters start on Thursday and end on Monday may not be exactly what you want. Other arrangements are possible—you bring the dog to the show and the handler simply goes in the ring for you, for example—but you'll have to know what you want and find a handler who's willing to go along with it.

How much money do you have to spend? How expensive a professional is will depend to a large extent on your goals. We'll discuss specifics on costs later in this chapter, but for now we'll point out that if you're staying in hotels and eating in restaurants most weekends, it may not cost a lot more to have a handler do it for you.

CAN AN AMATEUR BEAT THE PROS?

It happens every weekend, everywhere. The judges are supposed to be judging the dogs, and a good judge will look past your ineptitude. Some will even give you advice on how to better your performance. And the professional handlers do not always have the best dogs, even in the biggest shows.

But there are times when the amateur doesn't really have an equal chance. There is an odd symbiotic relationship between judges, professional handlers, and show-giving clubs. The clubs need entries to cover their expenses and turn a profit. Professional handlers bring anywhere from a dozen to three dozen dogs to a show, as opposed to the one, two, or maybe three most amateurs bring. Judges who tend to put up professionals over amateurs attract more professionals to a show. So the club is happy with the entries, and the judge gets more assignments, and the professionals keep coming. It's an incestuous sort of connection, but one that does exist. Not many judges do it, of course. And even some of the judges who do may not be conscious of what they are doing and why. You should simply realize that professional handlers have more power in the world of dog showing, and sometimes it pays off.

Judges who were once handlers themselves may tend to favor professionals because they know it means extra money in the pro's pocket. (Most professional handlers get a cash bonus for wins.) The owner handler only gets a ribbon, and doesn't depend on winning to earn a living.

This favoritism is another reason to keep records on judges. If you find that a judge gives the win to a professional even though the

Fancy That!

At the 1999 edition of Westminster, three of the final seven dogs in the Best in Show ring were owner-handled. The owners of the Saluki, CH Sundown Alabaster Treasure, JC, went so far as to drive their dog from northern California to the New York show. The dog never flies. That JC after the name, by the way, stands for Junior Courser, meaning the dog also performs in lure coursing.

dog is obviously mediocre, make a note to avoid that judge yourself, but recommend him or her if you ever hire a professional. There are politics in this game, and you can make an effort to recognize and avoid or exploit them.

How to Hire a Professional

If you have decided to entertain the idea of hiring a professional, first ask for recommendations. It's early in your career, and you might not know many people in the fancy, but ask those you do know, including the breeder of your dog.

Watch the pros at shows you attend. You want to see someone who has rapport with the dogs, who reaches down to pet them or ruffle their ears. The dogs should appear happy and focused on the handler. And of course they should be immaculately clean and well groomed.

The professional should practice good sportsmanship always. This person is your representative in the ring, after all. He or she should take both wins and losses without a large show of emotion. You can do the jumping up and down and screaming for wins from ringside.

If you are truly serious, make an appointment to meet with the handler you are considering. Handlers are extremely busy at shows, so you will probably have to visit the handler's kennel facility. You'll want to see it anyway if your dog is going to be spending any time there. The runs or kennels should be immaculate, and the whole facility should smell fresh and clean. There may be indoor/outdoor runs, where the dog has access to a small

Tips from the Pros

Pick a professional handler that has time for your dog. While a Toy handler is ideal, you need to know who will be handling the dog. Affenpinschers need to bond with their handler. They do not take kindly to being handed off to a stranger. If your handler is more interested in pushing another breed of dog and won't be handling your dog in the group, you're wasting your money.

—Sharon Irons Strempski, AKC exhibitor and breeder of Affenpinschers

Figure 5.2. Don't let those shiny trophies and silky ribbons lure you into doing anything you really don't want to do.

section of the outdoors during the day. Or the runs may all be indoors and the dogs taken out by the handler or, more likely, an assistant every day.

Good ventilation is essential in kennels. Dogs kept in close quarters are more likely to pass diseases from one to another. Good ventilation can literally help to clear the air.

Ask any questions you have. One detail to investigate is whether the handler is already representing a dog in your breed. The handler is only one person, after all, or at most half of a partnership. Having more than one dog in a breed means that conflicts will occur at some shows, and your dog may end up being handled by an assistant or by another professional handler whom you haven't met. Some handlers will take one bitch and one dog of a breed, knowing there will be no conflict unless both dogs win through. This is reasonable and normal. Even if your dog were the only individual of the breed in the handler's string, conflicts could still occur in the group ring or because of the timing of various breed classes.

If all looks good and you're sold on the idea of hiring a professional, read the next section for details and costs.

AGREEING ON SERVICES AND COSTS

There are a lot of different arrangements you can make with a professional handler—everything from you bringing your dog to each show and the handler simply taking over for the ring appearance, to full-time boarding of your dog with the handler. You have to decide what's right for you, and you must be reasonable about your goals. If you want to keep the dog at home and drive to shows, you're probably not going to be able to make the top ten in any of the ratings systems. Whatever you decide you want for your dog is fine, but it has to match with your goals.

If your dog will be staying at the handler's kennel, you need to agree on some details. The handler would probably like to feed the same food to all the dogs, but if you are loyal to a particular brand or diet, say so. The handler should be willing to accommodate your wishes. Also ask about any supplements the handler may use. Some are devotees of a whole range of additives. You must do research if necessary, realize that more is not always better (too much calcium can actually result in deficiencies of other minerals, for example, and calcium is one of the favorite supplements), and make your wishes known. You must be able to trust this person to do as you request.

The handler should also take care of any medications or preventives you use for your dog. Anything from monthly flea and heartworm preventives to daily medicines should be discussed. The handler may bring up the subject of tests and treatment for internal parasites. This is another potential hazard of keeping dogs in close quarters and traveling to a lot of show sites.

You should discuss what will be done if your dog should suddenly need veterinary care. The handler will have an ongoing relationship with a

Watch Your Step

Do not let anyone talk you into more than you want to do with your dog. If it's more important to have the dog at home than to be in the top ten in the ratings, well, it's your dog. Some hired handlers and some breeders, excited over a dog that's starting to win, will push for more showing.

Tips from the Pros

Get recommendations from people you trust and who have the same values as you do. Try to get a look at how the handler keeps his setup at shows. See how he and his associates interact with the dogs in their care. Visit his facilities at home to get an idea how the dogs are cared for. Check to see what experience the handler has had with your particular breed. If you are paying for professional services, make sure that this is a true professional with adequate facilities at home and on the road and a proven track record of winning. Discuss the "fine print"—not only regarding the handler's fees and other expenses, but what liability he will assume.

—Lilian S. Barber, AKC exhibitor and judge,
author of *The New Complete Italian Greyhound*

veterinarian in his or her area, and you may want to meet that veterinarian. You will be billed for any veterinary services.

And of course you should discuss what will happen if there is a conflict between your dog and another at ringtime. Which will the professional handler handle?

Finally, the handler should carefully spell out all the costs involved in the showing plan you have set forth. The rate for handling may range from $50 for a young handler just acquiring a reputation to $75–$100 for an established professional. Specialty shows and National Specialties can cost

Watch Your Step

One thing you definitely want to avoid is artificial enhancement of your dog. There are unscrupulous handlers who will do illegal surgery to improve the set of a tail, correct a crooked bite, or supply a missing testicle. Such "win at all costs" attitudes are ridiculous, since conformation is supposed to be choosing which examples of the breed are worthy of contributing to the gene pool. The results of surgery cannot be passed along to offspring.

even more. The handler usually gets a bonus for any group placements or Best in Shows, sometimes even for breed wins. If there is any purse money being offered (some shows do provide cash awards), it goes to the handler. There are charges for boarding, grooming, and travel. The travel at least is divided between the owners of all the dogs being taken to a particular show.

All charges should be discussed in advance. Remember, one of the requirements of the Professional Handlers Association is that the handler have a rate card and offer it to clients.

When you have agreed on the details, you should both sign a contract spelling it all out.

Is This Still My Dog?

If you decide on lofty ambitions for your dog, you may find that the only time you actually see the dog is on television, trotting around the ring somewhere across the country. You can take comfort in the fact that show careers are usually short, and the dog will retire home to you. Or you can adjust your ambitions and bring the dog home. It's up to you.

Remember

○ UKC does not allow professional handlers.
○ If you are too nervous to show your dog well, not physically up to the task, or don't have the time, you may want the services of a professional handler.
○ Amateurs can beat the pros, although some judges may make it difficult.
○ Investigate any professional handler you are considering using.
○ Spell everything out in a contract if you are hiring a professional.
○ You can always change your mind and bring the dog back home.

Part II

Basic Training

Your partner in this sport happens to be a dog. So you need to take the responsibility for both of you. For your dog's sake, you'll need to provide lots of socialization, reliable identification, and regular checkups. A good conformation class can help both of you get over those novice jitters. Setting reasonable goals early will help keep you levelheaded amid the excitement of this new undertaking.

For your own deeper understanding, learning how dogs progress through dog shows can save you from embarrassment and missed opportunities. Learning what moves your dog physically can help you understand why an Afghan doesn't trot like a Collie and how to better show off your dog when moving.

There's a lot to learn about this sport of dogs, and you may want to skip over some of the information here. No problem. Come back and check it out at your leisure.

6

Homework

Before you even begin your career in conformation, you have three large responsibilities to yourself and the sport: Know what conformation is about, set reasonable goals for yourself, and always practice good sportsmanship. You have the added responsibility to your dog of understanding his or her likes and limits.

You're probably excited about this new undertaking and anxious to attend your first show . . . or your next show, if you started without us. You may even have sent in your next entry already. Just be aware that not being prepared or not understanding some of the things that go on at a dog show can sour either your dog or yourself or both on the experience.

UNDERSTANDING YOUR SPORT

To familiarize yourself with the basics, you should certainly obtain and read the conformation rules and regulations for the kennel club you will be showing under (AKC and UKC are the two main clubs in the United States, and some of their regulations are quite different). But that won't be enough. You'll probably have questions, and words set down on paper can't quite describe what being in competition with your dog is really like. You should plan on using a couple of shows as research sites for your fact-finding mission.

Attend *without* entering your dog. In fact, leave your dog at home. By not competing, you will be more able to concentrate on the events going on around you. By not having your dog, you will be able to wander unencumbered from ring to ring and free to talk with competitors (when they are not busy, of course). If you first become familiar and comfortable with the surroundings of a dog show, your dog is likely to enjoy the experience more when you actually begin competing.

Talk to people at ringside. Ask what is going on if you don't understand it. Keep in mind that not everyone will know a lot more than you. Some may even cheerfully provide completely incorrect information. Be polite and keep asking different people. Don't force yourself on people, especially if they are accompanied by a dog and could be readying for their turn in competition.

Also take some time away from the ring to wander among the exercise pens, crates, and motor homes of exhibitors. Especially if they have already had their turn in the ring, exhibitors relaxing at their "campsites" may have more time and energy to talk with you. Most are eager to promote their sport.

If you are shy, even just standing and watching ringside for a few hours will give you a different look at a sport than sitting home and reading rules will do. But do try to talk with people. You all have dogs in common, after all.

After attending a show or two as a spectator, if you still have serious questions, we hope that you will find your answer some-

Fancy That!

A large show, especially a multiday affair, can resemble summer camp or a rock festival. There are campers, tents, and often parties. People are doing something they enjoy and having a good time. Join in.

Figure 6.1. While the judge is busy with other dogs, this canine competitor gets an encouraging chin scratch from his owner.

where in this book. But if you still need information, you can call the kennel club and ask. Both AKC and UKC also have Web sites, which also could prove helpful (see appendix A for addresses and phone numbers).

Before you enter competition, or early in your career, you're likely to be taking training from someone. You should consider your trainer as a valuable resource for information about your sport. Politely ask questions when time permits. If you really want to indulge in deep and searching conversation, maybe you can arrange to take the trainer to lunch.

UNDERSTANDING YOUR DOG

To show well, you must also know your dog. Of course you will learn the physical mechanics of grooming and presenting your fine example of the canine species. But we are talking here of understanding your dog for him- or herself.

Some dogs are natural-born "hams" and thrive on attention, standing taller if someone applauds and giving it their all because they enjoy the experience. Others may be willing but shy and will need to be gently coaxed along. One dog may hold it all together and gait beautifully on a loose lead, whereas another may need constant reminding to hold his head up while moving.

Practice and an increasing appreciation of the canine physique will reveal your dog's physical strengths and weaknesses. But only a solid relationship will help you understand the mental aspect of your dog. Such an understanding is crucial if you hope to get the most out of showing.

By experiencing as many different things as possible with your dog, you will not only gain a deeper understanding of his or her psyche, but you will also lay down a good foundation for dealing with anything unusual that might happen in the show ring. Many conformation exhibitors also compete in one or more performance events with their dogs. Obedience is popular (and useful). Fears that a dog taught to sit in the obedience ring won't stand in the conformation ring have proven groundless. Dogs understand the difference between the two events. Appropriate breeds also take part in field trials, lure coursing, and other sports based on their heritage.

You want your dog to be bright and personable in the ring. You don't want a dog that's so geared up as to be out of control. You should know what is necessary to achieve the right level of controlled energy. With a high-energy dog, especially one that also competes in one of the demanding performance sports such as herding or agility, and thus has built up some serious stamina, you may need to schedule a good outing the day be-

Tips from the Pros

Looking at the British, who are dyed-in-the-wool dog lovers, the question becomes: What is it that makes these dogs so comfortable in public places? Are British dog owners raising their pups any differently, socializing them differently?

The answer is that the dogs are extremely well socialized and trained right from the start, going to obedience class after they've received their vaccinations. Virtually everyone in the UK trains their dog, no matter what the dog's size. The dogs are therefore under better control and create fewer problems. This makes close encounters of the canine kind far more enjoyable both for the dogs and the people involved.

—From Darlene Arden, *The Irrepressible Toy Dog* (Howell Book House, 1998). Used with permission.

fore a show to take the edge off the dog. This is a tricky business and one of the places where good understanding of your dog is essential. You don't want the dog so tired that he or she doesn't have any spark.

Try different levels of pre-event activity while you are training and appearing in matches to learn what works best for your dog.

SETTING REASONABLE GOALS

Most dogs are shown in conformation in the hopes that they will become champions. Earning a championship gives you the right to prefix your dog's name with the abbreviation for champion; for example, CH Tudor's Wild as the Wind (a lovely Doberman who won Best in Show at Westminster and also earned a UD, a high-level obedience title).

Registration certificates, whether issued by the AKC, the UKC, or some other kennel club, have nothing to do with a championship other than that a dog must be registered to compete. "Papers" mean only that the dog has been bred from purebreds of the same breed. They are no guarantee of health or quality.

Although breeders often sell puppies as either "pet quality" or "show quality," this is at best an educated guess. Most puppies are sold at the age of six to twelve weeks. At this tender age, judging how they will develop as mature dogs is exceedingly difficult. Studies have estimated that roughly one out of every one hundred "show quality" pups becomes a champion.

A lot goes into making a champion. A dog may be an unbelievably beautiful specimen of the breed but simply hate the show ring. Such a dog will not show spark or personality and will frequently be beaten by dogs of

Watch Your Step

Beware of anyone who guarantees you a championship. No one can make such a guarantee unless something shady is going on. You want a breeder who is enthusiastic but honest. After all, you're hoping this person will become your mentor in the sport.

lesser physical quality but greater "presence." This is a major impetus for being sure that your dog's experiences both in training and in showing are unfailingly positive.

Some owners don't have the temperament for showing either (see chapter 3). They just don't have the perseverance to keep coming back after a close loss to one dog or another.

Expenses, discussed in chapter 4, may be a problem. Entry fees, travel expenses, and the rest mount up quickly. There is an equal (and possibly equally expensive) investment of time. Four-day show clusters and long drives to and from events can require time away from home and work. Those lucky enough to have a show within an hour or two of home most weekends should count their blessings and realize that others may need to travel four hours or more any time they want to show.

Bad luck can also come into play. You may be looking forward to a show with a judge that your research has shown loves your type of dog and one you know will be absent your hottest competition. But your dog *blows coat* the week before the show, or injures a paw the day before, or your car breaks down in the middle of nowhere on the way to the show. Such things do happen, and you must be tough enough to shrug them off and try again.

Setting high but realistic goals for you and your dog is important to your enjoyment of the sport. A goal beyond your reach will quickly result in disappointment, discouragement, and probably a disgusted exit from the world of dog showing. A goal too low will be too easily accomplished, but at least it can be adjusted upward without major trauma.

Remember, every dog should be a champion in his or her owner's eyes. Maybe you'd like to learn more about your chosen breed, work to be more confident in public, make some new dog-enthusiast friends, and bring

Talking Dog

Nearly all dogs do some shedding year-round. But twice a year many breeds go through a heavy shed, losing the bulk of their undercoat in a short period. This is what is known as *blowing coat*. For a time, the dog has an uneven patchy-looking coat and is hardly fit for the show ring. This often seems to occur at the worst possible time.

Figure 6.2. Even in the less formal world of European showing, notice how each of these handlers is focused on his or her dog. (Photo courtesy of Dr. Bernd Guenter)

home some of those enticing pieces of colored silk called ribbons. Maybe a championship awaits you, or maybe not—you will have a better idea about your chances with some experience behind you.

Goals often change with experience. Winning that first blue ribbon often sends exhibitors to higher goals, maybe with a second dog. The "show bug" bites some people very hard. Always keep in mind that this is a sport, intended to be fun and rewarding for you and your dog. Don't become so focused on winning or getting your first major that you forget to have fun. There is always another day, another show.

PRACTICING GOOD SPORTSMANSHIP

Dog showing is a social event, and being snubbed is always hurtful. Always congratulate the winner, whether it happens to be your friend or someone you didn't think had a chance. You can make catty comments in private with friends later if you must, but out in public be the model of civility. Otherwise someday it may be you standing alone with a blue ribbon while others turn their backs and walk away.

Watch Your Step

One popular magazine devoted to dog showing ran an article titled "Judge Bashing: A Sport for the Novice." It's true that newcomers to the sport, who may hardly know their breed standard, are often very free with their uncomplimentary assessments of judges. Don't indulge in this "sport."

In public at least, and preferably in private as well, don't make disparaging remarks about fellow competitors, judges, show-sponsoring clubs. Be thankful that people are willing to give so much of their time to host, judge, and compete at a show. Once you are no longer a novice, do your part by volunteering to help when you can. In fact, stewarding is a good way to get a close-up look at dogs in the ring. As part of your study of conformation, you may want to consider putting in some time as a steward. Although you can't discuss anything with the judge while he or she is actually judging, there may be time between classes, and there's certainly lunch. Explain that you are new to the sport and trying to become a model exhibitor without making a lot of mistakes. Most judges will appreciate your efforts.

Be nice to everyone. You never know where your next friend is going to come from.

BE PREPARED!

For most people, getting started in conformation is not a planned event. You have a friend who asks you to go to a show for company and find it's a thrilling place to be. Or you take your dog to a fun match on a whim and—here's the one that hooks a lot of people—the judge hands you a ribbon! The impulse is to jump right in and start showing. But *that's* the way the sport loses a lot of people. Without preparation, the show experience can be mind-numbingly confusing, and the losses can be crushing. (Estimates of the length of a show career—the person's, not the dog's—range from five to ten years.)

Because there is so much to absorb, you might want to choose two shows a couple of weeks apart and use them as your open-air university.

Tips from the Pros

Learn the rules! You should know what classes go when, the order of competition, the point system, etc. If you want to play the game, you have to know the rules, just like anything else. Very important. Watch and listen, you will learn so much this way.

Read as much as you can about what you want to do and about your particular breed. If you know what the breed is supposed to look like, their faults and good points, you'll better understand how to present your own dog to its best advantage. Have the dog trained *before* you go in the ring. Be ready.

—Karen A. Brancheau, StoneFox Kennels

The first week read chapters 10 (the progression through the classes) and 23 (your setup at a dog show), then go to the first show and pay close attention to these topics. The second week read chapters 14 (stacking), 15 (gaiting), and 16 (baiting), then go to the second show and examine how handlers present their dogs in the ring. Or, if this doesn't seem logical to you, make your own breakdown and study plan. Just don't try to learn it all in one weekend.

Remember

○ You must understand both the rules and the goals of your sport.
○ Attend some shows without your dog so you can focus on learning the basics.
○ Talk to as many people as you can—you never know where the next pearl of wisdom or future good friend will come from.
○ Understand your dog's mental makeup and take it into consideration when planning your show career.
○ Set your goals high enough to be challenging, but not so high that they are unattainable.
○ Always practice good sportsmanship.
○ Always be prepared.

7

Check It Out

One of your primary responsibilities when preparing to show a dog is the health and well-being of your own dog and every other dog and person at the show. How often have you attended a conference or flown off to a meeting and come home with a cold or the flu? Whenever a group of people gets together, they generously pass germs to one another. The same can happen with large groups of dogs.

Dogs have the added potential of biting another dog, or even a person. "Not *my* dog," I can hear you exclaim. But it does happen, sometimes fueled by raging hormones, sometimes by nervousness. And while you might be certain your dog won't be the aggressor, he or she could be the victim if you don't exercise due caution. Take heed of the old Boy Scout motto: Be prepared.

VETERINARY CHECKUP

When you sign an entry form for a show, you are certifying that your dog is in good health and current on all vaccinations.

There is some controversy over vaccinations right now. Traditionally, many vaccines have been given annually. Rabies could be given every year or every three years, depending on regulations in your state. Some vaccines—Lyme disease, bordatella—are optional, given only at the owner's request. Often vaccines are given in combination, such as DHLPP (distemper, hepatitis, leptospirosis, parainfluenza, parvovirus). Many long-time participants in conformation recommend that vaccines be given twice annually, every six months—for added protection around all those other dogs, they say. But some in the veterinary community are now questioning the wisdom of even annual vaccinations. They maintain that protection actually lasts much longer, and we may be doing damage by overvaccinating our dogs. No solid long-term immunological studies have ever been done to prove the point one way or another.

So where does this leave you and your dog? Confused, along with the rest of us, more than likely. You can discuss the controversy with your own veterinarian, but be aware that veterinarians are in an awkward position on this topic. Annual vaccinations are often the only thing that brings in people and their pets and gives the veterinarian a chance to assess pet health. You, of course, are more conscientious.

One logical course you can take is to have your dog's blood checked by your veterinarian for titer levels. This gives an actual indication of how well protected your dog is against a specific disease, and may help you decide how often to vaccinate.

Watch Your Step

No sick dog should ever be brought to a dog show. There is no excuse for this behavior. If you have a sick dog that requires your care, you stay home with the dog and skip the show. That's all there is to it.

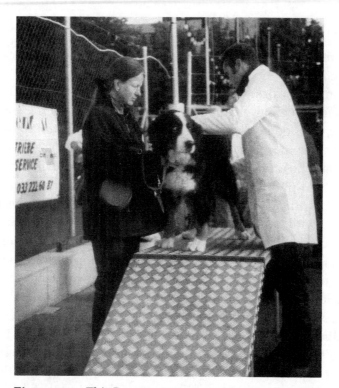

Figure 7.1. This Bernese Mountain Dog and handler are at an FCI show in Europe, where dogs receive veterinary checkups as they enter the show grounds. (Photo courtesy of Dr. Bernd Guenter)

There's more beyond just vaccinations, of course. Just as you should consult your physician before taking up a strenuous new sport, your veterinarian should do a thorough checkup before your dog begins in conformation. Many breeds are unfortunately prone to maladies such as hip dysplasia, luxating patellas, spinal disorders, and eye problems. Some dogs will try so hard to please that they will endure intense pain rather than disappoint their owners. Be sure your dog is sound before ever setting foot in a ring.

Tell your veterinarian what your plans are. Inquire about *CERF* and *OFA*—these registries track eye problems (or lack thereof) and orthopedic disorders (or lack thereof). Early detection of some problems can greatly help in improving the dog's long-term quality of life. And if you should progress to breeding, all breeding stock should be cleared of genetic defects before being used in any breeding program. (For more on breeding,

Talking Dog

CERF stands for Canine Eye Registration Foundation. Results of eye exams for hereditary problems can be registered with the foundation. OFA stands for Orthopedic Foundation of America. They started out registering results of hip exams but have expanded to cover many more genetic problems.

see chapter 27 . . . but don't even think about it until you've gained *a lot* of experience in your chosen breed.)

RELIABLE IDENTIFICATION

Even dogs that will never take part in any organized sport should be reliably identified. Accidents, by definition, are unexpected. Car crashes might spring open a door, meter readers may not latch a gate, home remodelers are notorious for leaving front doors wide open. Dogs do get out. Make sure they have the best possible chance of getting back home.

Your dog should be licensed with your local animal control organization. That tag, a current rabies tag, and an ID tag with your address and phone number should be worn regularly on the dog's everyday identification collar. If you object to the jingling of the tags, there are little pouches that wrap over the tags and secure them tight to the collar, or you can simply wrap a rubber band around them.

Many fanciers of long-coated breeds refuse to keep collars on their dogs for fear of damaging the coat. As an aficionado of lavishly coated dogs, I haven't found it to be a problem, but if you decide to forgo a collar, other forms of identification are even more crucial.

Tattooing has been popular for some time. If the tattooed number is the dog's AKC registration number, the AKC will track that number to the last-known registered owner. But many times a personal number, most often your driver's license or

Fancy That!

Where I live, canine identification is emphasized. One local shelter microchips all dogs before adopting them out. And my county of residence offers free licensing for life for any dog that is microchipped and spayed or neutered.

your social security number, is tattooed on your dog's inner thigh. However, someone finding your lost dog can't simply call the federal government, give them your social security number, and get your phone number. And only police can legally track your driver's license number. So for a tattoo to be effective, it has to be registered with an organization such as the National Dog Registry. The hope is that anyone finding your dog will, first, look for a tattoo and, second, know enough to call the registry. The reality is that many people have no idea how to track a tattoo, and a lot of animal shelter workers are reluctant to roll a dog over to examine the inner thigh for tattoos. Tattoos also are prone to fading and being covered under the dog's coat.

Fancy That!

Did you know that the AKC has an identification program called Companion Animal Recovery Program or Home Again? This registry is open to all companion animals, the only national database to accept all permanent forms of ID (most often microchips or tattoos) from all vendors. There is a 24-hour 800 number for people to call to find out if a found animal is enrolled.

The most recent technological innovation for identification is the microchip. This marvel, the size of a grain of rice, is injected into the dog between the shoulder blades, where the musculature will hold it in place. Each chip is coded with a unique number. A scanner passed over the dog's shoulders picks up the information and provides a readout. The manufacturer of the microchip can link the readout to you. There is no fading, as there is with tattoos. The problem here has been that several chip manufacturers are in competition, and their products are not all compatible. Also, not every shelter possesses and uses a scanner, though the situation has improved. Most scanners can now read most chips, and the chip manufacturers have issued free scanners to animal shelters across the country.

Your best bet is to use as many forms of identification as you can.

SOCIALIZATION

Your dog will encounter many people, other dogs, and new situations in the sport of conformation. Early socialization can help make this a pleasant experience for both of you.

If you get your dog as a puppy, take the time to accustom him or her to riding in the car, walking amid crowds, crossing busy streets (safely on leash, of course). Puppy kindergarten classes are quite popular now and are a wonderful way for your pup to meet other pups and people. Although some worry about puppies in groups being susceptible to disease, the risks of undersocialization are much greater. The more safe experiences you can give a puppy, the better the grown dog will be able to cope with new things.

If you acquire an older dog, you should take the dog into different situations and watch any reactions. You may learn that the dog has a problem with loud noises or shies away from people approaching with outstretched hands. You will have to work on these difficulties with great patience, and you should enlist the aid of a trainer interested in problem solving.

Dogs in the show ring undergo a hands-on examination from the judge. A dog that growls or attempts to bite may be excused from the ring that day or even banned from the sport entirely. And with good cause. A dog with such a temperament has no place in the ring or in a breeding program. Be sure that your dog is relaxed about being handled by all sorts of people.

Another bit of training, though not strictly socialization, is very important for the show dog: familiarization with a crate or exercise pen or both.

Figure 7.2. Even in the crowded ring conditions at Westminster, these shelties are all attending to business.

Tips from the Pros

The key is to make the crate the dog's bed and the best place in the world that he can be, so pup should only get his best treats and a favorite toy when he's in the crate. . . . The added bonus is that the crate is an ideal place for your dog in the car. . . . Putting your dog's crate in the car will assure him of a safe place, rather like having a child in a car seat. . . . The best part is that if you're traveling, the crate becomes the dog's bed in a hotel or motel room. Wouldn't you like to travel with your own bed?

—From Darlene Arden, *The Irrepressible Toy Dog*
(Howell Book House, 1998). Used with permission.

At almost any type of dog sport, including conformation, you will need to wait for your turn to compete. You could stand around with your dog on leash, but this would leave both of you tired by the time your turn arrived. A crate or exercise pen can serve as a home away from home. Your dog can relax—many in fact nap until their performances. You are free to visit the restroom, check out the raffle or vendors, or sit and relax yourself. If you will be traveling to shows and staying overnight, a crate may gain you entry to lodgings that otherwise would not accept your dog. Crates can also be useful at home, especially in housebreaking puppies or keeping dogs quiet while they convalesce from illness or injury.

Don't expect your dog to walk into a crate and lie there contentedly if you have not done your part in training. Even an exercise pen, though less confining, requires that your dog not jump up on the sides or try to leap out. Talk with your trainer about a program for familiarizing your dog with a crate and pen.

CONDITIONING PROGRAM

Once you know that your dog is healthy (and your own health is reasonably good), you should begin a conditioning program together. There is a lot of movement involved in showing a dog, and you don't want your dog or yourself to be gasping for air while trying to make it around the ring one more time. You also want your dog to show good musculature under the judge's hands.

How you set about conditioning will depend on your dog's size, breed, and current condition, your own inclinations, and the opportunities available to you. For those who have appropriate water available, swimming is an excellent workout, with both cardiovascular and full-body musculature benefits.

Undoubtedly, the most often used style of conditioning is roadwork, where you exercise your dog by having him or her join you as you jog along a road, sometimes for miles a day. Soft ground will be kinder to your dog's feet and legs than pavement (the same applies to you). Do not begin a program of roadwork until your dog is at least a year old. Until that time, the dog's bones are still growing and forming and could be damaged by the repetitive pounding of roadwork.

If your dog is a large, active breed, you may need a bicycle to keep up. Several companies manufacture devices for attaching a dog to a bike safely. One such device is called the Springer, available from www.dog-training.com/springer.htm. It attaches the dog to the side of the bike low on the frame so that the dog's movement will not unbalance you. Another device, the K9 Cruiser, available from www.adogsbestfriend.com/k9cruiser.html, can attach one or two dogs to a bar extending behind the bike.

Speaking of safety, always consider safety first. Discuss your conditioning program with your veterinarian and/or trainer, and always take weather, particularly hot weather, into account.

Remember

○ A dog should always have a complete veterinary checkup before starting any sport.
○ All dogs should have reliable identification at all times.
○ Dogs must be socialized early and often, for the benefit of all.
○ Crate training offers many benefits, both at shows and in the home.
○ A well-thought-out conditioning program will have you and your dog ready for the exertion of the ring.

Boot Camp

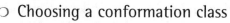
A lot of people just starting out in the fancy take handling classes. But there are handling classes and there are handling classes. Some are excellent and can put you months ahead of other novices by taking some of the mystery out of dog showing. Others seem to be held only to stroke the ego of the instructor, who appears intent on keeping the fancy as mystifying as possible so he or she can retain the position of power.

There are also seminars, one-time events rather than ongoing classes. Professional handlers or judges, or simply experienced exhibitors, may offer these seminars. And of course there are books, though it's hard to learn the finer points of a physical activity by reading. You might even be lucky enough to find a video dedicated to showing your breed.

However you advance your learning, keep your eyes, ears, and brain open. Keep what makes sense and seems to work and discard the rest.

CHOOSING A CONFORMATION CLASS

Let's be honest right from the start—there may not be a choice of classes in your area. In fact, there might not even be a class within an hour's drive of your home. Or the local kennel club or training group may offer the only classes around. If these are your circumstances, make the best of them. Go to the only class available. Maybe it will be fantastic, but you never know. Even if it isn't, it will provide your dog with a facsimile of the show experience. Dogs lined up nose to tail is not an experience you're likely to encounter anywhere else but the show ring and show class. So even if you're not learning a lot, your dog could be. Concentrate on making it a happy event for your dog and you'll come out ahead.

If the only classes available are in obedience, or "puppy kindergarten," then enroll your puppy in kindergarten or your dog in subnovice obedience. Use positive training methods even if the instructor doesn't. (See some suggestions for books in appendix E.) Being in class will get your dog out there with other dogs—this alone is reason enough to go. A little basic obedience will impart some good manners to your dog, something you'll find valuable in living in the same house together. And teaching your dog to sit will *not* ruin it for the show ring!

Watch Your Step

Not all classes and instructors are equal. Be certain that the teacher is familiar with your particular breed and how it is presented. If it becomes apparent that the instructor doesn't know much about your breed or doesn't even like it, look for a different class.

—Lilian S. Barber, AKC exhibitor and breeder,
author of *The New Complete Italian Greyhound*

Fancy That!

An owner of Alaskan Malamutes competes in a variety of sports. Far from confusing her dogs, she notes that if she comes into sight carrying training collars, the dogs all sit because they know the best behaved will get to go first. But if she is carrying show martingales, the dogs all stand and pose. And if she's carrying harnesses, look out! The dogs go wild because they know they're going to get to run and pull. They have no problem recognizing the equipment associated with each activity and the appropriate actions.

If, however, you live in an area where classes are abundant, you have the happy task of choosing one. How do you do that? What criteria do you use?

One good way to start is to ask people you meet at fun matches for their opinions of local classes. You will find that in dog showing, everyone seems to know, or at least know of, everyone else—at least within their breed and often within an entire group. So mention the instructor of the possible classes and see what responses you get.

If classes are offered continuously, drop in and watch how a class is conducted. Are the handlers laughing, chatting, and having a good time? More importantly, are the dogs eager, wagging their tails, and having fun? If so, this is a good class for you! Even if the instructor can't tell you precisely how best to show your dog—some instructors are familiar with the finer points of their own breed only—you and your dog will absorb good attitude, get used to the feel of the "ring," and make some friends in the sport.

If, on the other hand, class participants are silent, the instructor operates like a drill sergeant, and the dogs are kept in show poses for ten or fifteen minutes waiting their turn, flee! Nothing will turn a dog off of showing faster than the tension

Tips from the Pros

A good handling class can be very helpful. Get a recommendation from a top handler or a good breeder/handler. Some classes are taught by excellent handlers and some are taught by whoever's available. A good class is also helpful as practice ring experience.

—Bill McFadden, AKC professional handler

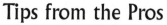

Tips from the Pros

Local handling classes are good for education of the dog if he's a novice. They mostly give you the basics, but they can't give you the finer points of showing a dog. . . . The problem now is we do not have the process of assistant handlers learning the fine points of taking care of dogs and learning from a handler. We have lost a lot of fine points on conditioning and handling. There are a lot of handlers out there now who, in my opinion, were not given the right education.

—Tom Glassford, former professional handler, AKC rep

and boredom of this sort of class. Better to get your training in fun matches than to risk teaching your dog that showing is a bad thing.

A lot of classes will fall somewhere between these two extremes. As long as the dogs appear happy, a class will probably be a valuable learning experience for both of you.

WHAT YOU SHOULD LEARN

What you learn at conformation class will depend to some extent on the quality of classes available to you. In any decent class, you can teach your dog to be comfortable in close quarters with other dogs and people. If you find that the instructor doesn't have much to offer you in the way of solid information, you can concentrate on teaching your dog to bait in the ring. It may sound strange, but many dogs are so keyed up in the presence of all those other dogs that they have no interest in food, even tidbits that they would beg for hours for at home. So, settling them into their surroundings enough to begin showing interest in bait is a valuable accomplishment.

Never let anyone tell you that you must correct a dog mercilessly for moving a foot when in a stacked pose. Again, this is a sure path to crushing the spirit of a dog. In the ring, attitude is vital. How many times have you heard a judge say, "He just asked for it"? Presented with an entire class of superb dogs, the judge will give the nod to the one that sparkles. If you have a dog that dances in the ring, treasure that attitude and do nothing to stifle it.

In a good-to-mediocre class, you should receive pointers on better ways to move and stack your dog. Maybe you never realized that the way

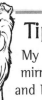

Tips from the Pros

My mother, when I was in Junior Showmanship, used to prop a mirror up along the house and then there were big sliding doors, and I would run back and forth with the dog so I could see myself moving the dog in the mirror and glass doors. Lots of people take on a bent posture when moving, especially when starting out, and it just doesn't look good.

—Taffe McFadden, AKC professional handler

you use your leash annoys the dog by hitting her in the ear. Or you're moving a little too fast or too slow. Or you need to learn to move in a straighter line to avoid throwing your dog off stride (a common problem with novices).

One skill you might learn in a class is the "handler's glide." Most good handlers do not bounce up and down a lot when they jog or run to gait their dogs. They keep their knees bent and glide, in a less exaggerated version of Groucho Marx's famous walk. It's an acquired skill.

In stacking, although each breed has its minor (or sometimes major) peculiarities, many of the basics are the same. Listen to whatever advice you are given about where to put your leash or if to take it off, how to hold a tail, where to place each foot, and on and on. The mechanics are important, but it's just as important for your dog to be happy. Keep both in mind.

Of course a class offers the opportunity to get to know others in the fancy. Some will be beginners like yourself, in which case you may find that you console each other over your gaffes in the ring and celebrate any ribbons won. Others may be old-timers, in class to acclimate a new dog to ring conditions. You won't know who these people are or if they might be future friends unless you talk to them. The social aspects of the fancy are very important.

But if you are lucky enough to find a really *good* conformation class, you can learn worlds more. You will still have to do plenty of study on your own, but a good instructor will point out each dog's strong points and show the handler how to accentuate them (without annoying a judge—judges do not like to be played for fools). The instructor will also discuss each dog's faults and how to minimize them. Don't daydream when it's not your turn.

Pay careful attention to every comment. This exercise can speed your ability to discern the good and bad in dogs, to have an "eye" for dogs.

THE POINTS OF THE DOG

The points of the dog that can be discussed generally follow the points of the breed standard and might go something like this: general appearance; size, proportion, substance; head; neck, topline, body; forequarters; hindquarters; coat; color and markings; gait; and temperament.

General appearance is one of the most important aspects of a dog. All the parts must fit well together to create a pleasing picture. A dog with the most perfect head but a neck that's a little too short and a body that's a little too long may look entrancing from the front, but will seem "off" from the side. A dog with not as fine a head but better proportion overall will probably win over the dog with the wonderful head (see figure 8.1).

There are so many ways that all the parts of the dog *cannot* come together well. If the length and angles of the front legs don't match the

Figure 8.1. By looking up at the handler, this dog makes the neck appear shorter and flings the ears upright rather than bent near the tip.

Talking Dog

Crabbing, or *sidewinding*—the two are pretty much synonymous—is one of the most common movement faults in dogs. When viewed from the rear, the dog appears to be moving slightly sideways (hence the terms). The rear legs are swiveled to the outside or the inside of the front legs. Although well-built dogs will sometimes do this out of habit, it can be the sign of a dog whose rear reach exceeds its front. To avoid having the back feet interfere with the front feet, the dog cants its body sideways and moves the rear on a different track from the front. It can also be a far-too-frequent sign of poor handling, with the handler pulling the dog from a straight-ahead gait.

length and angles of the back legs, the dog will have some sort of movement fault. These go by a confusing plethora of names—*clipping, crabbing, daisy skimming, padding, paddling, sidewinding,* and lots of others.

Size, proportion, and substance can be crucial. In some breeds, there are maximum and/or minimum height limits, and a dog can be dismissed from the ring if *measured out*. The judge or other exhibitors can request measurement of a dog. In the UKC, Toy Fox Terriers are routinely weighed before each show and must be within stated limits.

"Head" is the major focus of some breed standards and seemingly of minor importance in others. The Saluki standard, one of the shortest overall, gives just four lines to description of the head, while the Boxer standard takes nearly an entire page to describe the head. Even in the General Appearance section, the standard states, "The chiseled head imparts to the Boxer a unique individual stamp. . . . The broad, blunt muzzle is the distinctive feature, and great value is placed upon its being of proper form and balance with the skull. In judging the Boxer, first consideration is given to general appearance, to which attractive coloring and arresting style contribute. Next is overall balance with special attention devoted to the head." So if our mythical dog with the perfect head were a Boxer, it's possible he or she would win out over a more complete dog, especially if the judge was a "head freak." Knowing which are the most important points of your breed standard—head in Boxers, but "expression" in Bichon Frises—and which judges concentrate intensely on those points can help your career.

And so it goes, through all the points of the dog. A good conformation class (or breeder or mentor) should be able to identify the best aspects of your dog and explain ways you can show them to best advantage. Say your dog has a good head and a fabulous neck but an imperfect tail set. If your dog will hold a stack no matter where you place yourself, then stack your dog and move to stand directly behind his or her tail. The judge walking up the line will get the dog's head and neck full on and have a slightly obstructed view of the tail end. This is not going to fool the judge, but it will create a better first impression, and first impressions are powerful things. There is a plethora of handling tricks like this, and everyone else uses them, so you may as well too.

Good instruction can also help you in gaiting the dog. There are so many variables—speed, loose or tight lead, even which lead to use, your own way of moving. And exactly how you do things could be different depending on whether you are moving away from or coming toward the judge (see figure 8.2).

Figure 8.2. Note the looseness in the lead as this handler gaits her dog.

Tips from the Pros

Follow the instructor's directions. Don't get angry at or argue with the instructor if the instructor corrects you. Practice daily at home.
—Sharon Irons Strempski, AKC exhibitor and breeder of Affenpinschers

OTHER LEARNING OPPORTUNITIES

Conformation classes and mentors aren't your only hopes for learning more of the intricacies of the sport.

Seminars can be an excellent opportunity. Often they are presented by judges or professional handlers with years of experience in the show ring. Some are given lecture style and some are hands-on, you-and-your-dog affairs. Either is valuable, but the latter can gain you priceless advice.

There are also sometimes breed-specific seminars, often given for the benefit of judges wishing to know more about the finer points of a breed. (Note that judges must apply for approval for each separate breed they wish to judge.) If one of these should come up for your breed, go to it if at all possible. Some of it may be in a seemingly foreign language beyond your current understanding, but much of it will be useful, plus you will have an opportunity to meet other people truly dedicated to your breed.

So how do you know when a seminar will be coming to your area? Belonging to your local kennel club will almost guarantee that you are kept updated on any doggy educational opportunities. Upcoming seminars are also listed in the *AKC Events Calendar* and in the UKC's *Bloodlines* magazine.

Fancy That!

There is even an online event organizer that specializes in dog-related seminars and conferences. You can find it at www.puppyworks.com.

Seminars are not inexpensive. Some can be downright break-the-bank expensive. If it means giving up a couple of weekends of showing (but not giving up dinner for the month), go to the seminar. You won't have the chance all that often. There are dog shows nearly every weekend, and seminars are few and far between. You never know what might happen. Your dog could be one the presenter especially likes, and you will get lots of attention and advice. Or you could be just another face in the crowd to the presenter but meet another novice who becomes your best dog show buddy. There are lots of possibilities for good things happening. At the very least, you will have the chance to meet others, most probably from your local area, involved in the fancy, at all levels of expertise.

While you're waiting for a seminar, there are videos and books. In fact, there are a *lot* of videos and books. Before you buy a lot of things sight unseen, see what your library has available. Then check out your local bookstores. It's always better to be able to flip through a book and see if it seems useful to you. Some stores even have sample copies of videotapes you can run.

If there's no place nearby that has the books you think you might want, try Amazon.com. For many books, Amazon provides synopses from the publisher and other sources, as well as reviews from readers. At least you can get some idea about how others have felt about the book. There are other online sources, but Amazon often supplies the most information about each book. You can also search for other dog book sites—there's quite a variety.

You can also mail-order books. Often if you order through a catalog, you can return any items that don't measure up. Direct Book Service offers the *Dogwise Catalog* (see appendix E). They also handle videos. And they also have a Web site at www.dogwise.com.

Remember

○ Any class—as long as the dogs are kept happy—is better than none.
○ Ask for recommendations if you have a choice of classes.
○ Go and watch how a class is conducted and if it seems right for you.
○ A class should at the least acclimate your dog to the conditions of the show ring.
○ A really good class can explain the finer points, both good and bad, of your dog.
○ Classes provide the chance to meet others in the fancy.
○ Seminars can be very valuable learning experiences, and you should attend those in your area.
○ Books and videos can be helpful or not—choose carefully.

Anatomy Class

Although some faults are obvious in a stacked dog, many more can show up when the dog is moved, or *gaited*. Understanding how the dog's physical parts come together to create movement will help you analyze the gait of your own and other dogs. Realizing your dog's strengths or weaknesses when moving can also help you show more effectively.

In the conformation ring, dogs are shown at a trot. The trot can be shown effectively within the confines of the ring, and it is considered the gait of choice for demonstrating coordination and the interrelationship of the bones and muscles. For some breeds, the trot is the natural preferred gait; for others, it is not.

To understand what makes good (and bad) movement, you have to understand anatomy. Learning canine anatomy will also acquaint you with many of the mysterious terms you will hear around the ring, such as *hocks, stifle,* and *shoulder layback.*

Tips from the Pros

A lot of people forget about how their legs are supposed to be straight up and down and underneath them. There's no way a dog can give you a good topline and look good if the legs are not positioned under him.

—Tom Glassford, former professional handler, AKC rep

BODIES IN MOTION

Somewhere in a science class in the course of your education, you probably heard this one: "A body in motion tends to stay in motion; a body at rest tends to stay at rest." Movement is actually a balancing act, a delicate compromise of propulsion and equilibrium. In the case of a dog at a trot, the balancing act takes place on two feet or, at times, one foot. In a further complication, the front feet and back feet have to coordinate smoothly to avoid interfering with each other.

Even a novice exhibitor should realize that different breeds move differently at the trot. A breed developed to chase gazelles on the open plains will not, and should not, trot exactly the same as a breed meant to follow vermin down their holes. Exhibitors and judges need to keep a breed's function in mind when critiquing movement.

You may have heard another popular phrase applied to dogs: "Form follows function." Function dictates structure, which dictates movement. Variations in shoulders, feet, hocks, stifles, even ribcages, necks, and tails, can mean a longer reach, stronger drive, more level topline, and on and on. Some combinations promote endurance, others favor agility, and some result in flat-out speed. An Alaskan Malamute designed for speed would not look like an Alaskan Malamute—it would look like a Siberian Husky—and would not be capable of the heavy freighting for which it was developed.

Many breed standards are woefully lacking in any description of desired gait, and sometimes even of the major contributing anatomical components. A standard that goes into great detail about color, coat, and head says nothing about what the dog is actually meant to be. All breeds could benefit from a clear description of desired gait based on the structure required for the dog to perform the work it was meant to do. Perhaps then breeders would not be striving for a one-size-fits-all, ring-attractive flashy, and far-reaching trot.

Talking Dog

A common fault of the front legs is *out at elbows*. A rib cage that is too wide forces the shoulder blade to slope outward too much and the elbows stand out from the body. In reaction, the dog also usually *toes in*, adopting a pigeon-toed stance.

THE FRONT HALF OF THE DOG

Before we can see how the dog works, we need to know how the dog is built. See figure 9.1 for the skeletal structure. Refer back to it as necessary throughout this section.

In many ways, movement of the front half of the dog hinges on the shoulder. Obviously, all the bones of the forelegs descend from the shoul-

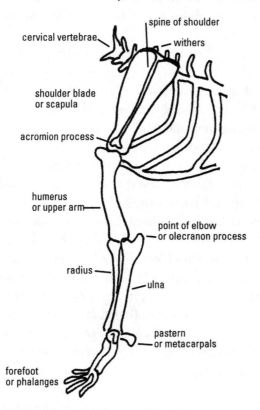

Figure 9.1. Skeleton of the forequarters

der blade, and most of the muscles attach to some portion of the shoulder blade.

Because the dog lacks a collarbone, the shoulder blade is held in place only by muscles. To stabilize this arrangement, the dog developed the acromion process. If you feel down the shoulder blade, you can feel this bony prominence at its lower end. Like a hub on a wheel, this outcropping provides greater room for attachment of the heavy muscling that holds the joint together.

Muscles run both over and under the scapula, forward into the neck, and back over the ribs. They hold the shoulder blade tight to the body, turn the neck from side to side, and lift and extend the forelegs.

To assist in smooth movement of the shoulder blade, the first four ribs of most breeds are flattened at the sides. Ribs begin to curve outward, or "spring," only from the fourth rib on. Dogs built for high-speed performance, such as the sighthounds, rely on free rotation of the shoulder blade. Observed from the front, these dogs are markedly narrower over the area of the forelegs, widening out from the fifth rib back to provide the necessary lung capacity for intense activity.

If you could view the dog's skeletal structure from the front, you would see that the shoulder blades slope outward from top to bottom. Too much or too little outward tilt can interfere with effective movement.

The shoulder blade is also set at an angle to the vertical when viewed from the side, with the bottom more forward than the top to a greater or lesser degree. Exhibitors should be aware that this angle can be changed *slightly* by different positions of the dog's head and front feet. If the head is raised and the feet are set forward of their normal at-rest position, the brachicephalicus muscle is tensed and the bottom of the shoulder blade is rotated forward. (The top of the shoulder blade maintains position, acting as a pivot point.) Although the change is slight, it might impart a degree or two of apparent slope to a shoulder blade.

In most dogs, the shoulder blade can rotate approximately 15 degrees forward and 15 degrees backward. Sighthounds

Fancy That!

The AKC does not write breed standards. Each national parent club writes the standard for their breed and submits it to the AKC. The parent club is free to change the standard to make it clearer or to actually make changes in how the ideal breed specimen should look.

require considerably more rotation for their ground-covering gallop and have been shown to be capable of as much as 70 degrees of combined rotation, compared to the 30 degrees of the less gallop-oriented breeds. Sighthounds also usually have steeper shoulders with less layback, which is good for sprinting but not endurance trotting.

"Layback" is discussed frequently around the ring and in conformation classes. Misinformation abounds. Many fanciers aren't even clear on what points are used to estimate layback. See figure 9.2 and read on to learn.

Use your hands to feel for the point of the shoulder (the leading edge of the humerus) and the spine at the top of the shoulder blade. Visualize a line between these two points and compare it to vertical. The angle between the two is the degree of layback. Although you may read breed stan-

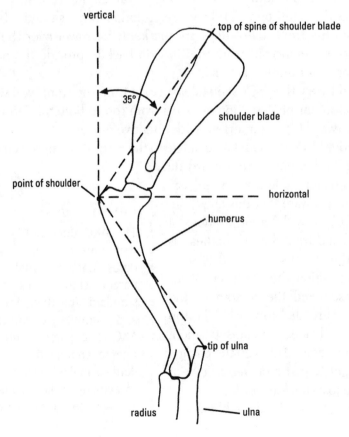

Figure 9.2. Estimating shoulder layback

dards specifying a layback of 45 degrees, this is rarely attained in real life. Most dogs range from 20 degrees (for a very straight, upright shoulder) to 40 degrees (for a very well laid back shoulder).

A steep shoulder means that to keep the hind legs from interfering with the front while at the trot, the dog will either take short steps (exhibiting lack of reach) or will raise the front off the ground to lengthen the stride (giving an up and down motion to the withers). Neither of these strategies produces the most efficient endurance trot. But steep shoulder blades are useful for speed (antelope and cheetah share this characteristic with the sighthounds) and effective for pulling heavy loads. The Alaskan Malamute compromises between an efficient trot and weight-pulling ability with moderately laid back shoulders. The Siberian Husky, focused more on speed than heavy loads, has shoulders that are well laid back.

The breeds requiring an endurance trot to do their work—many of the herding breeds, such as the Bearded Collie and Shetland Sheepdog, the Dalmatian meant to trot alongside carriages, and numerous of the sporting breeds—are all noted for standards requiring well-laid back shoulders. Some even specify that mythical 45 degrees. This greater angle increases reach, minimizes up and down movement of the withers (which is wasted energy), and decreases pounding as each foot contacts the ground.

No dog should be penalized for failing to exhibit an endurance trot if it is not a breed intended to do its work while trotting freely.

Because the forelegs carry most of the dog's weight, they are mainly columnar, to provide good support. Of course, a mental picture of a Bulldog will spring to mind to contradict this. But the Bulldog was specifically bred to be impossible to bowl over, with an abnormally wide base of support and low center of gravity. Form follows function.

The elbow joint, where the humerus, radius, and ulna come together, is extremely stable. When in a straight upright position, it is nearly locked, reliably providing support.

Where the elbow falls in relation to the body may also be dictated by function. For most breeds, the elbow is visible just below the lower line of the chest. But in dogs that go down holes and dig, the elbow sets higher, above the level of the chest, or keel. This allows the Dachshund to rest on the chest, with the front legs completely free to dig.

Many of the Terriers were also developed to go to ground in pursuit of vermin. Some of them have short legs, but some have only the humerus, or upper arm, shortened. Not only does this assist in digging in holes, but it is also responsible for the "Terrier front." The entire front leg appears to be one straight line, swinging like a pendulum from the shoulder. Although this is pretty, and correct for the Terriers, it would be woefully inadequate for, say, a draft breed or an athletic working breed.

In the average trotting dog, the angle formed by visualizing a line from the point of the shoulder to the tip of the ulna and comparing it to a horizontal line drawn from the point of the shoulder will combine with the shoulder layback angle to total 90 degrees. So in our illustration of estimating shoulder layback, this second angle would be 55 degrees.

Continuing down the leg, the bottoms of the radius and ulna connect through some small bones to the four metacarpals. Though people don't think of it this way, the metacarpals, also known as the *pastern,* are the major portion of the dog's foot. The pads on which the dog stands are actually only the dog's toes.

The pastern should be angled to help absorb the shock of footfall when the dog is moving. Too little angle and the leg will be prone to "knuckling over," with the joint flexing in the opposite direction and straining the muscles. Too much angle and the pastern "breaks down," bending too far and forcing the muscles and ligaments, rather than the bones, to carry the weight of the dog's front. Breeds with large shoulder blades and long upper arms, such as the German Shepherd, require greater angle in their pasterns. A short pastern provides an advantage in less expended energy to move the joint and contributes to endurance.

Finally, at the bottom, the phalanges, or toes, provide the base of support. Once again, different functions call for different forms. A long *hare foot* is good for bursts of speed and a bounding gait, while a compact *cat foot* is better for endurance and a smooth trotting gait. So the Doberman, a good endurance trotter, is known for dainty feet, while the speed-burner Saluki has long, elegant toes.

THE CONNECTION OF FRONT TO BACK

The midsection of the dog transmits the drive and power of the hindquarters of the dog to the forequarters. It is also crucial to the coordination of front and rear movement.

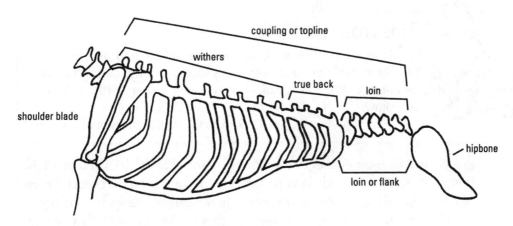

Figure 9.3. The connection of front to back

Terms used relating to this area have very specific anatomical meanings, although they are often used less than correctly. Study figure 9.3 and the following text.

The anatomical definition of *back* in the dog is four vertebrae between the withers and the loin. If you want to refer to the topside of the dog from the neck tailward, the terms to use are *backline* or *topline*.

From the last rib to the front edge of the pelvis at either side is the *loin* or *flank*. The length of this area—an important factor in determining gait—depends on the length of the overall body, the length and slant of the rib cage, and the tilt of the pelvis. The rearing muscles, essential for movement because the front must be lifted before the legs can move, are attached to the seven vertebrae of this section of the dog. Because there is no support from any other bones, at least a slight arch is necessary to impart structural strength. Even dogs supposed to exhibit a level topline can be felt to have a small arch through this section of the spine and should not be penalized for this necessary adaptation.

For efficient movement, the front, midsection, and rear portions of the dog must be in balance. Too short a loin impairs flexibility and restricts the gait. It's hard to picture a dog taller than it is long. But it's not hard to picture a dog appreciably longer than tall, though even the low-slung Corgi is not particularly long in the loin.

For a dog meant to trot, a longer body has advantages. The rear feet can have greater reach and drive without interfering with the front feet. But only

to a point. The most efficient movement requires that the back feet reach the front feet. Too long a body, and particularly too long a loin, prevents this and can result in a slack backline that bounces in movement, dissipating energy.

Most trotting dogs are rectangular, slightly longer than they are tall. This allows minor inequalities between the forequarters and hindquarters to be better balanced out, and gives the dog stamina at the trot.

THE REAR HALF OF THE DOG

Now we come to the remainder of the dog's anatomy. See figure 9.4 for the skeletal makeup of the canine hindquarters.

Just as the front half of the dog hinges on the shoulder, the rear half depends largely on the pelvis. The length and angle of the pelvis play a large part in the effectiveness of the rear legs' movement.

Length of the pelvis can sometimes be judged by the projection of the ischium beyond the set of the tail, often especially visible in the Terriers. A prominent ischium indicates a longer pelvis. A longer pelvis can serve as the base for stronger muscling of the hindquarters.

The angle of the pelvis is measured from the horizontal. Here, an angle of about 30 degrees is considered average and effective for a good trot. A steeper angle, say 45 degrees, is more effective at providing lift to the front end of the dog, good for making quick spinning turns or running uphill. But the steeper slope impedes the backward reach of the hind legs. Dogs with flatter-than-average pelvises (angles of less than 30 degrees) have an extended backward reach. So, the angle of the pelvis can be assessed by watching the rearward extension of the legs while the dog is trotting (see figure 9.5).

In the sighthounds, the hindquarters should be wider than the forequarters to allow the rear legs to reach past the front legs in their double-suspension gallop.

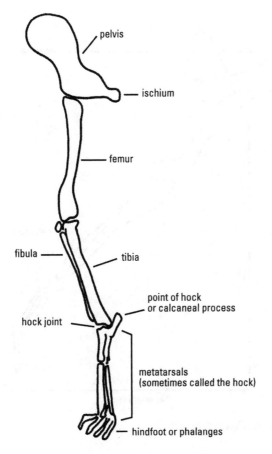

Figure 9.4. Skeleton of the hindquarters

The *croup* is the section of the topline above the rear legs, from behind the loin to the base of the tail. The angle of the croup does not impact gait, but does determine tail set. People will argue this point, but the problem is mainly one of semantics—the angle of the pelvis is instrumental in determining gait, but the angle of the croup is a separate issue.

Working down from the pelvis, the femur fits into the socket joint of the pelvis. This is the joint where hip dysplasia occurs, when the ball of the femur does not sit securely in the socket. Unlike the forequarters, the hindquarters are linked securely bone to bone. Because the joint is not sheathed entirely in muscle, the rear legs can rotate outward—the front legs cannot.

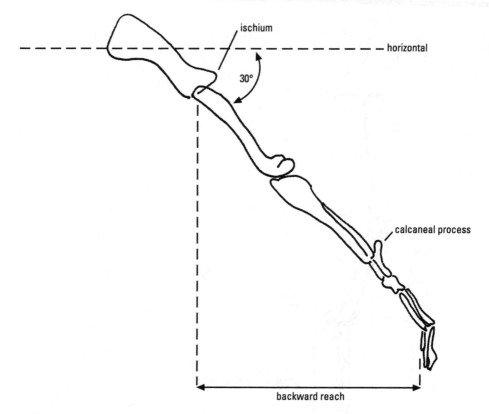

Figure 9.5. Pelvis slope and backward reach

The femur curves down to the knee, or stifle, joint. As with our own knees, this is a complex joint held together by ligaments. The angle of the connection of the femur to the tibia and fibula below should be roughly the same as the angle of the connection of the humerus to the shoulder blade when the dog is standing. This provides equal bases of support for the front and rear (see figure 9.6).

Because the rearing muscles attach at the stifle joint (and to the ischium), the angle of this joint is intimately related to function. A straighter joint provides more pulling power and greater efficiency in harness, so it is seen in breeds such as the Alaskan Malamute and the Bernese Mountain Dog. Well-angulated stifles, on the other hand, promote speed, leaping ability, and the flying trot of the German Shepherd.

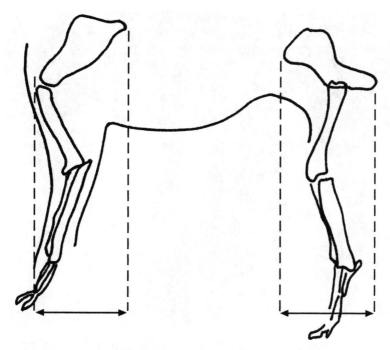

Figure 9.6. Equal bases of support

The tibia and fibula descending from the stifle joint are known collectively (and confusingly) as the *second thigh* or *lower thigh*. At their lower ends, these bones connect to the metatarsals in the hock joint. Note that the hock is the joint, not the straight section below the joint. You will hear the term "hock" used to refer to the metatarsals, as in "position the hock perpendicular to the ground," although this is not anatomically correct.

So, remembering that the hock is the joint, both its angle and its distance from the ground impact on the gait. Hocks far from the ground (meaning, in effect, long metatarsals), as seen in the cat and the Greyhound and Afghan Hound, are excellent for initial bursts of speed, but not so good for endurance. Low hocks (also referred to as "well let down") are better for endurance.

The hock joint must be well angled to produce a smooth trot and also to allow the rear legs to fold for traveling down tunnels. Most dog breeds have well-angled hocks. Chow Chows are an exception, and their unique stilted gait is a direct result of their nearly straight hocks. Bulldogs also have only slightly angled hock joints and have their own distinctive gait.

Figure 9.7. The hindquarters of a Boxer, also illustrating the equal bases of support front and rear, with the shoulder layback just visible.

At the rear of the hock joint, the calcaneal process juts up and is connected near the bottom of the femur by a muscle-tendon combination. When this arrangement pulls on the calcaneal process, the foot is pushed back on the ground. The length of the calcaneal process impacts on foot speed. A long calcaneal process (referred to as a *narrow hock*) means slower foot movement. But length of calcaneal process and height of hock from the ground can combine to provide a blend of speed and endurance. A longer calcaneal process can compensate, at least partially, for a high hock, offering increased endurance to go with speed.

Just as with the front legs, the metatarsals descend from the joint to the phalanges (see figure 9.7).

HEADS AND TAILS

Although not part of the propulsion system, the tail and the neck and head assembly do play a part in how the dog moves. The dog controls its center

Tips from the Pros

To be in balance, the most important thing is to teach your dog to go on a loose lead. A dog that's doing it on his own pulls it together and looks so much better.

—Bill McFadden, AKC professional handler

of gravity by raising and lowering the head and neck. Many standards give a nod to this, as for example the English Setter standard stating, "Long forward reach and strong rear drive with a lively tail and proud head carriage. Head may be carried slightly lower when moving to allow for greater reach of forelegs."

All the muscles used to move the leg forward are connected somewhere among the seven vertebrae of the neck. So position of the neck and head is strongly related to movement of the front legs.

This is a primary reason for showing a dog on a loose lead. Artificial faults can be created by forcing a dog's head up while gaiting, and a judge may suspect you of attempting to conceal actual faults with your actions.

The tail also serves as a stabilizing rudder. As the dog's speed increases and the head and neck lower, the tail often elevates, helping to shift the center of gravity forward. It can also provide lateral stability by moving side to side. According to one author of a book on canine gait, dogs lacking tails tend to stand wider in the rear to compensate for the lack of the balancing mechanism the tail provides.

NOT ALL DOGS WERE MEANT TO TROT

There has been a sad tendency, still occurring, to breed dogs for a "flashy" movement in the ring, a sort of generic "show trot." For many breeds this is simply *not* correct movement. An Afghan hound that trots like a Collie will not be able to perform the astounding ground-covering gallop representative of the breed.

So why are some people breeding for what is actually incorrect? Because it is rewarded in the ring far too frequently. There are many, many judges who know the breed standards well, abide by them in the ring, and judge what they see before them on the day. Others are bowled over by

Tips from the Pros

The trot is the normal gait seen in the show ring. It is a two-time movement and is the simplest of all. Moreover, it shows up faults more than any other gait. It is a free swinging movement from shoulders and hips; the elbows, stifles, hocks, pastern, and pads all play their part and coordinate perfectly with each other. . . . The well-proportioned dog is propelled along with equal propulsion by the fore limbs and the hind limbs. The gait should appear to be smooth and ef-fortless.

—Hilary Harmar, *Showing & Judging Dogs* (Arco, 1977)

flash and style and hand out ribbons for all the wrong reasons. Rather than changing a breed to suit these judges, exhibitors should avoid showing under them and stay true to their standard.

And, indeed, many standards should be given a serious look. Examin-ing old photographs of some breeds will show you how much they have

Figure 9.8. With a side view of this Boxer, you can see how the legs work in diagonal pairs, the left front and right rear driving while the right front and left rear are off the ground.

Watch Your Step

Old-time dog show enthusiasts hark back to a time when dogs were not raced around the ring but moved at a speed appropriate for their breed. Though some judges do ask handlers not to race, others seem to feel the need for speed and reward the flashiest dog.

changed, and not always for the better. A breed that cannot conceive or deliver on its own, such as the modern Bulldog, has been taken to an unhealthy extreme that would not exist in nature. A variety of veterinarians, breeders, anatomists, and judges agree that moderation and balance are key. Forgetting that form should follow function, we corrupt the natural symmetry and beauty of the dog.

For more on what the judge is looking for, and how to move a dog, see chapter 15.

Remember

○ Form follows function.
○ A breed should move appropriately for the work it was meant to do.
○ The correct slope of the shoulder blade is crucial to good movement of the front.
○ The midsection of the dog—the loin—coordinates front and rear movement and transmits power from the rear to the front.
○ All the angles of the rear leg, starting from the pelvic angle, impact movement of the rear.
○ The head, neck, and tail are used to change the center of gravity and keep the dog balanced.
○ Not all breeds should exhibit an endurance trot.

10

The $64,000 Pyramid

In This Chapter

○ The progression of the classes
○ Explanation of placements
○ Beyond the classes
○ Points and how you get them
○ The mathematics of a championship

Before you ever get to a show with a dog you've entered, under-stand this chapter. Without knowing when you should be ready to come back into the ring, you may miss an opportunity to shine. It isn't just the class winners that need to stand by, and people don't always have the time to give explicit instructions to an inexperienced novice.

THE PROGRESSION OF THE CLASSES

In chapter 19, we look at the classes offered by the various reg-istries. All of these classes are divided into dogs (males) and bitches (females). A show progresses through the classes in the same order every time (see figure 10.1).

The dogs always go first. Sounds terribly chauvinistic, and it is, at least to some degree. But the boys, being boys, would be very

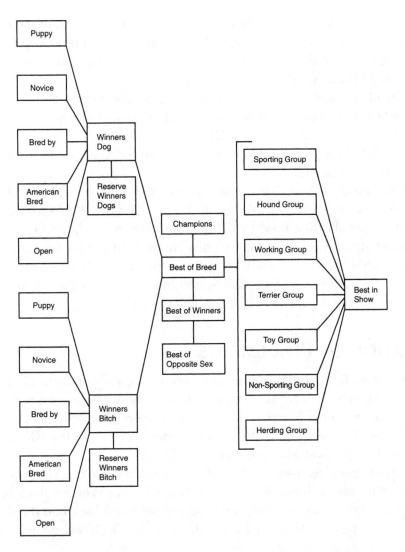

Figure 10.1. Chart of the progression of an AKC show

distracted if the girls went first and left their scent all over the ring. The girls, being girls, are more in control.

So, in an AKC show, the male Puppy classes go first, followed by the male Twelve- to Eighteen-Month class, male Novice class, male Bred-by Exhibitor class, male American-Bred class, and finally male Open class. (Note that there may not be entries for every class at a show—obviously a class with no entries will not be judged.) The winners of each of the classes are then brought back into the ring to be judged for Winners Dog. The entire progression of classes is then repeated for the females, then the winners are brought back in and judged for Winners Bitch.

Canada does it slightly differently, going Junior Puppy, Senior Puppy, 12–18-Month, Canadian-Bred, Bred-by Exhibitor, and Open. (At Specialty shows, a Veterans class can follow Open.)

At a UKC show, the classes simply go from the youngest to the oldest. Again, the boys go first.

The American Rare Breed Association (ARBA) starts with Six Months to Nine Months, then Nine Months to Fifteen Months. Novice comes next (but it's optional), then Bred-by Exhibitor, American-Bred, and Open. They also offer Breed Club Class and Certificate of Aptitude for Championship in the United States, which will be further explained in chapter 19.

The FCI offers only four classes, and the first one of these is optional. They are Intermediate, Open, Working, and Champion.

EXPLANATION OF PLACEMENTS

In each class, there are four placement awards, logically enough, First, Second, Third, and Fourth. As we just explained, the first-place winners from each class are called back to compete for Winners Dog (after all the male classes) and Winners Bitch (after all the female classes). In the UKC, these are called simply Best Male and Best Female.

If your dog placed second in a class, do not wander off. You may have further duties to perform. Should the Winners Dog or Winners Bitch be the first-place dog from your class, your dog will be called back into the ring to compete for Reserve Winners Dog or Bitch (or, in UKC, Reserve Best Male and Reserve Best Female).

Only the Winners Dog and Winners Bitch earn any championship points. The Reserve Winners are chosen in the event that the Winner is not entitled to the points. The dog may have been entered in the wrong class, the dog brought into the ring might not be the dog listed in the catalog, or a clerical error may have occurred. For whatever reason, the points would then be awarded to the Reserve Winner. You certainly wouldn't want to miss such an opportunity.

Once the Winners and Reserve Winners have been chosen, only the two Winners need remain at ringside. In AKC, they will now be brought back again to compete against each other as well as any champions (male and female) that are entered. From this elite group, the judge will choose Best of Breed (or Best of Variety), Best of Winners, and Best of Opposite Sex.

Best of Breed (or Variety) is awarded first. In the judge's opinion, this is the single best example of the breed (or variety) in the ring on that day. Only this dog (male or female) will continue on into group judging, as a representative of his or her breed or variety. You will sometimes see Best of Breed shortened to BOB.

Best of Winners is chosen next. Only the Winners Dog or Winners Bitch can take this award, so "better" of winners would actually be grammatically correct. But Best of Winners it is.

Finally, Best of Opposite Sex is chosen. If Best of Breed is a male, Best of Opposite Sex will be female. It could be the Winners Bitch or one of the champions. Of course, if Best of Breed is a female, Best of Opposite Sex will be a male.

At AKC specialties, the judge might have the option of selecting one or more dogs for a Judge's Award of Merit. This is an acknowledgment that there are more dogs worthy of recognition than there are traditional placements.

Fancy That!

Ribbon and rosette colors are mandated by the registries. For regular classes, AKC uses
- First—Blue
- Second—Red
- Third—Yellow
- Fourth—White
- Winners—Purple
- Reserve Winners—Purple and White
- Best of Winners—Blue and White
- Best of Breed or Variety—Purple and Gold
- Best of Opposite Sex—Red and White

Talking Dog

As far as most folks in the United States are concerned, "CH" means the dog is an AKC champion. But "CH" can also indicate a UKC champion, with GR CH referring to a UKC Grand Champion. A dog with AKC and CKC championships is referred to as Am Can CH, and a dog with an FCI championship is an Int CH.

Things proceed differently in the UKC. The Best Male and Best Female are judged for Best of Winners, who then must stand by while two other classes take place. The Champion of Champions class is open only to dogs that have already earned their UKC Champion title. All male and female Champions are judged, the top dog is awarded Champion of Champions, and a second dog is designated Reserve Champion of Champions. The Champion of Champions then stands by with the Best Male and Best Female while the Grand Champions class is judged. (To understand how to earn this title, see chapter 26.) This class, open only to Grand Champions, is held simply to choose the best of the Grand Champions to go on and compete against Best of Winners and Champion of Champions for the title of Best of Breed.

BEYOND THE CLASSES

Once breed judging (the classes) is finished, group judging begins—that is, if there is going to be group judging. AKC specialties and UKC shows are often single-breed affairs. For these shows, judging ends with Best of Breed (or Variety), Best of Winners, and Best of Opposite Sex.

For shows with group judging, the starting time for group judging is listed in the catalog, but the order of the groups is often left to be announced on the day of the show, based on how judges finish their classes. Some other long-established shows have their own schedules. Two-day shows often hold group judging until the afternoon of the second day. Westminster holds group judging in the evening of both days. Whenever the judging is done, the Best of Breed (or Variety) dogs come together to compete against the other breed representatives in their group.

The AKC uses seven groups—Sporting, Terriers, Hounds, Working, Toy, Non-Sporting, and Herding. Other registries may use slightly different schemes. See appendix C for a complete listing of breeds and their groups. The UKC rarely uses group judging at all.

Tips from the Pros

Learn the rules! You should know what classes go when, the order of competition, the point system, etc. If you want to play the game, you have to know the rules, just like any other sport.
                                —Karen A. Brancheau, UKC exhibitor and breeder

In the groups, the judge awards Group First, Second, Third, and Fourth. Any group award is an honor, but only the Group Firsts come back to compete for Best in Show. One dog is chosen for the honor of Best in Show. No other placements are made.

POINTS AND HOW YOU GET THEM

Championships are based on points. Different registries award points differently and add them up to a championship differently, but the basic idea is the same.

The AKC issues a new Schedule of Points each year. The country is broken down into regions. The number of points awarded are based on the number of dogs competing, with the number varying in the different regions and according to the popularity of a breed. A relatively rare breed, such as the Flat-Coated Retriever, for example, will require fewer dogs competing than a more popular breed, such as Cocker Spaniels, for the same number of points. A region such as California, with large show entries as the norm, will require more dogs than a less populated region such as Wyoming for the same number of points.

A sample Schedule of Points is shown in table 10.1. Notice that it will take at least 13 Golden Retrievers to make 2 points in dogs (15 in California—numbers may be different in other regions). If there are 13–21 male Goldens entered (and shown—only dogs actually showing count toward the totals), it will be a 2-point show. It only takes four English Setters to make the same 2 points (five in California).

The UKC uses a simpler system, with only two point schedules. Point Schedule 1 applies to all breeds without Varieties, and Point Schedule 2 is for breeds with Varieties (see table 10.2).

If your dog wins more than his or her class, you add together the points for the wins. For example, if your female Keeshond won the Veteran class, went on to take Best Female of Show, and capped it off with Best of Show, she would earn 10 points for winning the class, 15 points for Best Female, and 10 points for Best of Show, for a total of 35 points.

Canada uses an incredibly simple system. Table 10.3 shows the CKC's complete point schedule.

The AKC and CKC schemes for points beyond class winners are less straightforward. The Winners Dog and Winners Bitch both win points

Table 10.1. Sample AKC Schedule of Points (Division 8: Colorado, Idaho, Montana, North Dakota, Oregon, South Dakota, Utah, Washington, Wyoming; Division 9: California)

D = Dog B = Bitch	1 point		2 points		3 points		4 points		5 points	
	D	B	D	B	D	B	D	B	D	B
DIVISION 8										
Retrievers (Flat-coated)	2	2	3	4	6	7	7	8	10	9
Retrievers (Golden)	3	4	13	14	22	23	32	35	50	56
Retrievers (Labrador)	3	4	12	14	21	24	31	42	50	75
Setters (English)	2	2	4	5	7	8	8	10	10	15
Setters (Irish)	2	3	6	9	10	16	14	20	21	28
Spaniels (Cocker) Black	2	2	5	6	7	10	9	13	12	18
Spaniels (Cocker) Parti	2	2	6	6	9	10	11	12	16	15
DIVISION 9										
Retrievers (Flat-coated)	2	2	4	6	6	9	9	11	14	15
Retrievers (Golden)	4	6	15	18	25	30	34	38	52	54
Retrievers (Labrador)	3	4	11	14	19	23	42	59	84	126
Setters (English)	2	2	5	7	7	12	12	19	20	33
Setters (Irish)	2	3	7	8	11	13	16	21	26	36
Spaniels (Cocker) Black	2	2	5	6	7	9	9	12	13	17
Spaniels (Cocker) Parti	2	2	5	7	7	11	9	14	13	20

based on how many dogs and bitches compete in their class. These points are theirs to keep, but they could gain even more.

If either Winners goes on to take Best of Breed, the champions of both sexes competing are counted as dogs defeated, in addition to the dogs from the regular classes. This could result in more points being awarded. Similarly, if either Winners takes Best of Opposite Sex, the entered champions of the same sex are counted in figuring the points to be awarded.

Table 10.2. Sample UKC Schedule of Points

Point Schedule #1—All Breeds Without Varieties

Classes	Points Awarded for Win
Puppy (6 mo.–1 yr.)	10
Junior (1–2 yr.)	10
Senior (2–3 yr.)	10
Veteran (3+ yr.)	10
Breeder Handler	10
Best Male	15
Best Female	15
Reserve Best Male	0
Reserve Best Female	0
Best of Winners	10

Point Schedule #2—All Breeds with Varieties

Classes	Points Awarded for Win
Puppy (6 mo.–1 yr.)	5
Junior (1–2 yr.)	5
Senior (2–3 yr.)	5
Veteran (3+ yr.)	5
Breeder Handler	5
Best Male of Variety	8
Best Female of Variety	8
Best Male	10
Best Female	10
Reserve Best Male	0
Reserve Best Female	0
Best of Winners	12

Table 10.3. Sample CKC Schedule of Points

Dogs Competing	1	2	3–5	6–9	10–12	13+
Points Allocated	0	1	2	3	4	5

One of the Winners will definitely be named Best of Winners, and this too could have an impact on the number of points. It's often said that the Best of Winners will "take the bitch's (or the dog's) points." This is misleading. No one "takes" anyone else's points. If, say, the entry of bitches was

Watch Your Step

Only the FCI specifies a minimum age higher than the age for entering a show in order to earn championship points. Only dogs at least 15 months old can earn a CAC or CACIB. The AKC has, in fact, gained something of a reputation for creating "puppy champions" who never go on to win as adults.

small, but the entry of dogs was large, the Winners Bitch may win only 1 point, while the Winners Dog wins three. Now say that the Winners Bitch goes Best of Winners. She is now deemed to have beaten every dog competing in the classes by beating the best of them, the Winners Dog. She therefore receives the higher number of points—3—the same as the Winners Dog. The Winners Dog still receives his 3 points as well. They are not stolen by the bitch. In the CKC, all the dogs defeated directly or indirectly are counted up to determine the number of points awarded.

Following the same idea, if a Winners Dog or Winners Bitch goes on to take a Group First in AKC competition, thus beating the winners of every breed in the group, the Group First receives the highest number of points available to any of the breeds in the group. A Winners Dog or Winners Bitch who takes Best in Show is awarded the highest points available to any breed taking part in the show.

The CKC has another table to offer for figuring points from group placements (see table 10.4). All placements, first through fourth, might earn points.

THE MATHEMATICS OF A CHAMPIONSHIP

With the AKC, a dog requires 15 points to become a champion. But of course it's not that simple—at least two of the wins must be "majors," under two different judges.

A major is a show where at least 3 points will be awarded. There are 3-, 4-, and 5-point majors, all spelled out in the Schedule of Points. Because the points are based on the number of dogs competing (not just entered), and the major is necessary for the championship, you can see how impor-

Table 10.4. CKC Group Points

Number of Dogs Competing at Group Level	Points for Dogs Placed			
	First	Second	Third	Fourth
13+	5	4	3	2
10–12	4	3	2	1
6–9	3	2	1	1
5	2	1	1	1
4	2	1	1	0
3	2	1	0	0
2	1	0	0	0
1	0	0	0	0

tant it is to compete if you have entered (unless you have a truly serious reason, such as medical necessity). Pulling your dog could *break the major* and rob some dog of the chance to achieve the last major win he or she needs for a championship. Someday, that dog could be yours!

The UKC, with many more points available from a single show, requires a dog to earn at least 100 points under no fewer than three different UKC judges. The dog must also win at least two Best Male or Best Female of Shows, under two different judges.

The CKC requires at least 10 championship points earned under at least three different judges. No matter how many dogs a winner defeats, no more than 5 points may be awarded in a single show.

Remember

○ Classes always run in the same order, and males always go first.
○ First-place, and sometimes second-place, dogs from the classes will have further showing to do.
○ Most registries offer group judging.
○ In the AKC, points are based on number of dogs competing, in accord with schedules based on popularity of a breed and region of the country.
○ AKC championships require major wins—show your dog if you have entered, or you may break the major.

11

Taking It on the Road

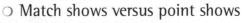

In This Chapter

- ○ Match shows versus point shows
- ○ How to find shows
- ○ Choosing a show
- ○ Managing your bookings

You've conditioned, socialized, practiced, and groomed. Your dog is the picture of health and well-being, and you're pretty sure you can survive in the ring without passing out. You're ready to take it on the road and enter a show!

You'll need to know when and where upcoming shows are, of course. And you can't enter them all, so you'll need some way to choose. See chapter 19 for how to actually enter a show once you choose one.

MATCH SHOWS VERSUS POINT SHOWS

We explained about the various sorts of match and point shows in chapter 1. Here we will consider which you should enter.

If you have only been practicing on your own, it would be wise to enter at least a couple of match shows. No matter how hard you may try, you cannot duplicate the show experience without rings and judges and other exhibitors and spectators. Match shows are for your benefit as much as your dog's.

You can certainly be pleased if your dog wins a ribbon at a match, but don't take any wins or losses too seriously. The judges at matches are often there to gain experience, the same as you. Instead, concentrate on getting the feel of the ring, making your dog comfortable, and trying to control your own nerves. Before and after your own time in the ring, watch how others perform. Don't be shy about talking to other exhibitors. You may be lucky enough to run across a long-time exhibitor who has brought some puppies for practice and could be invaluable to your learning experience. Or you may start a friendship that will last through the coming years. People are generally more relaxed at match shows, though you may find that they leave early if there is no group judging to keep them there.

Don't be in too much of a rush to enter the real thing! Entry fees at points shows are considerably higher—you want to be ready to get your money's worth. But much more important, others form impressions of you and your dog every time you appear before judges in these serious shows. You could easily give yourself a bad name through sheer inexperience. You might also disrupt another handler in the ring—an innocent mistake on your part, but one that may not be forgiven. It pays to be as prepared as you possibly can be.

Fancy That!

The AKC uses a completely different set of colors for ribbons awarded at match shows or for nonregular classes at points shows.
- First—rose
- Second—brown
- Third—light green
- Fourth—gray
- Special Prize— green with pink edges
- Best of Breed—orange
- Best in Match— pink and green
- Best of Opposite Sex— lavender

HOW TO FIND SHOWS

Dog shows are put on by licensed and member kennel clubs and breed clubs all across the country and world. For smaller all-breed or specialty shows, some clubs use a show secretary to handle the paperwork. This may be a member of their own club or someone they hire locally. But many clubs use a licensed superintendent to handle the masses of paperwork associated with these events. These superintendents handle printing and distribution of the premium list, taking the entries, printing the catalog, reporting the show results to the kennel club, and all the other myriad details associated with running a dog show.

Some AKC show superintendents are now online, and you can visit their sites not only for lists of upcoming shows, but also for judging panels, premium lists, and results of already-completed shows. Right now, Jack Onofrio Dog Shows is at www.onofrio.com, Jim Rau Dog Shows is at www.raudogshows.com/rau1.html, Roy Jones Dog Shows is at www.royjonesdogshows.com/, and MB-F shows can be found at www.infodog.com. Some sites also take advertising (see chapter 26 for more on advertising).

You can also learn about upcoming shows in many of the dog magazines. All UKC shows must be listed in the UKC magazine *Bloodlines*. The AKC lists shows in the *Events Calendar*, containing *all* AKC events, including seminars you might find useful. The more general dog magazines, *Dog World* and *Dog Fancy*, and training magazines, such as *Front & Finish* and *Off-Lead*, include show listings, though they may not be comprehensive. Some areas also have their own local events newspapers. Here in the Pacific Northwest, it's the *Eventer.* If you are taking classes, your instructor and classmates will likely know all the regular shows well in advance. Likewise if you belong to your local kennel club or breed club. Dog shows generally occupy the same weekend year after year, so are wonderfully predictable. Just as the Kentucky Derby is the first Saturday in May, your local cluster may be the first weekend in March. Some of the large dog food companies put out show calendars, listing the shows available each weekend (and more) throughout the year.

Fancy That!

A mere handful of show superintendents run nearly all the AKC points shows in the United States as a profit-making enterprise. You can write to one or more of them and ask to be put on their mailing list. They will send you the premium lists for upcoming shows. If you don't enter very many shows, your name will be removed from the mailing list. (See appendix A for a list of show superintendents.)

CHOOSING A SHOW

When you first start showing, you will probably be inclined to simply go to the shows closest to your home. And that's fine. But as you and your dog compete together, you will find that you have preferences.

Even before gaining much experience, you may realize that your dog prefers either outdoor or indoor shows. Many of the larger breeds naturally prefer being outdoors on grass. It's more familiar to them, they have better traction for gaiting, and to many, it's an enjoyable walk in the park. Some of the toy breeds, who spend more of their time indoors and rarely set foot on grass for fear of dirtying their luxurious coats, are nervous in the great outdoors and prefer indoor shows.

Indoors there is generally less space, much more noise, and possibly slippery floors. Be prepared for all of these. You will have to work far in advance to desensitize your dog to sound and crowding. At the event, keep in mind that the mats you find in the ring are there to keep your dog from slipping. Don't hog them yourself.

Outdoors, of course, there is weather to contend with. Dog shows are *not* canceled because of adverse weather conditions, short of something as extraordinary as a tornado. Be prepared to keep your dog and yourself clean, warm, and dry.

With a little experience, and help from other exhibitors, you can begin to choose shows by their size and the competition you are likely to encounter. Maybe you know that a dog that's been beating you weekend after weekend is looking for a major and probably will skip that small show out in the mountains. Or friends may tell you that your fiercest competitor never goes on the "Raisin Circuit."

Tips from the Pros

For a novice exhibitor I would recommend showing at every possible show. Don't listen to others who tell you under whom to show or not to show until you have had a chance to feel things out for yourself. You and your dog both need the experience anyway.

—Lilian S. Barber, AKC exhibitor and breeder, author of *The New Complete Italian Greyhound*

Talking Dog

A series of shows on consecutive days in the same location is a *cluster*. A series of shows on consecutive days in the same general area is a *circuit*. Both often have nicknames of some sort. The Raisin Circuit is several shows in the Fresno, California, vicinity, an area known for, of course, raisins. The Turkey Circuit takes place every year around Thanksgiving in turkey-raising country.

CHOOSING A JUDGE

As you gain more experience, you may begin choosing among shows by who will be judging your breed. This information is included in premium lists.

You may not have any opinion of judges when you begin, but you will quickly form some. Try not to simply react to winning or losing. Each judge, being only human, has some detail of the breed standard that he or she considers a little more important. A judge could be a "movement freak," a "head man," a "coat specialist." He or she might focus on topline, angulation, expression, or "bravery." To try and figure out what a judge is looking for, you may want to make notes after each class. Consider the placements and try to understand what the judge saw in each of the chosen dogs. You will hear plenty of ringside comments on this subject, but don't take them as gospel. Unless you know and trust the source of the comments, form your own opinions.

If you are fortunate enough to attend a show where verbal critiques are made by the judge, pay close attention to as many as you can. Look at the dog as you listen to the judge's remarks, and try to see what he or she is talking about. Seminars where dogs are presented and discussed in much the same manner are also valuable.

As you gain experience in showing, watch judging, attend seminars, and talk to breeders and handlers, your "eye" will develop. You will learn to see details in dogs, both good and bad, that you would not have noticed before. You can make a better assessment of your competition and enjoy a fuller understanding of the judge's reasoning. Of course you aren't always going to agree with the decisions made by the judge. But whether you agree or not, you can better decipher what each judge is looking for and start to recognize preferences for certain types by certain judges.

Once you reach this point, you can begin to choose shows based on who is judging your breed. If your dog's head matches the breed standard down to the tiniest detail, but he or she is not as strong in other areas, showing under a judge who concentrates on heads will give you an improved chance of gaining a ribbon. This may sound a bit odd, even slightly dishonest somehow, but it's really just smart. You have nothing to do with a judge's predispositions—they exist whether you show your dog or not. Being aware of them and turning them to your advantage is just being a smart competitor. (Should you begin to consider breeding your dog, however, you must consider the whole dog, whether or not ribbons have been won and a championship or even multiple championships attained. Chapter 27 provides more information on breeding considerations.)

When you have gained some points toward your dog's championship, you will need to keep in mind the judges who awarded you those points. Nearly all the registries require some minimum number of judges who must award points before a championship can be attained. In the AKC, you could gain five times the necessary points, but if they are all from the same two judges, you still do not have a championship. There is no point going to more shows under the same judges unless you just like collecting ribbons.

The same consideration comes into play for AKC (or SKC or CKC) exhibitors who need a "major" to finish a champion. Some shows historically draw large entries and offer a good chance that the requisite number of dogs will be competing. Others don't. Ask your fellow exhibitors and classmates for advice.

MANAGING YOUR BOOKINGS

In some parts of the country, it seems there are shows to choose among nearly every

Fancy That!

The UKC uses somewhat different colors from AKC for their placement ribbons, as follows:

- First—blue
- Second—red
- Third—green
- Fourth—yellow
- Best in Show—purple, gold, white
- Reserve Best in Show—purple and gold
- Best in Multibreed Show—purple, pink, white
- Reserve Best in Multibreed Show—purple and pink
- Total Dog Award—red, white, and black

weekend, while in other areas, showing involves long drives to distant cities. Both situations have their hazards.

With plenty of shows available, you may be tempted to spend both days of every weekend in a ring somewhere. As a novice exhibitor, your dog probably isn't ready for such a rigorous schedule. Rein in your enthusiasm. You definitely do not want to sour your dog on showing so early in your career.

You generally have to enter shows a month or more in advance (except for UKC shows, which often accept entries on the day of the show), so sit down and plan out your show schedule. If you want to attend both days (or sometimes the three or four days) of a cluster, plan to take the weekends before and after off from showing. Do something completely different to keep your dog fresh.

Some dogs really value a routine. For these canines, you may want to try a schedule of showing every Saturday and taking Sundays off (or vice versa). Dogs are amazingly good at calculating time, and days of the week, and will fall right into the routine.

If your family does not share your interest in dog showing, you also have their feelings to consider. You may find yourself in the doghouse along with the dog if you spend too much time on your hobby. They just won't understand your fascination with those bits of blue silk. Either find a way to involve them to some extent—maybe your spouse is a golfer and would enjoy trying out each area's courses while you're settled in on the show grounds, or an angler who would be delighted if you explored each area's trout stream or bass lake potential—or keep your schedule at a level that keeps everyone happy.

Watch Your Step

The expenses of showing a dog can mount up more quickly than a Buffalo snowfall in February. Gasoline, always high in the summer, prime dog showing season, meals, hotels, entry fees, show clothes, and all that equipment! But it's probably not as pricey as a cruise or an Aspen ski vacation, and you get to be with your dog!

Obviously, with a lot of shows going on around, you will have a much greater opportunity to choose the best judges, conditions, and so forth for your dog.

If your circumstances are the opposite, with few shows and long drives to many of them, you are more likely to attend everything within reach. The only real choice will be how far is too far to travel. This situation inevitably means either the added expense of a motel room or very early mornings to get up and on the road. Or, if you are *really* into dog showing, the purchase of a motor home or van as accommodation on wheels for yourself and your dog. You still have to consider the stamina of your dog and the tolerance of your family.

Remember

○ Practice at match shows before entering points shows.
○ Don't take wins in the match show ring too seriously.
○ Dog shows are listed in many magazines and events newsletters.
○ Professional show superintendents can put you on their mailing lists and notify you of upcoming shows.
○ Know your dog's preferences about indoor versus outdoor shows.
○ Study judges to learn what they like and choose shows more wisely.
○ Don't overbook—plan your showing schedule.

12

For the Younger Set

In This Chapter

○ The basics of Junior Showmanship
○ The dog you show
○ Special AKC Junior Showmanship opportunities
○ Junior Showmanship in Canada
○ 4-H dog programs
○ Apprenticing

Although younger handlers often compete with the adults quite successfully—a teenager showing in Group at Westminster wowed the crowd one year—they also have some opportunities all their own.

Many professional handlers began as competitors in Junior Showmanship. You may not want a career in dogs, just an interesting pastime, but you never know how things might turn out. For those aged 10 to 18, this special class is another chance to compete, and to be judged on your ring knowledge and expertise rather than the physical attributes of your dog. For those showing with the UKC, a career can begin at the tender age of 2, assisted by an adult, with ribbons for all. And even UKC-registered mixed breeds can serve as the dogs being shown. Canada also starts them young, at age 4.

Local 4-H clubs offer a lively assortment of canine events, including fitting and showing and groom squad. The big event of the year in each locale is often held in conjunction with the county fair.

Apprenticeships with professional handlers are probably open to those beyond their teens and twenties, but it's easier for those younger individuals unencumbered by families and bills to take the time and admittedly meager pay. There will be plenty of menial labor, but there should also be intensive instruction.

THE BASICS OF JUNIOR SHOWMANSHIP

Junior Showmanship owes its start to an enthusiastic fancier, Mr. Leonard Brumby. As a professional handler and officer of a kennel club, he realized that the future of dog sport resided in youth, and he decided that something needed to be done to promote participation by youngsters. He campaigned for this idea through the 1920s and succeeded in 1932, with the first-ever Children's Handling Class held at the Westbury Kennel Club Show. Handlers were under 14 years old, divided into classes of boys and girls. The following year there were two age divisions—under 15 and under 10.

The major dog show superintendent for the Northeast, George F. Foley, saw this as a good idea and began to encourage show-giving clubs to offer this new class. The Westminster Kennel Club was an early advocate, sponsoring the first Grand Challenge Trophy for the Children's Handling Class in 1933. Even then, the handlers had to qualify by earning a first place during the previous year. The trophy still exists today, though ever since the Professional Handlers Association took over sponsorship in 1949, it has been called the Leonard Brumby Sr. Memorial Trophy. It is now sponsored by the Westminster Kennel Club itself.

The name was changed to Junior Showmanship in 1951. It was still sponsored by individual kennel clubs, and judging could be very uneven. The Professional Handlers Association helped resolve that issue by using their members to judge, based on the youngsters' handling skills. The AKC recognized the event in 1971, making all AKC-approved judges automatically eligible to judge. Rules changes in 1989 meant that judges no longer could question junior handlers on topics such as canine anatomy, dogs in general, or their breed in particular (though these sorts of questions continue under other rules, such as the CKC's). At this time juniors were also

Figure 12.1. Juniors, shown here competing for the finals, are still part of Westminster. The finals are held in the big ring right before the second evening's group judging. (Photo copyright and courtesy of Amy D. Shojai, author of *The Purina Encyclopedia of Dog Care*)

required to apply for an ID number. And because bitches in heat could not be shown, substitutions of dogs could be made if a veterinary certificate was provided.

Junior Showmanship is now a popular, widespread, highly competitive sport.

Classes

Classes vary widely among the different kennel clubs, so we shall go through each one separately to assure there are no misunderstandings.

The AKC is the most restrictive, offering only two classes and two age groups:

Novice is for juniors who have not won three first-place awards at AKC licensed shows.

Open is for juniors who have won three first-place awards in the Novice class. A junior winning the third first place may immediately move up to Open and compete again at the same show.

These classes may be further divided into

> *Junior,* for handlers at least 10 years old but under 14 years old on the day of the show
> *Senior,* for handlers at least 14 and under 18

Best Junior Handler may also be offered, bringing together the winners from the four classes to compete.

Because we ignore the section of the AKC entry form devoted to Junior Showmanship in chapter 19, we'll explain it here. On the front of the form, fill in your Junior Showmanship class and your name under Name of Junior Handler. On the back of the form, fill in all information in the box at the bottom, provided especially for Junior Showmanship (see figure 12.2). (The AKC entry form is shown in its entirety in figure 19.1.)

To apply for a Junior Handler ID number, necessary before you can show, write to the AKC. Give your name, address, phone number, and birth date, and request a Junior Handler ID number. You will use this number until you *age out.*

The UKC also offers four classes, but they are all based on age:

> *Pee-Wee* is for youngsters aged 2 or 3. Parents are allowed to accompany the child, and the class is not placed. All participants generally receive ribbons.
> *Sub-Junior* is for those at least 4 years old but under 8. The rest of the rules are the same as for Pee-Wee.
> *Junior* is for handlers at least 8 years old but under 13. Placements are made of first through fourth.
> *Senior* is for handlers at least 13 years old but under 18. Placements are made, first through fourth.

Talking Dog

Ageing out, to Junior Handlers, means reaching the age of 18. On the very day of their birthday, they are suddenly no longer eligible to compete in Junior Showmanship. Some go directly into an apprenticeship to become professional handlers in a few years.

Front of AKC form:

DOG (2) (3) SHOW CLASS		CLASS (3) DIVISION Weight, Color, Etc.
ADDITIONAL CLASSES	OBEDIENCE TRIAL CLASS	JR. SHOWMANSHIP CLASS
NAME OF (See Back) JUNIOR HANDLER		JR. HANDLER AKC #

Back of AKC form:

JUNIOR SHOWMANSHIP. If this entry is for Jr. Showmanship, please give the following information:

ACK JR HANDLER #   JR.'S DATE OF BIRTH
☐☐☐☐☐☐☐☐   ☐☐ ☐☐ ☐☐
NAME OF JUNIOR HANDLER: _____
ADDRESS: _____
CITY: _____ State: _____ ZIP + 4: _____
If Jr. Handler is not the owner of the dog
Identified on the face of this form, what is the
relationship of the Jr. Handler to the owner? _____

Figure 12.2. Junior Showmanship portion of AKC entry form

Only the winners of the Junior and Senior classes compete for Best Junior Handler.

The Canadian Kennel Club offers five classes, based on both age and experience:

Pee Wee is for youngsters aged 4 through 7. No placements are made, and ribbons are generally given to all participants.

Junior Novice is for handlers at least 8 years old but under 13, who have not placed first in four competitions.

Junior Open is for the same age group, but with four first-place wins to their credit.

Senior Novice is for handlers at least 13 years old but under 18, who have not placed first in four competitions.

Senior Open is for the same age group, but with four first-place wins to their credit.

Tips from the Pros

All dogs entered in the Junior Showmanship Classes must be UKC registered. United Kennel Club Permanently Registered, Limited Privilege or Temporary Listed, neutered and mixed breed (UKC LP program) dogs are allowed in Junior Showmanship classes. These classes are not to be divided by breed.

—From *Bloodlines Rules Special Issue*

Best Overall is an optional class for the winners of the four classes that are placed (Pee Wee does not compete).

The Dog You Show

For AKC Junior Showmanship, the dog must be owned by the Junior Handler or the parents, grandparents, siblings, aunts, or uncles of the Junior Handler (including, for these days of blended families, step-relations and half-relations). The dog must be eligible to compete in dog shows or obedience trials, making neutered dogs eligible for this class. In specialty shows, only the breed of the specialty may be shown. Bitches in season may not be shown.

With the UKC, any UKC-registered dog, including neutered and mixed breed dogs, may be shown by Junior Handlers. It is recommended, but not required, that the Junior Handler, or his or her immediate family, own the dog.

In the Ring

No matter which kennel club you are doing your junior handling under, the judging is supposed to be of your ability to show the dog, not the dog's conformation. So you need to be prepared and keep your wits about you. Always work to get the best from your dog. Even if he or she is misbehaving—and dogs do have their bad days, just like people—if you remain unflustered and keep trying to show the dog, your efforts could be rewarded. Junior Handlers who were sure they were out of the running because of their dogs' antics have won their classes because they didn't give up.

Because this is a competition based on handling, the judges sometimes ask for gaiting patterns or set up situations not generally seen in the regular conformation ring. Do your best to be ready for them. Although the AKC now officially discourages unusual patterns such as the "L" and "T" (see chapter 15 for discussion of gaiting patterns), judges use them, especially when they're having a difficult time deciding on their placements. They also might ask for dogs to be gaited side by side.

Because of all this, you must be prepared to show the dog on either side of yourself and to switch the lead from hand to hand. This requires practice. Switching the lead is done in the midst of a gaiting pattern, while you and your dog are moving, and must be quick and sure. You have the lead bunched up in your left hand so no loose ends are dangling. Bring your hands together, palms facing, with the right hand over the left fist. Curl your left fingers back out of your palm so that the lead is held by the fingers. Press those fingers into the palm of your right hand below the thumb. Open the fingers of your left hand so the leash is held between your two palms, then close the fingers of your right hand over it. You can practice this even sitting in front of the television.

Work your dog on the right side sometimes. I once witnessed an entire class asked to gait clockwise rather than counterclockwise, meaning all the

Figure 12.3. This junior handler has given herself plenty of room to set up and concentrate on her Petit Basset Griffon Vandeen. (Photo copyright and courtesy of Amy D. Shojai, author of *The Purina Encyclopedia of Dog Care*)

dogs had to be on the handlers' right. So even without intricate gaiting patterns, you may be asked to switch sides.

Never let anything come between your dog and the judge. This of course includes yourself—hence the need to switch sides—but it also includes other handlers and such physical obstructions as the exam table and poles for the ring entrance tents at outdoor shows. If you are at an indoor show and going inside the exam table would mean pulling the dog off the mats onto a slippery floor, then maybe being momentarily blocked is the better option. Otherwise, make sure the judge always has a clear view of your dog.

Always—we repeat, *always*—be alert to any instructions given by the judge. You might be asked not to use any "tricks" before your first gaiting pattern. Only the judge knows precisely what he or she means by this, but you may want to forgo using a *blind courtesy turn* or doing any *finger work* in this case.

Finger works are small hand movements while your dog is stacked, to emphasize good points. If your dog's topline is the best by far, running two fingers over your dog's back from the withers to the base of the tail, then looking up at the judge accentuates both the good point and your knowledge of it. The same can be done for heads.

Or the judge might ask that all the dogs be stacked with their fronts or rears facing the judge, or that two dogs be gaited against each other—in which case you may have to show the dog on your right if you are unlucky enough to be the handler on the judge's left. The dogs should be next to each other on the inside, the handlers on the outside.

In addition to listening for instructions from the judge, you must be aware of his or her location at all times. Learn to shift your eyes and catch a glimpse of the judge in your peripheral vision—your major attention should always be on your dog. At the far end of the up and back, or the turn onto the final diagonal of the triangle, it is acceptable to look at and "spot" the judge for a moment to align your movement directly toward him or her. This is where you are showing off the dog's front, after all, and you want the judge to have a good straight view.

Keeping an eye subtly on the judge also lets you know exactly when the judge's attention is on you. If the judge watches handlers all the way to the end of the line on their circle after the individual exam, you might gain an edge by free-stacking your dog while you still have the judge's eye, rather than just stopping or trying to formally stack your dog.

Talking Dog

A *blind courtesy turn* is an alternative to an about face at the far end of the up and back. It keeps the dog in good view of the judge at all times, but requires the cooperation of the dog. While you make a left about turn, the dog makes a small clockwise circle in place, so that you both end up facing in the opposite direction.

One time you want to make definite eye contact with the judge is when he or she first walks down the line of dogs at the beginning of the class. Your look—and a smile wouldn't hurt—is a sort of formal greeting to the judge. This is standard ring procedure. Making eye contact at the *end* of the class, when the dogs are again stacked and the judge may be making the final decision, is *not* standard ring procedure. It is sometimes used by professional handlers, a sort of stare down meant to say, "I know and you should know that I'm the winner," and it can be read by the judge as an attempt at intimidation. You might try it if the judge seems to be having a hard time making placements, but be aware that it can backfire.

An additional consideration is your clothing and hair. If you wear your hair long—and we don't care if you're male or female—pull it back in a ponytail or fasten it back in some other manner. You don't want it falling in your face, maybe into your dog. It will not make a good impression on the judge. As far as clothing is concerned, sweats, jeans, and baggy pants are definitely out. You are trying to present yourself as a serious contender. For boys, at the very least slacks, shirt, and tie, and adding a jacket will probably make a better impression. For girls, dresses, pant suits, or skirt and blouse are all acceptable. (See chapter 20 for further clothing considerations, and realize that the UKC is much less formal in their events.)

SPECIAL AKC JUNIOR SHOWMANSHIP OPPORTUNITIES

Every year, junior handlers race to qualify to compete at Westminster. Entering requires the junior to have placed first in the Open Junior or Open Senior classes on at least eight occasions throughout the year. Entries for everything, including Junior Showmanship, close very quickly at Westmin-

Tips from the Pros

We stress going and watching shows to our junior handlers. Every dog we show—probably 15 a show—every one is shown differently. Some you have to show with the lead up, some with the lead down. Pick out a respectable handler to watch.

—Tom Glassford, former professional handler, AKC rep

ster, so the junior must have the wins in hand and ready to submit before Westminster entries open. Fewer than one hundred entries are accepted.

Preliminary judging is done during the day, concurrent with breed judging. Two judges each preside over approximately half the entry, often one taking the larger dogs and one taking the smaller. The classes are large, and the judge will often take them half at a time so other dogs and handlers can relax until it is their turn. Each judge can select four finalists to send to the Best Junior Handler competition. This takes place on Tuesday evening, prior to the start of the second night's Group judging. It's in the big group ring, often with many from the press in attendance. Perhaps some year they'll see fit to televise it as part of the coverage of Westminster.

Pedigree once sponsored the World Series of Junior Showmanship, but that was changed in 1996 to the Pedigree Junior Showmanship National Invitational. Pedigree provides awards at twenty shows around the country, but the biggest prizes are reserved for two December shows. The Open Junior class winner at the Long Beach Kennel Club Dog Show receives a trip to the World Dog Show to compete in Junior Showmanship. The winner of the Open Senior Class at the Bay Colony Cluster in Boston receives a trip to the Crufts Dog Show in Birmingham, England.

In addition, many local and national kennel clubs offer annual awards for junior handlers. And the Owner Handlers Association provides trophies for the top ten member junior handlers each year.

JUNIOR SHOWMANSHIP IN CANADA

In addition to actual Junior Showmanship, the CKC offers the Junior Kennel Club, which is sponsored by a regular kennel club for fanciers younger than

18 years of age. It operates as an actual kennel club, with elected officers and a club constitution, and can hold social events and CKC-sanctioned matches. Holding a match, with all the organization and volunteerism that goes into it, is a highly educational experience.

Junior handling in Canada favors gaiting patterns that require switching hands on the lead and courtesy turns. Judges may still ask questions of the handlers and can even ask handlers to swap dogs if necessary to make a final decision. Juniors should be rewarded for remaining calm, using good techniques, and exhibiting good sportsmanship in difficult situations, such as a dog acting up or another handler running up on them.

Juniors who place (first through fourth) are awarded points:

> First—100 points
> Second—75 points
> Third—50 points
> Fourth—25 points

Throughout the year, the points are tabulated for each province or zone (the CKC draws up the zones). The top five juniors in each class division of each province or zone (more if there are ties in the point standings) are invited to compete at the Provincial/Zone Finals. A panel of three judges chooses the top handler in each of the classes, who then compete for Top Provincial/Zone Finalist. The winner (or the Reserve Finalist if the Finalist is unable) goes to compete at the National Junior Handling Competition. At the National, there are no class divisions—all juniors compete directly against one another. They are often asked to exchange dogs to further demonstrate their handling skills.

The CKC also offers a Junior Handling Competition in the sport of Obedience. Juniors can show in Pre-Novice (Sub-Novice in the AKC), Novice, Graduate Novice, Open, Utility, and Brace or Team. They are judged on their teamwork and gentleness in their handling.

4-H DOG PROGRAMS

4-H programs aren't just for raising livestock. They offer a variety of programs involving dogs, including "Fitting and Showing," the 4-H equivalent of conformation. There are four divisions for membership:

Primary—first and second grades
Junior—third, fourth, and fifth grades
Intermediate—sixth, seventh, and eighth grades
Senior—ninth through twelfth grades *or* not having reached the nineteenth birthday before January 1 of the current year

All members must be enrolled in the dog program to participate in 4-H dog shows. The 4-H'er must care for a dog, whether it is their own or one they have borrowed or leased. Dogs may be of any age, any breed or mixed breed, and may be spayed or neutered, even blind, deaf, or physically handicapped so long as they have a veterinary statement that participating in the program will not have any adverse effects.

The 4-H ground rules, covering all divisions of the dog program, are as follows for Washington State:

1. No alcoholic beverages.
2. No drugs.
3. No smoking or chewing tobacco.
4. No abuse of animal.
5. No coaching of children while they are in the ring or showing their dog.
6. Adults may not groom or school dog while on the grounds. Designated adult may *help* members with the project.
7. The ring is off limits to everyone except working show personnel.
8. Approach the judge for information only, not to dispute his placing, and only after judging is completed.
9. A visibly ill animal can be dismissed from participation by show personnel.
10. All exhibitors will participate in herdsmanship if offered. (*Note:* Herdsmanship is equivalent to benching of dogs.)
11. Leaders will ask any members of their club to leave grounds with their dog if behavior is unacceptable.
12. Only dogs entered in novice and higher classes may be off leash at any time and these only in the show or practice ring.
13. At a benched show, there is to be no eating or drinking in the benching area.
14. Prong and choke collars and muzzles are not allowed.

15. Dogs may be shown with minor, noncontagious ailments. A veterinarian's certificate is strongly recommended.

16. No 4-H'er may go barefoot. No thongs. Stockings must be worn with sandals.

17. Anti-social or uncontrollable dogs will be sent home.

18. Exhibitors must dress tastefully, no shorts or bare tops. Improperly dressed exhibitors will be asked to change or leave.

19. No running or rowdy behavior.*

Other state regulations are similar. All exhibitors receive a ribbon, based on the Danish scoring system. Blue ribbons require 80 to 100 points, red ribbons are for 60 to 79 points, and everything below that earns a white ribbon. Judging is based on

- Personal appearance, including clothing and hair
- Patterns—all exhibitors are asked to perform a T pattern and may be asked for another as well
- Stacking as appropriate for the breed (those showing mixed breeds must state on the entry form what breed their dog most resembles)
- Questions—each exhibitor will be asked five questions, one each about anatomy, breed history or standard, general care, AKC general knowledge, 4-H general knowledge
- Grooming
- Baiting
- Courtesy turns (optional)
- Equipment—use of or type of show lead
- Ability to relax dogs when told to do so by the judge
- Set up (equivalent of free stacking)

There is also a separate fun event in which teams of 4-H'ers are given a dirty dog and a set amount of time in which to bathe and groom the dog. The technique during the competition, especially keeping the dog unstressed, and results of the grooming are judged. The dogs are often shelter dogs, which are then put up for adoption.

*From "Guidelines for Washington State 4-H Dog Program," Cooperative Extension, Washington State University, 1988.

**WASHINGTON STATE DOG PROGRAM
FITTING AND SHOWING SCORECARD**

Class _____ Lot _____ Date _____

Show Name_____ Exhibitor No. _____

Judge's Name_____

	MAXIMUM POINTS	NET SCORE
Part I. FITTING (50 points possible)		
Dog (40 points possible)		
Clean, well-brushed, and required body scissoring done	10	
Ears clean and properly trimmed	10	
Teeth clean	10	
Legs, feet, and toenails properly trimmed	10	
Handler Appearance (10 points possible)		
Properly dressed and groomed	5	
Courteous, observes ring courtesy	5	
Part II. SHOWING (50 points possible)		
Gaiting (10 points possible)		
Group gaiting	5	
Individual gaiting	5	
Stacking (10 points possible)		
Stacking in line-up	5	
Individual stacking	5	
Ring Procedures (15 points possible)		
Line spacing and ring etiquette	5	
Dog between judge and handler	5	
Ring patterns and showing bite	5	
General Knowledge (5 points possible)		
Parts/anatomy	1	
Breed history and standard	1	
Care and health	1	
AKC general knowledge	1	
4-H	1	
Ring Presence and Poise	10	
TOTAL SCORE	100	

Comments: _____

_____

_____

Figure 12.4. Washington State Dog Program Fitting and Showing Scorecard

Watch Your Step

Do not let your eagerness to advance in the sport of dogs blind you to any unsavory practices of a professional handler. Unfortunately, illegal surgeries, faking, and other shenanigans do take place. Extricate yourself from any such situations.

APPRENTICING

Obviously opportunities for apprenticing are limited—be sure you have a very strong interest in making dogs your profession before seeking one. Professional handlers occasionally have an opening for an assistant, and owners of large breeding kennels often hire kennel help. In either position, you will be paid little and expected to perform many menial chores such as cleaning runs and feeding and exercising dogs. But you will also have the chance to learn from the pros. Many young people graduate from Junior Showmanship to an apprenticeship to a career as a professional handler.

To look for opportunities in your area, go to local shows and strike up conversations, especially with people there with several dogs. You can also contact the Professional Handlers Association for a list of pros in your area, and your national breed club for local breeders.

For a less formal learning opportunity, join the Owner Handler Association of America. There are local chapters in many areas, holding training classes and educational programs. The stated purpose of the group is to encourage and promote the sport of owner handling and training of purebred dogs.

Remember

- ○ AKC Junior Showmanship is for those aged 10 to 18 years.
- ○ AKC juniors must apply for a Junior Handler ID number.
- ○ UKC Junior Showmanship is for those aged 2 to 18.
- ○ CKC Junior Showmanship is for those aged 4 to 18.
- ○ The judging of Junior Showmanship is based on the handling of the junior, not the conformation of the dog.

○ The junior handler's clothing and hairstyle must be neat and appropriate for the ring.

○ 4-H offers competition in Fitting and Showing for those in first grade through twelfth grade.

○ 4-H'ers are judged on their grooming and showing of the dog, as well as basic knowledge.

○ Young people truly interested in dogs and dog showing can look for an apprenticeship, either formal or informal, to further their education.

Part III

Mechanical Skills

If you're ready for some hands-on instruction, here it is!

First there's grooming—only the very basics, because trying to cover all the different coat types and breed trims takes at least a book by itself. If your breed requires extensive grooming, you'll need a mentor to show you the ropes. But all dogs should be clean and free of mats.

Stacking, gaiting, and baiting are the nuts and bolts of showing a dog. Some lucky people seem to be naturals at all of this, but for the rest of us, all these skills must be acquired. Lucky for us, conformation classes and fun matches give us plenty of opportunities to practice.

The last chapter here (chapter 17) pulls together the basics of how to conduct yourself at a show, and warns of some of the transgressions that can get you thrown out of the ring. You'll also find the growing controversy over cropping and docking here.

13

Grooming for Success

In This Chapter

○ Coat types and how you handle them
○ Knowing when you need help
○ Combs and brushes and much, much more
○ Ears and nails and teeth and toes

Grooming is an essential part of dog care whether or not you ever venture into the show ring. But grooming for the show ring can be a bit different from simply grooming for health—especially if your dog is a Poodle or Schnauzer or Kerry Blue Terrier or any of a dozen other breeds.

Obviously we can't give detailed grooming instructions for every breed here. Even books specifically about grooming often cover only a limited number of breeds. So we will discuss the basics in equipment and how-to and leave you to learn the details of your breed.

Whatever you do, don't practice your new grooming skills on your dog the night before a big show. Even just combing or brushing can damage a coat and make it unfit for the show ring. Rely on professional groomers (and choose them wisely, too—not all groomers have any idea of how to groom for conformation) until you learn more.

COAT TYPES AND HOW YOU HANDLE THEM

There are three basic coat types: short hair, long hair, and wire hair. But within each category there are many variations. Even short-coated dogs may have thin slick coats or short but thick coats that may need to have undercoat stripped out. Wire coats are very precise in their requirements—brushing can ruin these coats, and so can the wrong shampoo. Long hair may be single or double coated, stand-off or flat.

We certainly can't cover all coat types in depth, but here are some examples from various breed standards.

Pointer coat is simply described as "short, dense, smooth with a sheen," whereas the German Shorthaired Pointer gets more specific: "The hair is short and thick and feels tough to the hand; it is somewhat longer on the underside of the tail and the back edges of the haunches. The hair is softer, thinner, and shorter on the ears and the head. Any dog with long hair in the body coat is to be severely punished." The German Wirehaired Pointer standard is more specific by far: "The functional wiry coat is the breed's most distinctive feature. A dog must have a correct coat to be of correct type. The coat is weather resistant and, to some extent, water repellant. The undercoat is dense enough in winter to insulate against the cold but is so thin in summer as to be almost invisible. The distinctive outer coat is straight, harsh, wiry and flat lying, and is from one to two inches in length. The outer coat is long enough to protect against the punishment of rough cover, but not so long as to hide the outline of the dog. On the lower legs the coat is shorter, and between the toes it is of softer texture. On the skull the coat is naturally short and close fitting. Over the shoulders and around the tail it is very dense and heavy. The tail is nicely coated, particularly on the underside, but devoid of feathers. Eyebrows are of strong, straight hair.

Tips from the Pros

Asked for a list of essential equipment, Affenpinscher exhibitor and breeder Sharon Irons Strempski mentioned a VariKennel crate first, but every other item related to grooming: small grooming table, stripping knife, stripping stone, plain scissors, scissors with teeth on one side, blunt tip "baby" scissors, slicker brush, pin brush, medium-tooth metal comb. Be sure you have the grooming tools you need for your breed.

Beard and whiskers are medium length. The hairs in the liver patches of a liver and white dog may be shorter than the white hairs. A short smooth coat, a soft woolly coat, or an excessively long coat is to be severely punished. While maintaining a harsh, wiry texture, the puppy coat may be shorter than that of an adult coat. Coats may be neatly groomed to present a dog natural in appearance. Extreme and excessive grooming to present a dog artificial in appearance should be severely penalized."

The Beagle description is as short as its coat: "A close, hard hound coat of medium length. Defects—A short, thin coat, or of a soft quality." The Samoyed is more coated and the standard more explicit: "The Samoyed is a double-coated dog. The body should be well covered with an undercoat of soft, short, thick, close wool with longer and harsh hair growing through it to form the outer coat, which stands straight out from the body and should be free from curl. The coat should form a ruff around the neck and shoulders, framing the head (more on males than on females). Quality of coat should be weather resistant and considered more than quantity. A droopy coat is undesirable. The coat should glisten with a silver sheen. The female does not usually carry as long a coat as most males, and it is softer in texture."

For the Cairn Terrier, coat faults take more space than coat description: "Hard and weather-resistant. Must be double-coated with profuse harsh outer coat and short, soft, close furry undercoat. Faults—Open coats, blousy coats, too short or dead coats, lack of sufficient undercoat, lack of head furnishings, lack of hard hair on the legs. Silkiness or curliness. A slight wave permissible." The Lakeland Terrier standard offers a "typical" terrier coat description: "Two-ply or double, the outer coat is hard and wiry in texture, the undercoat is close to the skin and soft and should never overpower the wiry outer coat. The Lakeland is hand stripped to show his outline. (Clipping is inappropriate for the show ring.) The appearance should be neat and workmanlike. The coat on the skull, ears, forechest, shoulders and behind the tail is trimmed short and smooth. The coat on the body is longer (about one-half to one inch) and may be slightly wavy or straight. The furnishings on the legs and foreface are plentiful as opposed to profuse and should be tidy. They are crisp in texture. The legs should appear cylindrical. The face is traditionally trimmed, with the hair left longer over the eyes to give the head a rectangular appearance from all angles, with the eyes covered from above. From the front, the eyes are quite apparent, giving the Lakeland his own unique mischievous expression."

Fancy That!

Many national or local breed clubs have booklets, videos, or even seminars on grooming. With electronic technology, they may even have information online, or a discussion group where you can ask questions and get advice.

The Maltese seems to have more coat than dog, as the standard describes it: "The coat is single, that is, without undercoat. It hangs long, flat, and silky over the sides of the body almost, if not quite, to the ground. The long head-hair may be tied up in a topknot or it may be left hanging. Any suggestion of kinkiness, curliness, or woolly texture is objectionable."

Obviously, you should read the standard for your breed. You will find a description of the desired coat, and possibly even grooming do's and don'ts.

In general—and this is very general—double coats are brushed from the skin out to avoid mats and remove any loose undercoat. Wire and terrier coats are often hand stripped, a technique that definitely requires training and experience. And short or hound coats are just gone over with a slicker or a hound glove. But some breeds are supposed to have "stand-off" coats, while others are meant to lie flat. Know what you are doing.

KNOWING WHEN YOU NEED HELP

If you have no experience grooming dogs, don't expect to just jump in and get your dog ready for the ring on your own. There's an art even to minor trimming, and without experience you may hurt your dog's chances through your inept grooming. At the very least, observe a groomer competent in show grooming working on your dog. Ask questions. Better yet, ask if you can pay for a lesson. An acquaintance in Scotland, just beginning to show his Standard Schnauzer, has already been told by a judge that he has a very nice dog, but he will go a lot further if the dog is professionally groomed before being shown!

If your breed is one that requires plucking, stripping, or extensive grooming, you definitely need to find an instructor of some sort. This might be the breeder of your dog—breeders are often involved in the show careers of their dogs' progeny and are willing to serve as mentors in many ways. It could also be a friend you have made at dog shows (possibly not even in your breed, but a breed with a similar coat), a groomer, or someone else.

Tips from the Pros

Have your breeder show you how to do it the first time. The Affenpinscher Club of America has an inexpensive breed booklet that has a section on basic grooming. Puppies go through coat changes so grooming may be different during that time. Attend a national specialty and watch exhibitors prepare their dogs.

—Sharon Irons Strempski, AKC exhibitor and breeder of Affenpinschers

Take pictures of specimens of your breed that you admire and study them for hints on grooming. You can also find lots of photographs in breed books and dog magazines devoted to showing.

But remember that grooming for show is far more involved than grooming for good hygiene at home. Even bathing your dog at the wrong time or with the wrong shampoo could ruin your chances. Seek help!

COMBS AND BRUSHES AND MUCH, MUCH MORE

Equipment for grooming is likely to take up much of your show kit. It will depend to some extent on the breed you are showing. Some of the larger pieces of equipment are a grooming table, forced-air dryer, and tack box.

There are several options for grooming tables. Two don't add to your need for space. One is a grooming table on wheels. This double-duty innovation serves as a dolly cart to move your equipment, then unfolds to an elevated table. However, many people ignore a table completely and simply use their crate as a grooming platform. Whether you choose a table or a crate, be sure that it provides a nonslip surface for the dog. Some attach a rectangle of carpet sample to the top of the crate. And there are some who simply groom the dog on the ground, although this will certainly depend to some extent on the size of your dog.

Only an actual grooming table will provide you the option of a grooming arm. This metal appliance fastens to the table and extends up and over one end to hold a short lead and slip collar. Putting the collar on the dog helps to hold him or her in position on the table while you groom (see figure 13.1).

Whether you use a table, a crate, or some invention of your own, do not leave your dog unattended on it. Accidents have happened.

Figure 13.1. This dog seems perfectly happy to relax on the grooming table. But his owner has stepped away just for me to take the picture and would not leave him there unattended.

Some breeds demand that you include some sort of dryer in your show kit. Especially if you're showing outdoors, feet and inquisitive faces and even bellies and tails can be wet after a walk around the grounds. And some coats simply demand last-minute primping.

You can use your own hair dryer if it includes a non-hot setting. Although human dryers were not meant for dealing with canine coats, they can handle small touchups. Or there are small hand-held dryers designed for dogs, more powerful than the average hair dryer. And of course there are the vacuum cleaner–like forced-air dryers. These powerful appliances literally blow the water off the dog. Be careful where you point them. In the close quarters of most grooming areas, you will not make any friends by blowing around papers or chalk or blasting other dogs with air.

Of course, all dryers require power, and you may have to work hard to find an outlet. Having a heavy-duty extension cord on hand may help, or you may simply have to wait your turn.

Clippers also require power. And that loose hair in close proximity to someone else's dryer could have you running for your life. Do your clipping

Watch Your Step

Chalk (or cornstarch) is a fact of life in the world of AKC showing. Though all artificial substances are supposed to be removed from the dog before entering the ring, dogs are chalked with great abandon. When brushed out, clouds of free-floating chalk may envelop nearby dogs and handlers.

at home, and if you must do any sort of last-minute touch-up, try to do it early, before the grooming area is crowded.

A tack box is essential. We don't mean you have to have one of those gleaming metal and wood trunks you may see at some professionals' setups. They're certainly beautiful and functional, but you can make all sorts of plastic housewares, cloth bags, and other less expensive items serve as tack boxes. The important point is to have some sort of container that will hold all your smaller grooming supplies, so that they are always packed and ready to go. This helps prevent forgetting small but essential items. Get in the habit of returning items to the tack box after using them and replacing expendable supplies before you run out.

Your tack box will contain an assortment of combs, brushes, scissors, cloths, grooming sprays or powders, and probably more. There's no way we can tell you what to carry—dog grooming is simply too variable. You will learn as you go along and soon have a tack box full of equipment you consider essential.

EARS AND NAILS AND TEETH AND TOES

Don't concentrate on the coat and forget the other details of the dog. Grooming encompasses the entire animal. The small things are important both for show and for health.

Ears should be checked regularly and cleaned when necessary. Drop-eared breeds with an abundance of hair in the ears—Cocker Spaniels are the prime example—are more prone to ear problems and need extra attention. Hair growing in ear canals can be plucked by hand to help provide better air circulation. Hot, bright pink ears should be brought to your veterinarian's attention. For the ring, grooming around the ears is particularly important for *feathered* breeds (see figure 13.2).

Figure 13.2. Sporting ear wraps to protect those long feathers, this dog waits patiently for a final grooming before the ring.

Nails, of course, must be kept clipped if they aren't worn down enough by the dog. Show dogs often have exceptionally short nails, as handlers feel it presents a neater picture. There are scissors-like clippers, guillotine-style clippers, and grinders. It's a matter of personal choice, though you should buy the best that you can afford.

A lot of dogs dislike having their nails clipped, and just as many humans dislike doing it. The job is made more difficult if your dog has black nails, making it impossible to see the quick. But you can learn to recognize the look of the nail as you are approaching the quick. Your veterinarian or groomer should be willing to demonstrate nail clipping.

Talking Dog

If the world of dog showing has its own language, the world of grooming is a distinct dialect. You may hear people speak of "hard coats" and "hound gloves," "furnishings" and "feathers," and much, much more. The glossary at the end of this book includes a small sampling of coat, color, and grooming vocabulary.

Tips from the Pros

Asked about how an exhibitor can put his or her best foot forward in front of the judge, the first answer of AKC judge, exhibitor, and breeder Lilian S. Barber was, "Make sure your dog is clean and well groomed. Teeth should be sparkling white and the nails trimmed."

Don't forget about dewclaws. A lot of show dogs have them removed at an early age, but they are mandatory in some breeds. If your dog has them, be sure to trim them regularly since they are not worn down by the dog.

Teeth must be kept clean. Even pet owners are now being told to brush their dogs' teeth regularly. Owners of show dogs often do more, regularly scaling the teeth of their dogs. This is not something to just decide to try on your own. You need to be shown exactly how to do this, and you must slowly accustom your dog to the idea.

Finally, those toes. Everyone remembers to trim nails, but not everyone remembers the bottom of the foot. Long-coated breeds in particular often have very fuzzy feet. The hair around the foot and between the pads should be carefully trimmed, both to make a neater presentation and to prevent mats from forming. Freeing pads of hair also improves traction. With scissors, as with nail clippers, buy the best that you can afford.

Obviously this chapter is not going to teach you how to groom your dog. Entire books are devoted to that subject. We hope we have given you some idea of what is involved and how to seek help.

Remember

○ Different coat types require different care.
○ Read your breed standard.
○ Seek help in learning how to groom your breed.
○ Keep all smaller supplies in a tack box so you always know where they are.
○ Pay special attention to cleaning ears, trimming nails, and clipping hair from pads.
○ Buy the best that you can afford—it will provide better service and last a long time.

Stacking Up

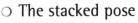
Have you ever watched a show and gotten shivers when a dog finished gaiting and, without any visible cue from the handler, snapped into the perfect pose, just daring the judge to find a more glorious specimen of dogdom? It is a breathtaking sight. Posing and free stacking both are things you and your dog can practice, but keep in mind that they are not the be-all and end-all of showing, and your dog's attitude may be more important.

We'll have plenty of advice from the professionals in this chapter. And you can even watch some handling without leaving your living room, with ESPN and Animal Planet now including dog shows in their programming, and USA Network covering the World Show in addition to Westminster. The more you can watch good dogs well shown, the better you will be able to understand the picture you are trying to present with your own dog. Do keep in mind, however, that not everyone you see on TV is presenting their dog to the absolute peak. You will see far too many severely tight leashes, handlers colliding with dogs, sidewinding dogs, and many other far-from-ideal things even on television.

THE STACKED POSE

Even if you do not plan to show your own dog, you should learn the basics of stacking and moving (see chapter 15) a dog. The experience will help you to know your own dog's faults and strong points and to see the good and bad points in your competitors' dogs. You will also be at least a little prepared for the day when your handler hasn't shown up by the time your class is being called into the ring.

Stacking is simply posing your dog. Most breeds follow the same principles in stacking, though there are some exceptions. Cardigan Welsh Corgis' front feet often point slightly out rather than straight forward, and German Shepherd Dogs in the AKC are presented with one rear leg forward under the body and one stretched back. Know if your breed has any pose peculiarities.

A good conformation class (see chapter 8) can really help hone your skills. And a mirror is essential, so you can see your dog from the judge's point of view. Other than that, it's practice, practice, practice—for the benefit of you *and* your dog.

In most dog shows, dogs are presented facing to your right because that is the direction in which they are gaited around the ring. So face your dog in that direction, presenting a dead-on side view to a judge standing on

Tips from the Pros

Training can start at five or six weeks. Work only two or three minutes at a time, morning and evening, but do it every day. Don't be too tough on the dog when teaching him to stand and stay, and don't tire or bore him. This is a good time to offer very small food rewards, but be careful that the treat doesn't get your puppy so excited that he loses concentration.

—Lilian S. Barber, AKC judge and exhibitor, author of *The New Complete Italian Greyhound*

Tips from the Pros

A dog that is looking good, and relaxed, is better than a dog with its feet placed mechanically correctly.

—Bill McFadden, AKC professional handler

the other side of your dog. Most people then raise the collar up directly under the ears and put enough pressure on the lead to keep it there. This is a useful technique—controlling the head certainly helps to control the dog—just keep in mind that it is vitally important for your dog to be *happy* in the ring.

SETTING THE FRONT

Most exhibitors set the dog's front feet first. Generally, you want the legs aligned with each other and straight under the withers (see chapter 9), with the feet facing forward. You will need to practice so that your dog understands that you will move his or her feet, and the dog is to leave them where you place them. If yours is a small breed, the stacking will be done on a table. You will need to practice on a table so your dog becomes used to the height and surface. That way they will show in a relaxed manner.

Don't just take hold of a foot and yank it where you want it. Many dogs are fussy about having their feet handled. They will probably resist your efforts and move once you let go. And you're not likely to get it straight anyway. Instead, gently take hold above the elbow and move the entire leg into position. Reach over, not under, the dog to set the outside leg. Frequent

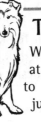

Tips from the Pros

When you have approximately one minute with the judge looking at your dog, you want it to be an artistic picture. It doesn't have to be correct, it's more like a painting: It will be etched in the judge's mind, so you want to leave a nice picture.

—Tom Glassford, former professional handler, AKC rep

Tips from the Pros

Most toys are put up on the table to have their nails trimmed and their ears cleaned. Most of them are then afraid of the table. They have to know it's two different things: They're up there for their nails and grooming, or they're up there for show. Play with them, give them bait, scratch their necks. Don't make it traumatic.

—Tom Glassford, former professional handler, AKC Rep

conformation seminar leader George Alston suggests that you treat your dog like fine crystal, always handling it gently and with care. This is excellent advice.

Small to medium-sized dogs can be stacked by "dropping" the front (or the rear). Place your left hand over the dog's back and then under the chest from the front between the legs. Lift the front end of the dog off the table or ground and let the dog back down so that both front feet touch at once. Remember to praise and make the dog happy.

SETTING THE BACK

Once the front legs are set, move to the back legs. But don't simply let go of a front leg, move over, and grab a rear leg. Let the dog know what is happening by keeping your hands on the dog. With a light touch, run your hands down the topline to the inside rear leg and grasp it at the second thigh, above the hock. Generally, rear legs are set up so that the pastern is perpendicular to the ground and the foot is slightly outside the front foot. Some advise that a line drawn on the ground from the front to the back of the dog should touch the outside of the front foot and the inside of the rear foot.

Again, small to medium-sized dogs can be stacked by dropping the rear. Reach your left hand between the back legs from the rear, lift, and lower to let both rear feet touch at once.

Once you have set the legs, use one hand to hold the dog's muzzle straight ahead and parallel to the ground. If yours is a breed with a tail to be presented, use your other hand to hold the tail in correct position for

Talking Dog

You will hear people say that the hock should be perpendicular to the ground. The hock is actually the joint and so can't really be perpendicular to anything. The pastern is the straight portion of the leg below the hock.

your breed, or take your hands away and let the dog do the showing. He or she may be better at it than you.

Do not obsess over the mythical "perfect" stack!

THE MAGICAL FREE STACK

At least once during your time before the judge, you will be asked to free stack your dog, letting the dog pose him- or herself. Some judges like to do this several times, sometimes asking that dogs they are considering be free stacked side by side (see figure 14.1).

The free stack is even more of an art than the posed stack, requiring a high level of cooperation from your dog. To see a master at work, watch Andy Linton free stack the Doberman Pinschers and Great Danes he frequently shows. Other handlers always mention Andy Linton when the subject of free stacking comes up. Many of them admit they learned to free stack, or at least to do it better, from Andy.

A good conformation class can certainly help you and your dog learn to free stack. But here are some techniques you can try on your own.

Tips from the Pros

People concentrate too much on making the dog stand with its feet just perfect and end up with a dog whose feet are in place but with the rest of the body looking like it would rather be anywhere else but there. The dogs that stand out when the judge is coming down a line are the ones that are relaxed and wagging their tail, not those properly stacked but unhappy.

—Bill McFadden, AKC professional handler

Figure 14.1. This handler has just completed her gaiting pattern and is urging her dog into a free stack under the judge's watchful eye. A second later the dog moved the left legs forward into a balanced pose.

Tom Glassford advises starting with the dog in front of you and about a foot away. Use one of your feet to keep the dog from creeping closer. Use bait to get the dog's attention, get the ears up and attention focused. Work on this, gradually increasing the distance to 3 feet, until the dog will hold its distance. Now concentrate on getting the back feet in correct position, trying to use bait, but placing them if you must. Continue working on this until the dog seems to understand. Then try to get the dog to lean forward—move the bait toward the dog then away, using a half-circle motion and trying to get the dog to reach for it.

Bill McFadden suggests a technique for keeping a dog relaxed but attentive at the same time—practice teaching them to catch liver. "They'll be on their toes and watching you, ears up because they're expecting it." Bill also notes that a dog expecting to catch will naturally want to be balanced, so is more likely to free stack correctly (see figure 14.2).

Figure 14.2. This Beagle is presenting an admirable free stack all on his own.

You can use bait in the ring (except in UKC shows) to try and persuade the dog into a better stack, but you'll only have a couple of seconds before the judge is on to something else. A gorgeous free stack may mean the difference between a win and second place. Be prepared.

PREPARATION AND PRACTICE

Experienced handlers agree that observing good handlers at work can pay off in better stacking and free-stacking technique. A specialty in your breed would be ideal, providing the opportunity to see many individual stacking examples of your breed. Pay careful attention to how the handlers go about achieving their stacks. It's best, when you are starting out, to just watch without attempting to compete.

Conformation classes get more qualified approval. Bill McFadden suggests getting a recommendation from a top handler or excellent breeder-handler in your area. The qualifications of teachers of these classes vary widely—some are taught by excellent handlers, who have a lot to offer, but some are taught by whomever a training club happens to have handy. Ask

Watch Your Step

Never let anyone convince you to use rough methods to stack a dog. Remember, the dog should look happy and relaxed. Yanking feet around, pulling on ears, and such is not going to help your dog's show potential.

around for classes near you. You can also ask to observe a class, and form your own opinion of the instruction being offered.

Tom Glassford feels that most handling classes are good only for educating novice dogs—getting them used to the atmosphere of a ring and the handling involved. He prefers seminars offered by professionals for the finer education of handlers. Local kennel clubs often sponsor such seminars, so be sure to keep in touch with your local club.

However you acquire your expertise, you and your dog must practice to hone your skills. This is one place where weekly classes can certainly be useful. Human nature being what it is, you are much more likely to practice if you have invested some money and know you are going to have to show what you've learned in front of others.

KEEPING COOL IN THE RING

One of the differences you will probably see while observing dogs being stacked is that some handlers keep their dogs posed throughout their entire time in the ring, while others keep an eye on the judge, ready to present their dogs, but let the dogs relax while the judge is occupied elsewhere. Which dogs do you think are going to look fresher and more relaxed when the judge comes down the line to make the cut? Look at the two parts of figure 14.3. It took this handler no more than a second to go from playing with the dog to having a beautifully posed dog.

Though it may not have any effect—opinions vary—you can also use ring time when the judge's attention is elsewhere to get the crowd on your side. Maybe it won't influence the judge, but some dogs get very up and animated when people are clapping and cheering as the dogs strut their stuff. Being the crowd favorite could work to your advantage.

Figure 14.3. Relax your dog while the judge is examining the rest of the entries. It should only take a moment to stack and be ready for the judge's attention to be back on you.

Tips from the Pros

Make sure you move as the judge goes over the front and rear so that you're not in the judge's way.

—Sharon Irons Strempski, AKC exhibitor and breeder of Affenpinschers

If you are going to try this, be very sure not to disrupt the other exhibitors in any way. That would certainly put you in disfavor. But in your own little space, you can play with the dog, give a good upside-down belly rub (spectators seem to love dogs rolling on their backs), or even do a few tricks if you know any. A dog sitting up and waving is pretty hard to resist, and you can toss a couple of treats as reward to work on that liver-catching ability. If nothing else, engaging in some play should keep your dog relaxed and happy. Just keep one eye on the judge and how things are proceeding so you will have your dog ready when the judge looks your way.

Remember

- ○ Stacking is posing your dog for presentation to the judge.
- ○ You and your dog must practice stacking for both of you to be reasonably good at it.
- ○ Remember that the dog's attitude is at least as important as where the dog's feet are placed—probably more so.
- ○ Small breeds are stacked on a table, and you must practice that way.
- ○ The free stack is a hands-off pose struck by the dog, with coaching from the handler. You will be required to free stack at least once in every ring appearance.
- ○ Use classes and seminars and observation to your best advantage.
- ○ Let your dog relax or even play while the judge's attention is on others.

15

At the Gait

Although the judge's examination of your posed dog is certainly essential, movement will really show how your dog is put together. In most instances, the judge will first have the entire class—or half the class if it is exceptionally large—*go around,* gaiting all the dogs at once. Then, after the judge has examined your dog, you will be asked to do an individual gaiting pattern and then perhaps a circle back to your position. The judge may send the whole class around again or pull some finalists out and send them around. A few judges like to make ring appearances into tests of stamina, sending dogs and handlers around and around.

Watching your judge examine his or her other classes will give you an idea of what to expect. But always be alert for instructions. Sometimes that extra lap around the ring will be to decide between your dog and one or two others.

Talking Dog

In the ring, dogs are shown—*gaited*—at a trot. It might be a slow, fast, or flying trot, but it's a trot. The command "Take them around" sends the entire class counterclockwise around the ring, usually the judge's first look at the dogs.

LEASH AND COLLAR MANAGEMENT

Exhibitors often appear totally unaccustomed to the idea of showing a dog on a lead. Perhaps it's a case of nerves, or they are more used to obedience competition, where the lead is held in the right hand, but they seem bewitched by this snakelike object, allowing it to flow from hand to hand or to flap about in the air.

Show leads are slender and quite malleable. Simply fold any excess into your left hand and keep it there. Only a single, unobtrusive line should extend from you to your dog. Practice tucking the lead away as you walk from stacking the dog to in front of the judge, until you can do it in your sleep (see figure 15.1).

Figure 15.1. Note that there is no lead visible other than the short section directly from handler to dog. Though taut, the lead is not holding the dog up.

You do not want the lead to throw your dog off in any way. You will undoubtedly see many exhibitors, even professional handlers, with a lead so tight that the dog is nearly trotting on tiptoe. Perhaps the dog gaits with his head held unattractively low, or the handler is trying to disguise some fault in movement. But unless a personal instructor has shown you some definite benefit with holding your dog so tightly, showing on a loose lead is preferable. Handlers, particularly inexperienced ones, can create the appearance of faults by holding a dog too tightly while moving.

Experiment with collar placement. Most exhibitors push the collar up high on the neck, just behind the ears. It requires at least a modicum of tension to keep it there. So long as your dog does not object to the slight pull, this position places the collar visually out of the way and allows a pleasing neckline. But if the tension on the lead causes your dog to lean away from you or put his head down and pull against you, try another strategy.

Also try different positions for the lead coming off the dog to you. Many place the lead-to-collar mechanism at the middle top of the dog's neck. But if your dog tends to lower his head, you might try having the leash come from under the dog's chin. It may encourage the dog to pick his head up. If you already use this up-from-under position and find that your dog shakes his head a lot, he is objecting to the leash hitting his ear. Try moving the attachment to the top.

Practice different positions of your arms until you find one that is comfortable for you and your dog. The leash hand is generally somewhere between waist and shoulder high, the elbow bent, the hand away from the body. The right arm, without a particular job to do, seems to give people more problems. Try not to fling it straight out as if you were a tightrope walker. Don't hold it out in front of you, or the dog may suspect that it

Tips from the Pros

Keep an eye on your dog when you're moving it. If the dog is not moving well or the lead isn't right, stop and make the necessary adjustment quickly.

—Sharon Irons Strempski, AKC exhibitor and
breeder of Affenpinschers

holds bait and bend his body to watch it, throwing off his stride. Do your best to let it swing naturally, not too vigorously, at your side.

As with most aspects of dog showing, you can benefit from seeing your performance on videotape. Though you may find watching yourself embarrassing, your goal is to simply fade into the background. Change anything that will distract attention from the dog to you.

Remember that bent-knee, low gliding gait we referred to earlier (yours, not the dog's)? You need to practice it until it feels natural to you. This somewhat peculiar gait lets you move around the ring quickly enough to show your dog well without doing a lot of bouncing up and down. Your body movement can be distracting to the dog, but most of all, you don't want to be moving the leash up and down as you progress around the ring. Some handlers advocate practicing with something like a set of keys attached to the end of the leash, rather than a dog, and working with that until you can glide smoothly around the ring without jingling the keys. Other handlers say it's rarely necessary for the exhibitor to do more than a fast walk. The long gaits of this flowing form of moving allow you to cover enough ground for the dog to trot while you walk. You won't see a lot of this in most rings, because many seem to feel it's a speed competition, but it does work. You can try it and see how it fits with your dog.

Speed Limits

If you're tired of being told to practice, maybe this isn't the sport for you! Because you're about to be told again. Not only does every dog have a particular speed at which he or she moves best, but also that speed may be different when viewed from behind than when seen from the side. The only way to determine these speeds—and to be able to reproduce them in the ring—is to practice.

Many people seem to think that faster is better. You see them racing around the ring, their dogs' legs a blur. You can even hear people say things like, "Judge so-and-so is a speed freak and really likes to see them go." Well, there may be a few judges out there who like to see how fast dogs can trot and handlers run. But there are many others who will either tell you to do it again, more slowly, or will simply ignore your dog, assuming that you are speeding around the ring to hide faulty movement.

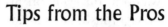

Tips from the Pros

You have to practice walking with the animal you are showing. Your speed will determine the dog's speed, and the dog will be his smoothest at his best speed. The amount of lead you give can almost control the dog in the line they will draw. You don't want to allow the dog enough lead so he can weave, but you don't want to string him up. Your gait will change with each dog you show.

—Taffe McFadden, AKC professional handler

Actually, most dogs do not move as well when forced to speed around the ring. They become erratic and may display faults not based on structure, but on trotting too fast.

Determining the best speed for your particular dog also depends on knowing your breed. If the breed standard for your dog specifies that the dog single-track, you may need to move a bit more quickly. Dogs' legs tend to converge under them more as they speed up. So your up and back, when you are moving directly away from and toward the judge, could be faster than your circle, or the middle leg of a triangle if you are asked to do one.

The circle and the trip across the far side of the ring in the triangle present the judge with a side view of your dog. In this view, the judge will be looking for reach and drive. For breeds specifying things such as a *hackney gait* (Miniature Pinscher) or a *flying trot* (German Shepherd Dog), the side view offers the judge the opportunity to check for these attributes.

It's important for you to realize that "reach" does not equal "speed." The dog actually will not be able to achieve maximum reach if you move too quickly, because there just isn't time for legs to extend to their fullest before needing to move in the other direction.

Fancy That!

The flying trot gets its name both from the fact that it is a speedy movement and that the dog is indeed suspended in mid-air for a time in each stride.

Try practicing at speeds you consider slow, medium, and fast until you can reproduce each speed fairly accurately. Then have someone videotape you from the front, rear, and side at each speed. This way, when you study the tape and decide which speed is most appropriate, you will be able to recreate it reliably.

Also take a quick look at how *you* move. If you watch experienced handlers who show dogs large or fast enough that the handler has to trot or run, you'll see that the handlers do not move on their toes and bounce up and down. Instead, they use a flat-footed run, trying to appear to flow over the ground. It requires a greater knee bend than more "normal" movement, and when you first try it, you will understand why handlers' knees often suffer.

If you are working on your own and don't have someone to coach you, first watch other handlers. Then watch an old Groucho Marx movie. That odd walk he does, crouching halfway to the ground, is an extreme example of what the handlers are doing.

No doubt about it, there's a lot to think about in moving a dog. You certainly want to know all the patterns you might be asked to perform, and have a lot of practice with your dog. And you want to watch the judge you will be showing under to see how he or she runs things in the ring.

The Patterns of Gaiting

First, the dog will be on your left side, with the exception only of segments of some of the more complex (and rarely used) patterns. You don't want a dog that lags behind—that hardly gives an impression of drive, power, and an "up" attitude. Dogs moving ahead of the handler at the end of the leash are always crowd pleasers. But you don't want the dog actually pulling against the leash—that disrupts movement. Seminar giver George Alston cautions that handler and dog should create a single picture; he feels that too much separation between them is distracting. The dog shouldn't crowd against you or veer away, but move in a constant path forward, whether it's straight or curving.

Take Them Around

Most judges will first send them around as a group to get an initial look at all the dogs. In large classes or groups, the judge may move half the group at a time. Pay attention—be alert for any instructions, particularly if you are at the head of a line.

The dogs and handlers will move in a circle counterclockwise around the perimeter of the ring. This is trickier than it sounds. You're expected to keep your place in line, not running over or passing the dog in front of you (unless for some reason they stop), nor impeding the dog behind you, and of course moving your own dog at his or her optimum speed.

If you need to move your dog faster than the dog in front of you, try to slow down while not in front of the judge to allow some space to develop. Use the space to move at your best speed while the judge's eyes will be on you.

Many judges will also send each dog around individually. Some will do this as they examine and move each dog. Some will examine and move each dog, then go back and have each handler take the dog around and to the back of the line. Some will make a cut and move only the dogs they are still considering.

Up and Back

This is also known as the out and back, or down and back. Whatever you call it, it's a line directly away from the judge, an about turn, and a line directly back to the judge (see figure 15.2). This allows the judge maximum time to check the dog's movement from the rear and front.

When you start practicing this pattern, you will realize how hard it is to move forward in a straight line. If you need to, practice on your own before practicing with your dog. You want the dog to understand right from the beginning that the idea is to move in a straight line.

With a large dog, you may need the help of an overhead line. If you are having problems with control, keep your show lead on the dog, but also attach a second line to the overhead line, with just a little slack. Practice moving up and down the line until the dog is not tugging on the overhead. Don't do the full up and back, because the overhead will not give the dog enough space to make the turn. Trot in one direction. Stop and praise the

Watch Your Step

Many of the dirty tricks of dog showing occur while the dogs are being gaited. Some handlers are quite skilled at stepping on the heels of the handler ahead of them, throwing the victim off stride or even yanking off a shoe. Others throw bait down so the dogs behind them will lunge for it.

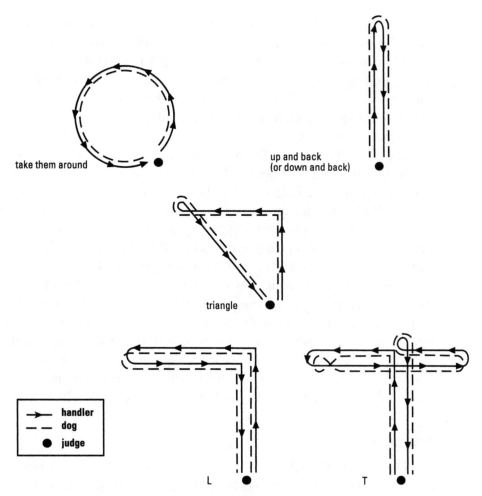

take them around

up and back
(or down and back)

triangle

handler
dog
judge

L

T

Figure 15.2. Gaiting patterns in the ring

dog. Turn around, being careful to keep the dog in position so the overhead line doesn't pull. Then trot back in the other direction.

Once you have stopped using the overhead line (or if you do not need to use one), practice the turn. It's interesting that obedience competitors, who heel their dogs in various patterns in the ring, practice all sorts of turns so that their movements do not disrupt their dogs, but many conformation handlers never bother practicing turns, even though they are supposed to be showing how well their dogs move. Don't be one of these nonpracticing handlers.

As you approach the far end of the ring, or as far as you're going away from the judge (small dogs sometimes use half or less of the ring), slow down to cue the dog that you will be turning. You don't want the dog confidently trotting along and slamming against the end of the leash because you have snapped a military about face and are speeding off in the opposite direction. Dogs subjected to such treatment could decide the ring is not such a fun place to be.

Also slow down some distance from the judge on your way back. You will be free stacking your dog, and you want some room to maneuver without running over the judge. Remember that you are presenting the dog—move so that your dog, not yourself, is heading directly toward the judge.

When watching televised dog shows, or big shows in person, you'll notice that many handlers have some sort of little ritual before they start the pattern. Some will walk over in front of the judge and make a little clockwise circle, ending it facing down the ring for the up and back. They feel that the circle helps get the dog oriented and moving. Others will give the dog a hearty pat and indulge in a second of play before starting off. Try different things to see what works best with your dog, then stick with it. Giving the dog advance cues to what is happening will help him or her perform. But be aware that the judge will not appreciate any ritual that takes more than a second or two—there are a lot of dogs to be looked at.

Triangle

An alternative to the up and back, the triangle gives the judge a full view of each dog's movement. The triangle is formed by moving directly away from the judge, turning 90 degrees left and moving across the back of the ring, then turning clockwise to come across the diagonal of the ring toward the judge (see figure 15.2).

Talking Dog

The little circle done by many handlers before gaiting the dog is called a *courtesy turn.* It lets everyone get in position and ready for gaiting, including the dog. Some judges, however, do not like it.

Most handlers will move across the back of the ring at a slightly faster pace to show off the dog's reach. Be careful to slow down for the looping 270-degree turn at the end. If you are showing a small dog, you may choose to make a sharp left to head into the final leg of the triangle. A larger dog cannot manage this and would be thrown off stride. For most larger dogs, the incomplete clockwise circle is a better option.

Be sure to look up and "spot" the judge as you start the final leg so that you will move the dog in a straight line to him or her. The judge is examining your dog's front, and any weaving on your part could create imaginary faults.

At the completion of the triangle, you will again be free stacking your dog. Plan ahead and leave room.

Other Patterns

These two more complex patterns—the "L" and the "T"—are used infrequently, but occasionally a judge will ask for one, particularly in Junior Showmanship, to examine a handler's competence. The judge of a champions class in which my dog was entered asked all of us to circle clockwise as a group—meaning the dogs had to be on the right—then used an "L" as his individual movement pattern. He'd seen many of the dogs before and wanted to see how they reacted to doing something different. Always be prepared.

Look at the "L" and "T" diagrams in figure 15.2 and you will see that these patterns require you to change the dog to your right side for some portion of the gaiting. The judge does not care how straight *your* legs are, after all, and moving across the end of the ring with the dog on your far side won't offer the judge much of a view.

The "L" demands that you do the first two legs of the triangle as usual, then move the dog to your right for the return across the back of the ring. Because most handlers and dogs are more accustomed to moving with the dog on the left, they switch back to that position for the final leg toward the judge. That means you will have to switch sides twice,

Fancy That!

FCI shows are somewhat more likely to use different gaiting patterns, and also to gait two dogs side by side.

so you had better be at least somewhat practiced at it. Or you can leave the dog on your right for the return to the judge.

For the about turn in the far corner of the ring, you do a counterclockwise about turn while your dog does one clockwise. Have your leash well gathered so you can make a smooth swap from left hand to right. Use a cue word such as "L-turn" to warn your dog that this is not a triangle (see figure 15.3). With a small dog, you may be able to do your left about turn and simply switch the leash from hand to hand and pass the dog to your right side.

Some handlers simply keep the dog on their right for the remainder of the pattern. If your dog moves equally well on either side, this is easiest. If you would rather switch back, you have two options. You can practice having the dog perform a right turn on his or her own ahead of you, so that you can then switch hands and come up on the dog's right. There is less hazard of tripping over each other this way than with a 270-degree turn as in the triangle, but with the added intrigue of switching sides in the midst of the turn.

The "T" begins the same as the "L," with a left turn and then a switch of sides in an about turn. But now after a trip across the back of the ring with the dog on your right, you make another about turn and switch the dog back to the left. The final turn can be a simple 90-degree left turn or a clockwise 270-degree circle (see figure 15.3).

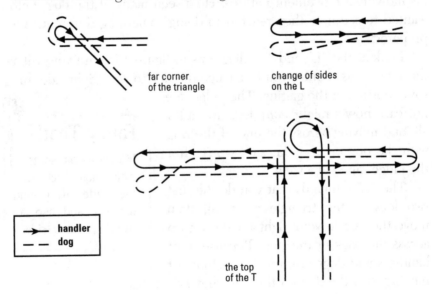

Figure 15.3. Details of complex turns

FINAL THOUGHTS ON PATTERNS

Even if you have never actually seen an "L" or a "T" used in the ring, practice them at least until you and your dog both have some idea of how to handle the turns. You never know what the next judge may ask for.

Certainly watch how the judge handles his or her ring so you will have an idea of what to expect. But don't be lulled into complacency. Always be alert for any instructions from the judge. You may be asked to repeat a gaiting pattern, move more slowly, or take some other definite action. You don't want to make the judge repeat instructions, though you may ask a question if you don't understand.

Be particularly alert as the judge finishes moving the last dog. The next action seems to be the most variable. Some judges may move certain dogs again, alone, in pairs, or in groups. Do not make any assumptions based on what happens. If a judge has already decided on the top dog but needs to sort out the others, the dog about to take first could be totally ignored at this point. Don't stop showing because you think your dog is out of the ribbons. You may be wrong.

WHAT THE JUDGE IS LOOKING FOR

Details vary, of course, depending on the view the judge is getting. But the best judges are looking for movement that indicates a structure best suited

Tips from the Pros

First get your dog moving happily on a lead. Walk him often and talk happily to him as you go along. When he has become accustomed to the lead, introduce a command like "Let's show." Once this command is given, your dog must learn to gait nicely at your side, moving in a straight line in whatever direction you want to go. Keep talking to him and keep corrections to a minimum. It helps to have someone watch you that can tell you what speed is best for your dog and how the two of you are looking as you move.

—Lilian S. Barber, AKC judge and exhibitor, author of *The New Complete Italian Greyhound*

to the job for which the dog was bred. Most of the herding breeds, for example, should exhibit a trot that covers ground effortlessly and could be maintained for hours. The trot is definitely their gait. Sighthounds, on the other hand, are born to gallop, and this appears in such things as more up and down "bounce" when they are trotting. Many of the toys, meant simply as companions, have an aspect of showiness to their trot, less efficient in actual movement but pleasing to the human eye. So first, you have to know your breed. Then realize that as you move around the ring, you present different views of your dog and thus different considerations to the judge.

Going away for the up and back or triangle, the judge has a rear view. This is the time he or she will be looking for straight pasterns, bent neither in nor out, single or double tracking as called for in the standard, correct tail carriage, and whether there is excess bounce to the hindquarters. Faults such as crabbing or sidewinding, where the dog's front half and back half are not aligned so that the dog's rear feet do not interfere with the front feet, show up best in this view. Certain breeds have particular characteristics, such as the roll of the Old English Sheepdog. There may be many more details, but these are the basics.

When you go around, or across the back of the ring, you present a side view. The judge has plenty to consider here, and speeding along too quickly will not benefit you (unless you are trying to hide faulty movement). The timing of the dog's front and rear feet is critical to effective movement and can be checked from the side. The reach of the front legs and drive of the rear—which can be shown without speeding around like a race car—and levelness of topline are evident from the side, as is head and neck carriage.

From the front—the "back" of the up and back or final leg of the triangle—the judge has the best view of how the neck, forelegs, and body come together. Elbows out, toeing in or out, and again sidewinding can all be detected from this perspective.

If a judge ever says anything about the way your dog moves, good or bad, pay close attention. There may be a problem your handling is causing that you could correct. Or you might hear the pleasant opinion that your dog shows very correct movement for the breed.

Remember

- ○ Show leads are held in one hand; the left unless the dog is on your right.
- ○ Collar position should not annoy or distract the dog.
- ○ Fast is not necessarily best—experiment until you find the speeds that show your dog to best advantage.
- ○ Know and practice all the patterns of gaiting.
- ○ Always be alert for instructions from the judge.
- ○ Judges are (or should be) looking for movement that is correct for the breed, not just the flashiest dog.

16

Taking the Bait

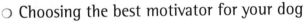

In This Chapter

○ Choosing the best motivator for your dog
○ Best use of bait
○ When bait is not allowed

First we will remind you that if you are planning to show under the auspices of the UKC, bait (as in food) is *not* permitted in the ring. Squeaky toys may or may not be permitted, at the judge's discretion. Only using your voice and snapping your fingers are regularly allowed.

With all other registries, food, toys, squeakers, and attention-getters of all sorts are a normal part of the show ring. Choosing the best attention-getter for your dog, and using it to best advantage, requires practice. This is the final bit of dog/handler ring behavior we will be coaching you on.

One decision you may as well make right up front—are you going to be a "bait spitter"? Although it is probably more prominent in obedience training and competition, some conformation handlers do hold bait in their mouths, either spitting it to the dog or removing it when they want to use it. Some people find nothing untoward

Watch Your Step

One thing you definitely don't want to do is give your dog a nice bite of some tasty morsel just as the judge wants to examine the dog's bite. Judges hate that.

about this practice, and some find it totally disgusting and nauseating. In obedience, it's meant to focus the dog on the handler's face. In conformation, that isn't as important, and it may be less off-putting for spectators if you choose to carry your bait in a pocket or pouch.

CHOOSING THE BEST MOTIVATOR FOR YOUR DOG

General wisdom dictates that food is the most important reward you can offer a dog, it being one of the necessities of life. This is true often enough for people to keep saying it. The majority of dogs *are* excited by special food treats. But there are those individuals out there who may eat or walk away from their food bowl. Sometimes they might accept a treat, but sometimes they'll just ignore your offering. Other dogs may like treats just fine when training at home, but they get so keyed up when in an actual show (yes, they certainly know the difference) that they no longer desire food. Some dogs not initially motivated by treats can be taught to anticipate and appreciate them.

Dogs in the Herding, Sporting, Working, and Terrier groups are often motivated with toys rather than food. They may play "fetch" as part of their conditioning program or be allowed to "kill the rat" after their performance.

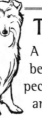

Tips from the Pros

A little trick—practice teaching them to catch liver because they'll be on their toes and watching you, ears up because they're expecting liver. A dog who's going to catch also wants to be balanced, so you get a better stack, more animation.

—Bill McFadden, AKC professional handler

They consider their toys highly desirable and will perk up at the sight of their squeaky mouse or tennis ball.

In large classes, some handlers will actually play with the dog with the toy while the judge is going over the other dogs. If doing this helps keep the dog relaxed and happy, it's a great idea. If the dog is going to wage a pitched battle to keep possession of the toy, better to wait until after the class is over—you aren't going to score many wins showing a dog with a squeaker clamped in his mouth.

During training, you should experiment with lots of different motivators to learn what works best for your dog. Just because every other Cavalier King Charles Spaniel you've ever seen loved dried liver doesn't mean this one will. Others may drool for salmon, and cheese is generally popular. Toys might include plastic squeakers, plush squeakers, balls, ropes, even the white pieces of plastic used with lure-coursing sighthounds. Try a variety, and if you find one that really appeals to your dog, save it for the ring and special training occasions.

Food Choices

When trying out possible treat choices, keep in mind that you need to be able to carry them in a pocket or bait bag, and the dog should be able to chew and swallow them quickly. (Judges don't want to have to stand around waiting for ages while a dog finishes crunching a hard treat.) But within these guidelines lie a plethora of choices.

Chunks of dried liver or steak cooked medium rare are popular among professional handlers. Both can be left in fairly large pieces and held so that the dog can chew off small pieces at a time, or cut into smaller pieces and tossed to the dog or in front of the dog to focus attention. Cheese offers the same choices for use.

Talking Dog

A *bait bag* is simply a pouch, usually lined with plastic, for holding treats. It might clip onto a belt or come with its own belt and fastener. It takes the place of pockets and may be more easily accessible.

Tips from the Pros

I teach my dogs a key word to perk them up. Whenever they get a treat, be it for going into their crates, doing a trick, just being cute, and so on, I cue that with the word "treat" or "cookie." All the dogs perk up at the sound of the cue or word. It gives an immediate great expression when the judge is looking at the dog and you have nothing—no bait, no toys. All I have to say to the dogs to get that great look is "Where's your cookie?" They stand up on their toes and perk right up. Of course, they always get the cookie—the reward is delayed, but they already understand this with training. So they always give me the expression I want when I ask for it. Sort of like Pavlov's dogs!

—Karen A. Brancheau, UKC exhibitor

Some people slice up hot dogs or sausages and microwave the slices till nearly dry. These little discs are nirvana to some dogs and can be tossed fairly well. Other people, perhaps harkening back to their dogs' Arctic heritage, dry fish such as salmon into tiny, tasty nuggets. Even non-sled dog types often go wild for this smelly treat. Those of us here in the Pacific Northwest can buy salmon "sticks"—a form of jerky—and slice them into tiny delectable morsels.

All versions of "people" food need to be kept refrigerated to avoid spoilage and food-borne diseases. RV-ers have their refrigerators to use. The rest of us carry picnic coolers.

Don't forget more exotic possibilities. Most dogs like popcorn. Also watermelon, although this could be hard to carry around the ring. There have been dogs that wanted waffles and those that begged for barbecue. Try different things until you find at least one that really excites your dog.

Nonfood Choices

As I mentioned before, the basic choices for nonfood bait are plastic or rubber toys with squeakers, plush or furry toys with squeakers, and balls. But there is more variation here than seems apparent, plus there are other less common possibilities.

Tips from the Pros

We play with the dogs with squeak toys because these are sometimes allowed in the UKC ring, at the judge's discretion. If the dog knows about the toy—I use a special one that they only get to play with in the ring—the dog will light up and think that the ring is a great place to be. They will show their hearts out for you, just to play a bit.

—Karen A. Brancheau, UKC exhibitor

Both the texture and "chewability" of the toy and the individual sound of the squeaker appear to be important to the dog. There are several completely different types of squeakers, and they produce a wide variation of sounds. Some seem to generate much more excitement than others.

If your dog does not already have a preferred squeak toy, visit a pet supply superstore and try out everything! Dogs are generally allowed in these establishments, so your dog can help make his or her selection. Buy several of the same kind if one makes a hit—toys get destroyed in the course of play and may no longer be in production when you need more.

For future reference, it may be helpful for you to know that you can buy replacement squeakers for rehabilitating toys. Plush toys in particular often outlast their squeakers, and a quick snip followed by a new squeaker and a few stitches can soon have a toy squeaking again. Squeakers can be found at vendor booths at dog shows and at some five-and-dime stores.

Also try out other toys while you are there. Yes, tennis balls may be all a retriever-type needs to be aquiver with happiness, but there are other choices of balls, and other things completely. Foxtails (balls with long fluttery tails), rope toys, and ball and rope combinations are just some of the possibilities. Whatever your ultimate choice, save it for only occasional training sessions and appearances in the ring.

BEST USE OF BAIT

Exhibitors use bait to get attention and expression. With males, bait is also often used to keep the dog's interest on something other than the judge checking for two normal testicles during the examination. Keep in mind that baiting is an *optional* activity. Yes, you may see everyone else doing it,

Tips from the Pros

Some dogs will bait with toys, others with food. Practice using bait at home before attempting it in the show ring. Some people just can't handle food bait, and some dogs won't take it in the ring. Find out exactly what gets your dog's interest.

—Sharon Irons Strempski, AKC exhibitor and
breeder of Affenpinschers

but if you can barely keep control of your leash, you may want to wait before attempting baiting. It doesn't automatically get good results—you have to work at it.

If you do choose to use bait, you will need readily accessible pockets or a bait pouch. You shouldn't have to take your eyes off your dog to search for bait—you should just be able to reach in and dig out a piece.

As mentioned earlier in a Tip from the Pros, teaching your dog to catch bait can improve the dog's performance. But with nearly all dogs, you will have to practice. Stand only a couple of feet from your dog, toss a small piece of bait in the air several times and catch it, then say "Ready" or some other cue and toss the bait in an arc toward the dog's muzzle. With most dogs unpracticed at catching, the bait will hit the dog in the head and drop to the ground. Grab the bait! The dog only gets it if caught in the air. If the dog is faster than you are, try standing the dog on a picnic table so that the bait drops well below it if not caught. Keep trying this and eventually most dogs will "catch" on. Some are never really good at it, but most will learn to make an effort.

Tips from the Pros

Your dog should be trained to respond to bait—food, a squeaky toy, or a clicker—long before you enter your first show. If your dog likes food, liver or some other treat will work, but only if you have trained him to give the correct, alert response. Some dogs get so nervous in the ring that food is uninteresting to them, so some kind of sound is better. Make sure this is not distracting to other dogs and exhibitors.

—Lilian S. Barber, breeder/exhibitor, AKC judge,
author of *The New Complete Italian Greyhound*

You can use bait to improve your dog's free stack. If you need to get the dog's left front leg more forward, move your bait to the dog's right. As the dog leans, the left foot will move forward. To move the right foot forward, move the bait to the dog's left.

If the dog is standing well, but just not "turning it on," try to get the dog up on its toes by tossing your bait in the air. Or encourage a forward lean by holding your bait and moving it in a half-circle almost to the dog, then away. Of course, the dog has to be used to this procedure before using it in the ring.

To direct the dog's attention away from you, show the piece of bait then toss it in the direction you want the dog to look. This used to result in a ring littered with bait, but judges are frowning much more on this than they used to. Do not toss food around unless you are going to pick it up, or risk the judge's displeasure.

Never give a dog a mouthful of bait right before the judge comes over to examine the bite. The judge does not want to wait while the dog chews, nor does the judge want to be overwhelmed with liver breath.

Also don't get in the bad habit of waving bait around as you gait the dog. The dog will crane his head around to focus on the bait, potentially

Figure 16.1. Note the various uses of bait in this photo. The second dog in line has just been examined and is being rewarded with a bite of bait, while the third and fourth dogs are being shown bait to gain interest and expression.

throwing off the gait. Some handlers do throw bait out ahead of the dog on parts of the gaiting pattern. Most only make the throwing motion in the ring to avoid littering the place with liver. You already have enough to think about without attempting this.

WHEN BAIT IS NOT ALLOWED

You know going in that you won't be using bait if you're showing with the UKC. But it's also uncommon with the FCI. And even some AKC and CKC judges frown on use of bait and will refuse to place dogs whose handlers use it. Always watch a judge's ring procedure before you are due to go in, and if you see a sudden absence of bait from handlers whom you know generally use it, put yours away as well. Some judges will even ask specifically that dogs be free stacked without use of bait.

When you cannot use food or toys, you still have your voice and your attitude. Use them! If you have trained the dog with cue words, recommended earlier, you can get a response from the dog simply by asking, "Where's your cookie?" Always remember to reward the dog when your performance is over, so that the cue words will keep their association with the desired object.

> **Fancy That!**
>
> "Bait" can be almost anything at all. One Siberian Husky showed well on almost every outing for the reward of leaping into his owner's arms at the end of each appearance.

And even without this training, making sure your own attitude is up and happy, and coaxing the dog in an excited whisper is often enough to get the dog alert and showing well.

Remember

○ Bait is not allowed in the UKC show ring.
○ Try different treats and toys to find which best motivates your dog.
○ Use a pocket or bait pouch to carry treats.
○ Teach the dog to catch for added alertness.
○ Don't leave food lying around the ring—pick it up.
○ Don't bait when you gait.
○ Remember to use your own attitude and voice.

17

The View from the Top

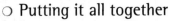
We've given you a lot to think about. There's much more to come. But before we get into the paperwork and paraphernalia of showing and take you to an actual show, we'll try to put things in focus thus far. If this is all starting to sound a little too complex, intense, and frightening, take heart! We're just trying to prepare you for whatever you might find out there in the fancy.

After we buck up your courage a bit, we need to introduce the topics of excusal and disqualification. These are the two punishments for breaking the rules of the show ring, one temporary, one permanent.

Finally, the cropping and docking controversy. If you are in a breed that is usually shown with cropped ears and/or docked tails, you may want to know both the implications of these surgeries and the effects on a possible international show career.

176

PUTTING IT ALL TOGETHER

All right, you've learned a little about the history of the sport, we've investigated some of the goods and bads of competition and sportsmanship, and we've taken a quick look at the time and money and temperament necessary for showing. In case your dog is well suited but you aren't, we discussed hiring a professional handler.

The basic training section stepped you through goals and taking care of the necessary medical, identification, and socialization issues and working on conditioning. We examined conformation classes and the anatomy of the dog. We made clear, we hope, how a dog show progresses through the classes, what the various awards mean, and how to earn and compute those championship points. We talked about how to find and choose shows, and the special activities available to those in their younger years.

In this section, we've practiced the actual mechanics involved in showing a dog—preshow grooming, stacking, gaiting, and baiting. We hope you've been doing all this, not just reading about it. Your head is probably spinning with information, and you might feel like a total klutz! Congratulations! You're a typical novice in the fancy. Only with practice and actual show experience will it all start to come together.

Your physical coordination at the sport, and your stamina, will improve as you continue to train and compete. Fortunately, you have to keep your dog in good condition, and that means you will be exercising yourself as well. Some judges do seem to make an endurance competition out of the ring, and you don't want to be near collapse if the judge says to "take 'em around" for the third or fourth time.

Mental toughness is also required. In any competitive sport, you have to be prepared for both the normal ups and downs of the game and for the unexpected. Old-timers can afford to chat at ringside, but you need to focus all your concentration on the task at hand. Don't worry about the competition. Focus on your dog and how the two of you are going to put your best effort forward.

Do your best to relax. It will help you and your dog. Take deep breaths, and above all, take your time. Yes, the judge may be waiting for you to finish stacking your dog, but you already know from past experience that hurrying will only mean you get flustered and actually take longer to get the job done. You also stand a good chance of upsetting your dog. Calm unhurried actions are best.

Tips from the Pros
Realize that most of the time the judge is looking at the dog, not you. Be able to laugh at yourself if you do something klutzy.
—Bill McFadden, AKC professional handler

If you have done any winning at all with your dog, put the picture of that win in your mind as you go into the ring. Feeling like a success will help you to stay calm and focused.

Do not fear the judge. Judges are people so enamored with the fancy that after what was probably a long career breeding and/or showing dogs, they have turned to judging to stay active in the sport. They are interested in the betterment of the breed, in choosing the dog that best fits the standard and still could perform its function. Yes, it is true, some judges seem to favor professional handlers or put up friends or those in positions of power. You will learn who they are, and you will avoid them. Don't obsess over it, and don't automatically blame your losses on a "political" judge. Maybe the other dogs *were* more deserving.

Your attitude toward your dog and the sport probably plays the biggest part in determining whether you'll have a long and happy career in the show ring or quickly turn bitter and burn out. If you find the politics and the limited number of wins available in each ring just too much, there are plenty of other dog sports available. In obedience, tracking, agility, herding, terrier digs, water rescue, and hunting tests, each dog is judged individually on a standard point scale. You can pass or fail, regardless of what the other dogs do. Ribbons and trophies may be awarded to the highest scoring dogs, but you can still have a successful experience and earn points or "legs" toward a title without beating other dogs. Only you can decide what's best for you and your dog as far as competition is concerned.

LISTENING TO YOUR DOG AND OTHERS

Your dog is listening to you all the time. If you are fidgeting with the lead, fussing with hairs out of place, shifting your feet, breathing shallowly, your dog knows you are nervous and wonders if he or she should be as well. You can avoid this, as we've explained above.

But you should also be open to the messages your dog is sending you. Dogs, as you should know, are wonderful creatures, often so willing to do what their people wish that they will suffer unhappiness and even risk personal injury. It is your responsibility to see that your dog is happy and healthy. More than a few excellent show prospects have been retired early because the dogs simply didn't enjoy the show ring. Their owners/handlers were willing to listen to the dog.

Although early socialization and proper training can go a long way toward preparing a dog for the show ring, some would simply rather stay at home. You will have to be attentive to understand how your dog is feeling about things. Then you will have to decide if you can jolly the dog into liking the ring, or if a few minutes of mild unhappiness is okay and counteracted by a good cuddle afterward.

You must be perceptive to know what your dog is thinking about dog shows; your human competitors will be much less subtle. In fact, you will likely receive plenty of unsolicited comments, many you wish you hadn't heard. If you listen to them all, you will undoubtedly find yourself soon

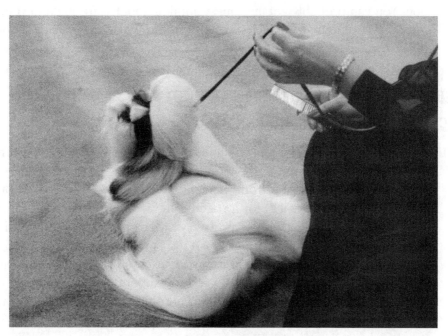

Figure 17.1. This little trooper has no problem relaxing in the ring.

depressed, insecure, and certain you will never win at a dog show. As we explained in the early chapters, you can listen to everything at a dog show, but you must have your information filters firmly in place.

After you have been in the sport a little while, you will start to recognize those exhibitors who always have something bad to say about the judge, the winner, the show-giving club, the weather, and any other topic that might come up. Ignore these people. You will never learn anything worthwhile from them because you'll never be able to separate a nugget from all those sour grapes.

You want to seek out those exhibitors who shrug off a loss and still pet the dog afterward. When asked why they didn't do better that day, they might point out a mistake they made in the ring, praise the attributes of the winning dog, or shrug and say the judge just doesn't like their type of dog. You can probably get an honest opinion about your dog and your performance from a person such as this. If nothing else, you have a model for how to behave at a show.

Fancy That!

The majority of UKC exhibitors prefer to show under the United Kennel Club because they feel the atmosphere is so much more relaxed. If you find yourself stressed out at dog shows, maybe you should give the UKC a try.

BEING EXCUSED OR DISQUALIFIED AND OTHER TRANSGRESSIONS

We need to discuss a few more unpleasantries before walking you through the paperwork and into the show ring.

A dog can be excused from the ring for a variety of reasons. Though it may be disheartening, it is for a specific show only, and the dog can come back and try again another day. In fact, at times it may actually be wiser to ask to be excused than to try and finish the performance.

One of the most common reasons for excusal is lameness. A dog may jump off a grooming table or just get too exuberant, and pull a muscle or twist a leg, and then limp in the ring. These things happen. You're out the money for the entry and travel, but it's only a temporary setback, and a limping dog isn't going to win anyway.

If, in the judge's opinion, a dog has been chalked, powdered, or dyed to conceal faulty coat color, or had any change or enhancement of the eye, lip, or nose pigment, the judge is to withhold any awards from the dog. The dog's handler will be advised of the judge's opinion, and the matter is reported to the registry (the AKC, UKC, etc.). The handler and/or owner of the dog may be subject to further discipline by the registry. In the case of the UKC, bringing grooming equipment into the ring is also subject to the same procedures.

Dogs must also meet any height, weight, or coloring guidelines stated in the standard. A judge or a competitor can request that a dog be measured or weighed during a class. A dog that falls outside the guidelines is not eligible for awards. In the UKC, the handler is notified and a note made in the judge's book. In the AKC, the dog is marked down as "Measured out—ineligible" or "Weighed out—ineligible." A dog found ineligible by three different judges is no longer eligible to be entered in that specific class. (Recall that some breeds are broken into several height divisions for showing purposes. So you may be able to show in another class.)

In the AKC, any colorings that fall outside the breed standard are treated the same way. Competitors may request a judicial opinion on another dog's markings, and the judge must write his or her opinion on an AKC form and disqualify the dog if the markings are deemed inappropriate. A dog thus disqualified by three different judges may not be shown again.

A much more serious transgression is any act of canine aggression in the ring or even on the show grounds. If a judge feels that a dog is menacing or threatening and cannot be safely approached, he or she can simply excuse the dog on the spot. If the dog actually attacks any person while in the ring, the dog is disqualified. Unlike the "three strikes and out" of an incorrect height or weight, this is a single strike and you're out. A dog disqualified for aggression is barred from any further showing unless the owner applies for and receives reinstatement from the AKC.

Under the auspices of the UKC, the judge reports any in-the-ring acts of aggression, but outside the ring any person witnessing an act of dog aggression is expected to file a formal complaint. The UKC, upon receiving such a report, notifies the owner, who then has two weeks to respond to the charges. After reviewing the facts, the UKC notifies the dog's owner of the decision. If the dog is found to have behaved aggressively, the owner must return the dog's UKC Registration Certificate. The names of the owner and dog are published in *Bloodlines* magazine.

A UKC judge may also excuse a dog if the handler is unable to control it, even if the dog is simply wildly exuberant rather than aggressive. The UKC also considers *double handling* a serious enough infraction to excuse the dog in question from competition.

You can also ask for your dog to be excused. If your dog is shy, and you have rushed him or her into the ring too soon, it may be better to ask to be excused before your dog really becomes frightened and totally ruins any possible show career.

The judge also has the option of withholding awards. If he or she doesn't feel that any dog in the ring is deserving of a blue ribbon, the ribbon is simply withheld. A red and yellow may be awarded, or all ribbons might be withheld if the judge feels the entry is really inferior. The judge could also award all the regular ribbons, but not select a Winners Dog or Bitch.

A variety of other circumstances can result in a disqualification. All male dogs are checked for having two testicles normally placed in the scrotum—anything less means disqualification. (These dogs are expected to be used in a breeding program if they have success in the ring, so being equipped for the job is considered essential.)

Dogs that have been surgically altered in any manner not specifically permitted by the breed standard can be disqualified. Some breeds are routinely cropped or docked (see the next section of this chapter for a discussion of these procedures), many have dewclaws removed. Anything beyond these stated specifics is illegal.

The human part of the team can earn a suspension through illegal activities. While suspended, a person may not show, sell, or breed a dog. As you can see, this is a very serious situation. A person can earn a suspension by showing a dog that has been surgically altered, substituting one dog for

Talking Dog

Double handling is the enlistment of a second unofficial "handler" outside the ring to attract the dog's attention and help keep the dog alert. This is against the rules of dog showing. You may see it happening right in front of you—I have. A perceptive judge will also see it and refuse to place the dog. (Note that double handling is routinely accepted in some European countries.)

Talking Dog

Unsportsmanlike conduct may seem like a wide-open and nebulous area, but as it relates to being suspended, it's actually pretty well defined. Yelling at a judge or competitors, using obscenities, refusing to accept a ribbon or throwing one on the ground, or failure to follow any of the normal dog show rules are considered unsportsmanlike and can be punished.

another, stating false information on any registrations, or being convicted of cruelty to animals. Unsportsmanlike conduct at a show can also earn a suspension.

Finally, the award you thought you won can be disallowed if the registry discovers your dog was not eligible for the class in which it was shown. The classes can be confusing, and you may have made an innocent mistake. You are not in trouble as long as you return the ribbon(s) or trophy when the registry contacts you. Any points you may have won will now be awarded to the Reserve dog. You might have entered a dog in Novice after winning three first places or a puppy in the wrong age class—these are the most common errors. Just get it right the next time, and still be happy for the win, even if it's no longer official.

THE CROPPING/DOCKING CONTROVERSY

A number of breeds are "traditionally" cropped (ears) and/or docked (tails). The justifications given for these procedures are that "hunting dogs with long tails are subject to tail injuries" and "drop ears are unnatural in a descendant of the wolf, and lead to increased ear problems with infections." Docking is often claimed to be painless.

Actually, most of this is quite untrue. A lot of docking actually goes back to an arcane British law that counted (and taxed) dogs by counting tails. So remove the tail and you removed the tax. The "hunting injuries" logic does not hold up because not all hunting breeds are docked. English Setters are known for their long feathered tails, and English Pointers are not docked. Yet veterinarians do not report any greater incidence of tail injuries in these breeds than in docked German Pointers or docked Cocker Spaniels. It is simply a custom that has been handed down over the years. Fanciers of docked breeds are wont to practically foam at the mouth at any suggestion that they are doing a disservice to their dogs and the practice should stop. But there doesn't seem to be any justification other than custom.

In some countries, veterinarians are no longer permitted to perform tail dockings. Other countries no longer allow cropped or docked dogs to be shown, or even to enter the country, in some cases. In the United States, the American Animal Hospital Association (AAHA) has come out with a position statement regarding both cropping and docking:

> Ear cropping and tail docking in dogs for cosmetic reasons are not medically indicated nor of benefit to the patient. These procedures cause pain and distress, and, as with all surgical procedures, are accompanied by inherent risks of anesthesia, blood loss, and infection. Therefore, veterinarians should counsel dog owners about these matters before agreeing to perform these surgeries.

AAHA hopes to convince the larger veterinary organization, the AVMA (American Veterinary Medical Association), to adopt the same resolution. Many veterinarians already refuse to provide these services.

Cropping is the more painful of the two procedures. At a period in its development when the puppy is forming its view of the world and humankind, it is put under anesthesia to wake up with those tender ears surgically sliced to an unnatural form, heavily taped, held upright by racks. Don't let anyone tell you this is not a painful procedure.

Watch Your Step

Boxer aficionados in the AKC are at war over the issue of cropping. Some owners tried to have the standard changed to include uncropped ears, but they failed. In a backlash, the national club then proposed, and the AKC has adopted, a standard change requiring judges to penalize any deviation from the current standard—making it well-nigh impossible to win with an uncropped Boxer.

As for more ear problems in drop-eared dogs, it is certainly true that Cocker Spaniels are the top breed for ear infections and other concerns. But other floppy-eared breeds, such as Flat-Coated Retrievers and Beagles, don't have significantly more ear problems than, say, German Shepherds and Collies. And if breeders desire upright ears, then they should breed for them, just as they breed for almond eyes or a scissors bite.

Because other countries are moving forward on this issue, and competitive U.S. exhibitors want to be able to compete internationally, the foreign bans are having a ripple effect in the United States. It is thus far small, but there are more dogs in natural ears turning up in U.S. show rings.

Before you choose a breed (if you have not already done so), check your feelings on this issue if you are considering a breed that is traditionally cropped and/or docked. Understand that, at least for now, showing, say, a Boxer in natural ears in a U.S. show ring will decrease your chances of winning. Someday, it may be different.

Remember

- ○ Be prepared for the normal ups and downs involved in any sport, including dog showing.
- ○ Take your time and focus on the job at hand.
- ○ Understand your dog and how he or she feels about the show ring.
- ○ Ignore other competitors who never have a good word to say about anything or anybody other than their own dog.
- ○ Know the reasons for being excused, disqualified, and suspended, and don't do anything to get yourself in trouble.
- ○ Don't have your dog cropped and docked because that's what's done without thinking about what you are actually doing and investigating the pros and cons.

Part IV

Paperwork and Paraphernalia

Sometimes it seems like dog shows must be run by the government—there are so many forms involved! First, your dog has to be registered. Then there's the entry form, with its dread decision of which class to enter. And there's confirmation of entry, judging schedule, show catalog, and that all-important armband. Read all about it, and you'll conquer the paper tiger with ease.

It's not all paper, though. There are clothes and shoes to consider, what you need to bring to a show, and how you can pack it in your vehicle. A handy checklist will help you out.

Finally, because most people are most familiar with the AKC, the last chapter here explores the differences between the AKC and the other registries.

Papers Aren't Just for Puppies

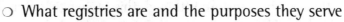

Before you can compete in conformation, your dog must be registered with at least one of the national or international registries, or kennel clubs. Among them, they cover every conceivable breed of dog. The UKC even welcomes mixed breeds for its performance events (not conformation). Many of the more popular breeds could conceivably be registered with each of the kennel clubs!

There are other registries not covered in this book—many single-breed clubs, other international registries, even other U.S. registries. But the kennel clubs described in these pages cover all the breeds you're likely to encounter.

What Registries Are and the Purposes They Serve

What does registration mean? Simply that a dog is the result of a mating of two purebreds of the same breed. There is no guarantee, actual or implied, of the quality of the dog's conformation, health, or temperament. Purebred dogs with "papers" have hip dysplasia, congenital heart problems, degenerative eye problems, epilepsy, rage syndrome, undershot jaws, uncertain temperaments, and on and on. So do dogs without papers. The registration itself has no bearing on anything other than the dog's status as a purebred.

So why must dogs be registered to compete? Because the kennel clubs track dogs and enforce rules through registration and membership. The clubs control how shows are run, so you play by their rules or not at all.

The breed of dog you have will determine your choices among the kennel clubs. Appendix C provides a listing of breeds and the clubs with which they can be registered (though this is changing at an ever-increasing pace, and the AKC especially seems to have decided to accept new breeds much more quickly than in years gone by, so you need to consult the registries for the most up-to-date information). Many breeds can be registered with several kennel clubs. You may want to register with AKC and UKC if both are active in your area, or register with AKC and get a CKC Event Registration Number if you live near the Canadian border. Some noteworthy dogs are shown to championships in the United States, Canada, Mexico, Bermuda, and beyond!

The U.S. Kennel Clubs

Although there are other registries operating in the United States, the ones we will cover to at least some degree in this book are

- American Kennel Club (AKC)—the oldest and largest dog organization in the United States, registering over 145 breeds of purebred dogs
- United Kennel Club (UKC)—an organization emphasizing performance events, but offering conformation, registering most European breeds in addition to those recognized by the AKC
- States Kennel Club (SKC)—newer organization, limited in geographic scope, emphasizing conformation and registering nearly every breed

- American Rare Breed Association (ARBA)—an organization formed to support those breeds not registered by the AKC, limited in geographic scope, and increasingly made redundant as other kennel clubs recognize more breeds

The American Kennel Club (AKC)

The American Kennel Club was formed in 1884. Its stated purpose, then and now, is to promote the interests and well-being of purebred dogs. It registers over one million dogs each year, making it the largest kennel club in the United States. Local kennel clubs across the country become members of the AKC, with each member club electing one delegate to serve as their voice in the affairs of the parent club.

The major functions of the AKC include

- Registering purebred dogs
- Setting rules and regulations for registration, dog shows, obedience trials, field trials, tracking tests, hunting tests, herding trials, and agility trials
- Sanctioning and licensing dog clubs to hold competitive events
- Recording the results of competitive events held under its rules
- Publishing the monthly magazine *AKC Gazette,* the Events Calendar, and the monthly Stud Book Register
- Funding the Canine Health Foundation for research into canine health issues

AKC defines a breed as "a relatively homogeneous group of animals within a species, developed and maintained by man." Humans have indeed created each of the many purebred dogs by using selective breeding to emphasize desired qualities, thus designing dogs for specific purposes. AKC divides breeds into seven groups, based largely on these purposes. Originally

Fancy That!

The UKC is owned and operated by a family of dog enthusiasts. As a private company, they can make decisions for themselves, and proved just that by aligning with AMBOR (American Mixed Breed Obedience Registry) to register mixed-breed dogs. With the demise of long-time owner Fred Miller, the UKC has been sold to Wayne Cavanaugh, who was once a vice president with the AKC, but moved to the UKC.

there were Sporting (hunting) dogs and Non-Sporting (everything else) dogs. Both of these remain, and Non-Sporting still includes breeds that just don't fit any of the other designations. Hounds and Terriers were broken out of the Sporting group to form their own large groups and joined by the Working and Herding groups. The only group determined by size is the Toys. A complete listing of AKC breeds and their groups can be found in *Rules Applying to Registration and Dog Shows*, available at no charge from the AKC and on their Web site.

The Miscellaneous Class also still exists, although the AKC is working toward eliminating it. Breeds included here are generally in the process of being fully recognized by the AKC. They may be shown in a separate class for each breed or a single class lumping them together. The premium list will specify. They may not go on to compete beyond their class.

Dogs in the Miscellaneous Class, as well as purebreds without papers (such as rescued dogs), may receive an ILP (Indefinite Listing Privilege). These dogs can compete in performance events and in the Miscellaneous Class in conformation shows offering a class for them. To receive an ILP, you must submit the appropriate AKC form and fee, along with clear photographs of the dog, and your request for registration must be approved. Some AKC shows now have reps present who will ILP dogs on the spot.

Some of the breeds in the regular groups are subdivided into "varieties" for show purposes. These divisions may be based on size, color, or coat type. One example is the Cocker Spaniel, which is shown in Black, ASCOB (Any Solid Color Other than Black), and Parti-Color varieties.

Watch Your Step

The AKC ILP program raises some hackles. Though it does allow more dogs to compete in performance events, it would be better simply to offer limited registration to all dogs. Many an owner of a mixed breed adopted from a shelter has been told, "Oh, you can ILP him as a Border Collie" (or Poodle or Border Terrier or whatever), though the dog is clearly a mix. This is, in effect, being encouraged to lie.

Breed varieties may be interbred and their offspring registered. Breed varieties are listed in appendix B.

As if this weren't confusing enough, some breeds can also use optional class divisions. These most often crop up at specialties or shows known for exceptionally large entries for some particular breed. If a class division is going to be offered, information will be included in the premium list. Permissible class divisions are also included in appendix B, but don't worry about them unless you receive a premium list specifying a class division for your breed.

There is some required reading before you begin participation in AKC (or any other registry's) conformation. The AKC will send you free, upon request, a copy of "Rules Applying to Registration and Dog Shows." Every time you sign an entry form for a dog show, you are affirming that you have read and understood these rules. Besides the legal requirement, there is a wealth of information. Much of it is included in this book, but reading two different versions may improve your understanding.

Be very clear about the transgressions for which a dog may be disqualified. Any dog that is disqualified can never again set foot in the show ring. A dog that is excused, however (say, because it limped while being gaited), may return to competition another day. (See chapter 17 for details.) Lack of familiarity with AKC's "Rules Applying to Registration and Dog Shows" could cause you embarrassment at best, disciplinary action by the AKC at worst.

Other required reading is the breed standard for your dog. Each breed has its own written "ideal," detailing how the perfect dog of the breed should look and move and the temperament it should possess. The standard will detail such things as height and weight; length, texture, and color of coat; set of eyes and ears; length of muzzle; structure of legs and feet; heaviness of bone; and on and on. Some standards are much more detailed than others. Some focus on head attributes, others concentrate on markings, and others zero in on other details. Each dog is judged

> ## Fancy That!
> ARBA uses the term "disqualification" somewhat differently, not necessarily meaning a ban for life. Know the details of rules and regulations for any registry you plan to show under.

against its own breed standard, rather than directly against the other dogs in the ring.

Although it places by far the most emphasis on conformation, the AKC does recognize other forms of dog sports, known collectively as performance events. These include

- Obedience
- Tracking
- Agility
- Field trials
- Lure coursing
- Herding
- Earthdog trials
- Carting trials

In all of these, in one way or another, the dog and handler perform a series of exercises, with judging based on the perfection of the performance. Some events, such as herding, rely partly on a breed's hereditary instincts. All performance events require training, practice, and teamwork between handler and dog. Try one—you'll like it.

United Kennel Club (UKC)

The UKC is the second oldest registry of purebred dogs in the United States, founded in 1898. Where the AKC is a mammoth "nonprofit" organization, the UKC is a family-owned, for-profit business. In addition to reg-

Tips from the Pros

You might not understand the nuances of conformation (breed) judging, but you'll have no trouble enjoying the performances in the Obedience ring, especially when you watch the more advanced dogs retrieving over a jump or doing scent discrimination exercises. And it may encourage you to get involved in further training your own dog.

—From Darlene Arden, *The Irrepressible Toy Dog* (Howell Book House, 1998). Used with permission.

istering many of the same breeds accepted by the AKC, it also registers many of the less common (at least in the United States) European breeds, and in the 1990s began registering mixed breeds for competition in obedience and agility. The focus of the UKC is more on performance events, but their conformation program has been growing. The UKC publishes a general dog magazine, *Bloodlines,* as well as *Coonhound Bloodlines* and *Hunting Retriever,* specifically for these scenthounds and gun dogs.

Because of its higher degree of interest in performance, the UKC encourages breeding based on soundness, working instincts, and temperament. They discourage inbreeding, feeling that most breeders are not familiar enough with the science of genetics to appreciate the potential for recessive genes carried by related parents producing defects in their offspring. Any dog that is the result of inbreeding has the notation "inbred" included on its UKC registration certificate.

For a long time, the UKC did not gather breeds into groups. Then, in the late 1980s, they experimented with the idea, using a more European breakdown of eight groups. But their shows mostly use the no-group strategy, concentrating on single-breed classes. Note that in their listing of breeds, they do not share AKC's insistence on reversing breed names. What the AKC refers to as Retriever (Golden) or Spaniel (English Cocker), UKC is content to call Golden Retriever and English Cocker Spaniel.

UKC ignores most of the breed varieties of the AKC. Cocker Spaniels of all colors compete together, as do Beagles of all sizes and Collies of either coat. They retain only the three size designations of Poodles and add a breakdown of Belgian Shepherd Dog into Groenendael, Laekenois, Malinois, and Tervueren. There are no optional class divisions.

Talking Dog

Inbreeding is the mating of two closely related dogs, such as mother and son or father and daughter. Though it can intensify desired traits, it can also intensify hereditary problems and result in litters of puppies afflicted with various maladies.

Fancy That!

The United Kennel Club hosts the "Premier" each year, one of its few all-breed dog shows, complete with group judging and Best in Show (adjudicated by a panel of three judges).

Although the UKC does not often offer group competition, they do offer two special classes beyond the breed classes. Rather than simply bringing champions in to compete against the Best Male and Best Female, as the AKC does, the UKC first judges a Champion of Champions Class and a Grand Champion Class. The first is open only to dogs that have earned their Champion title, and the first-place dog is awarded Champion of Champions, with a second-place Reserve Champion of Champions also chosen. A win with at least three dogs shown counts toward the Grand Champion title.

The Grand Champion Class is open only to those dogs that have earned their Grand Champion title (which they do by winning five Champion of Champions Classes).

The final class, Best of Breed, consists of the Champion of Champions winner, Grand Champion class winner, and Best of Winners (which is awarded only to either the Best Male or Best Female). No additional points toward a championship are awarded in this class, but the UKC does have a "Top Ten Show Dogs" point system, and dogs can earn points toward that.

Beginning in late 2001 or early 2002, the UKC will begin offering "Altered Champion" classes (though they may not call them exactly that) for dogs that have been spayed or neutered. These dogs will compete in exactly the same way as their "intact" brethren, and can earn championships of their own.

Before beginning to show with the UKC, you should obviously obtain and read a copy of the "Rules Special Issue." This comes out in December each year, and can be received as part of a subscription to *Bloodlines* (which will keep you informed of upcoming shows) or ordered separately. It contains the complete regulations for conformation, obedience, and agility. You can also receive on request the standard for an individual breed.

UKC licenses more than 6,000 events annually, with over 60 percent being performance events of one sort or another. In addition to conformation, they offer

- Obedience
- Agility
- Hunting Retriever trials
- Coonhound events such as Nite Hunts
- The Hunting Beagle program
- The Hunting Airedale program

To register with the UKC, you need an application, a three-generation pedigree for the dog, and three clear color photos of the dog in standing position, one from each side and one from the front. If the dog should show what would be a disqualifying fault in conformation, it will be registered only if spayed or neutered, and not be permitted to compete in the show ring. Dogs without a pedigree can be registered as mixed breeds, and compete in obedience and agility.

> **Fancy That!**
>
> The UKC is quite well known, particularly in the Midwest and South, for its combined conformation/hunt events for Coonhounds and Beagles. If you live in an area where these events occur, you can quickly meet many other enthusiasts by attending one.

States Kennel Club (SKC)

The SKC is one of the newest kennel clubs in the United States, formed in the 1980s. It uses the same groups as the AKC, but registers any breed recognized by the FCI (Federation Cynologique Internationale). To register, you need only to send a copy of your dog's registration papers from some other kennel club (AKC, UKC, CKC, FCI, or others) with the appropriate fee.

A copy of the rules regarding registration and conformation can be purchased from the SKC. The SKC supports a variety of performance events in addition to conformation, including

- Obedience
- Agility
- Herding
- Tracking
- Weight pulling
- Terrier trials
- Lure coursing

They encourage clubs to hold a variety of events in conjunction with dog shows. But the SKC has remained small and geographically limited, and seems likely to stay that way.

American Rare Breed Association (ARBA)

ARBA provides some of the aspects of AKC showing with some of the added aspects of FCI showing. They exist for the advancement of rare breeds in the United States and seem to be more active and organized now than they were in years past.

Dogs may be registered and shown with ARBA if they

- are a breed recognized by ARBA
- have a three-generation pedigree certified by a club or organization recognized by ARBA

ARBA also uses a blend of breed standards. For breeds originated outside the United States (the vast majority of breeds), the FCI-recognized standard is used for all breeds recognized by the FCI. For any breeds not recognized by the FCI, ARBA uses the standard from the breed's country of origin. For those breeds developed in the United States, the ARBA Show Committee selects the standard that it feels best represents the breed. ARBA allows changes to standards to be made only by the parent breed club in the breed's country of origin.

Judges at ARBA shows may come from the AKC, CKC, or FCI. They use a modified method of awarding Certificate of Aptitude Certificates (CAC-US) to the Winners Dog and Winners Bitch of each breed or variety. A Junior Championship of Beauty is earned by receiving four CAC-US from four different judges. A Championship of Beauty requires nine CAC-US from at least six different judges. Any dog that is the first of the breed to receive a Championship of Beauty is designated "A1 Champion."

ARBA uses seven groups: Companion, Herding, Hounds, Spitz, Sporting, Terrier, and Working. The breed names will be largely unfamiliar to many U.S. fanciers.

> ## Fancy That!
> ARBA's Web site (www.arba.org) provides pictures and descriptions of most of the breeds they recognize, so you can see what these European dogs look like.

If you want a taste of what it's like to show in Europe, without all the travel, try ARBA. With the Certificate of Aptitude Certificates, European breeds, and preference for the "L" as the gaiting pattern, you'll feel like you're in a whole different world.

INTERNATIONAL KENNEL CLUBS

Nearly every country has its own national kennel club, with Great Britain's (known simply as the Kennel Club) the oldest of them all. But Britain's quarantine keeps most foreign competition away from their shores—although the restrictions have already been loosened for other European countries, and may soon be relaxed for the United States and Canada as well. Rather than attempting to cover dozens of individual kennel clubs, we will look at the Canadian Kennel Club (simply because of our geographic proximity) and the Federation Cynologique Internationale, which includes much of Europe, Asia, and Latin America in its membership.

Canadian Kennel Club (CKC)

Canada's first kennel club, the CKC, was formed in 1888. It was soon challenged by the Dominion Kennel Club for national ascendancy, but when both clubs applied for incorporation under the Livestock Pedigree Act, the CKC won out.

The CKC uses the same groups as the AKC, but some breeds are shuffled into different groups, and some European breeds are included. Because the CKC recognizes the long border with the United States, U.S. dogs can compete in Canada without being registered with the CKC. They can instead receive an Event Registration Number by submitting a copy of the dog's U.S. registration certificate and a check for $53.50 Canadian with a written request for an ERN. This number allows U.S. dogs to earn CKC titles.

Should you wish to actually register your dog with the CKC, the dog will first have to be either tattooed or microchipped. Canada demands these identification methods for all registered dogs. The tattoo number must be one designated by the CKC. The dog must be registered in the United States with the AKC, and copies of the dog's AKC registration and certified pedigree (at least three generations) must be submitted.

A copy of Dog Show Rules, including Sanction Match Rules and a booklet of breed standards for one of the groups, can be ordered from the CKC (U.S.$3.21 each).

In addition to conformation, the CKC sponsors

- Obedience
- Tracking
- Field trials
- Working certificate tests

Federation Cynologique Internationale (FCI)

The FCI is different from the kennel clubs we have described thus far. Rather than having individual members or delegates from local kennel clubs, their members are the national kennel clubs of European, Asian, and Latin American countries. The FCI provides the very special and sought-after Aptitude Certificate of the International Beauty Championship (CACIB).

The FCI has jurisdiction only over shows for which the CACIB will be competed. Each member country receives at least four CACIBs each year, and can petition for an additional CACIB opportunity for every 5,000 dogs registered in their country's Stud Book. Only one CACIB may be awarded on any given day at any one site.

Ten new groups were adopted in 1990. They are

1. Sheepdogs and Cattle dogs (except Swiss cattle dogs)
2. Pinscher and Schnauzers—Molossian type and Swiss cattle dogs
3. Terriers
4. Teckels (Dachshunds)
5. Spitz and Primitive Types
6. Hounds (except sighthounds)
7. Pointers
8. Flushing dogs, Retrievers—Water Dogs
9. Companions and Toys
10. Sighthounds and related breeds

Each country indicates what group it wishes its native dogs placed into. Each affiliated country also submits its list of approved judges each year.

Four placements are made in each class. In addition, all qualified dogs receive one of the following ratings:

- *Excellent*—for a dog very close to the ideal specified in the breed standard and in perfect condition, with a "brilliant" demeanor
- *Very Good*—to a very "typey" dog, balanced in its proportions and in good physical condition, but with possibly some minor defects
- *Good*—a dog characteristic of the breed, but displaying nonhereditary defects
- *Fairly Good*—a dog of sufficient type, but without notably good qualities or not in physical condition

Only a dog placed first among those qualifying for a rating of Excellent may receive the CACIB. But this placing does not mean automatic award of the CACIB. It is given at the judge's discretion.

FCI-recognized breeds, their countries of origin, and the groups to which they belong are listed in appendix C. The member countries of the FCI are

Argentina	Ecuador	Italy
Australia	El Salvador	Japan
Austria	Estonia	Korea
Bahrain	Finland	Latvia
Belgium	France	Lithuania
Belorussia	Georgia	Luxembourg
Bolivia	Germany	Macedonia
Brazil	Gibraltar	Malaysia
Bulgaria	Greece	Mexico
Chile	Guatemala	Monaco
Colombia	Honduras	Morocco
Costa Rica	Hong Kong	Netherlands
Croatia	Hungary	New Zealand
Cuba	Iceland	Nicaragua
Cyprus	India	Norway
Czech Republic	Indonesia	Panama
Denmark	Ireland	Paraguay
Dominican Republic	Israel	Peru

Philippines	Singapore	Switzerland
Poland	Slovakia	Taiwan
Portugal	Slovenia	Ukraine
Puerto Rico	South Africa	Uruguay
Romania	Spain	Venezuela
Russia	Sri Lanka	Yugoslavia
San Marino	Sweden	Zimbabwe

Of these countries, an even dozen outlaw cropping and docking of dogs: Austria, Germany, Belgium, Denmark, Finland, Greece, Luxembourg, Norway, Portugal, Sweden, Switzerland, and Cyprus. Cropped or docked dogs may not compete in, and may not even be allowed into, these countries.

Note that the United States is not an official member country of the FCI. However, the FCI maintains a "gentleman's agreement" with the AKC, accepting AKC pedigrees in international shows of FCI member countries. If an American dog fulfills the requirements for an international championship, one of the show-organizing FCI member countries submits the application for the title. So U.S. dogs can become Int. CHs, though in a roundabout sort of way.

Remember

- ○ Your dog must be registered with at least one kennel club to compete in conformation.
- ○ You can register a dog with multiple kennel clubs and achieve titles with each of them.
- ○ Registration, or having "papers," is not a guarantee of quality.
- ○ The AKC is the oldest and largest U.S. kennel club.
- ○ The UKC is nearly as old, and registers a greater variety of breeds.
- ○ The CKC has a reciprocal agreement with the AKC, and you can get a registration number that allows you to compete in Canada without registering your dog with the CKC.
- ○ ARBA can give exhibitors a taste of European showing without leaving home.
- ○ The FCI offers a special championship at shows under its jurisdiction in member countries.

19

At a Premium

In This Chapter

○ The AKC entry form
○ Entry forms for other registries
○ Mailing entries in on time
○ Making changes

Sometimes dog showing seems to involve more paperwork than dogs. We've just discussed registration papers; now we'll take a look at the premium list.

All sanctioned shows, and many fun matches, provide a premium list to anyone interested in the event. Its name comes from the listing of premiums, or awards, to be available at the show. But it includes much more—and more important—information, such as

- Date of the show
- Location of the show
- Name of the sponsoring organization (Hurricane Ridge Kennel Club or Greater Boston Briard Fanciers, for example)
- Close of entries (the date and time by which your entry must reach the sponsoring organization or show superintendent)
- Times of opening and closing of the show (for each day, if it's a multiday event)

- Whether the show is held indoors or outdoors, and if it's benched or not
- Names of the judges and classes they are judging
- Prizes, ribbons, trophies, and sometimes cash being offered (the premiums)
- Directions to the show site
- Lodging information
- The entry form
- Classes being offered
- Any limitations on entries (sometimes there is a limit on the number of entries, sometimes only certain breeds are permitted)

Fancy That!

UKC shows sometimes allow day-of-event entries—see the section "The UKC Entry Form" later in this chapter.

It's a lot of information to take in. Take your time and read through the premium list until you know what it's telling you. Pay particular attention to the close of entries. Though it's only one brief line, easy to miss, it's an essential piece of information. Entries *must* be received by this date and time, usually $2^1/_2$ to $3^1/_2$ weeks before the show date. There are *no exceptions* to this cutoff date.

Allow plenty of time for your entry to make its way through the postal system. It must be *received* by the close of entries, not just mailed. Attempting to use a postmark or certified mail receipt to show that you mailed the entry will not get you anywhere if it wasn't in the hands of the superintendent or show secretary on time.

If there is any limit on entries, it will be noted in the premium list, and you will need to get your entry in even earlier or risk being turned away.

All the remaining benched shows have limits on entries, as do many obedience trials held in conjunction with conformation shows. Send your entry as early as possible for these events.

THE AKC ENTRY FORM

If you have a show's premium list, you have the entry form. The AKC entry form is notoriously confusing to newcomers. We will walk through it line by line in a moment. First, some general information.

If you make a copy of an entry form rather than filling out the original, be sure to copy and fill out the front and the back. You *must* use an AKC entry form or a copy of it, and you must use a separate entry form for each show and for each dog entered in a show.

When filling out the entry form, use a typewriter (if you still have one) or print *very clearly*. You are responsible for all information being complete, accurate, and legible. If the show superintendent or secretary can't read your writing, you could be a very unhappy competitor. You could win the whole show and not earn any championship points because no one could decipher your name and address or your dog's registration number. If you are entering online, check before submitting to be sure that you haven't made any typos. Transposing numbers in your address and your dog's registration number could have the same unhappy effect.

Also refrain from providing any additional information. For example, you cannot write on an entry form

> Please enter my dog if it's a major.

or

> Please enter my dog only if Briarwood's Foo-Foo's Delight is not entered.

This is a definite no-no. Do not write anything not specifically called for on the form. Doing so can result in your entry being rejected.

The entry forms for the AKC, SKC, and CKC are nearly identical, so use the following instructions and figure 19.1 for all of them. You don't have to be a rocket scientist, but . . .

1. *Club name and date.* The name of the organization sponsoring the show, and the date of the event, must be on the top of the form. If you are using a form from the show's premium list, this information is already there. But if you found out about the show late and don't have time to get a premium list, you can use another show's entry form by gluing a small piece of paper over the show date and sponsoring club and writing in the correct information. Remember, many superintendents handle multiple shows each month, and they won't know which show you're trying to enter if you don't tell them.

NOTICE: PLEASE PUT BREED & NAME OF SHOW ON CHECKS. I ENCLOSE $_____ for entry fees.
IMPORTANT: Read Carefully Instructions on Reverse Side Before Filling Out. Numbers in the boxes indicate sections of the instructions relevant to the information needed in that box. (PLEASE PRINT)

BREED	VARIETY (1)	SEX

DOG (2) (3) SHOW CLASS	CLASS (3) DIVISION Weight, Color, Etc.	

ADDITIONAL CLASSES	OBEDIENCE TRIAL CLASS	JR. SHOWMANSHIP CLASS

NAME OF (See Back) JUNIOR HANDLER	JR. HANDLER AKC #

FULL NAME OF DOG	

□AKC REG. NO. □AKC LETTER NO. □ILP NO. □FOREIGN REG. NO. & COUNTRY Enter number here	DATE OF BIRTH
	PLACE OF BIRTH □USA □Canada □Foreign Do not print the above in catalog

BREEDER

SIRE

DAM

Exhibitor's Code _____

ACTUAL OWNER(S) (4) _____
                              (Please Print)

OWNER'S ADDRESS _____

CITY _____ STATE _____ ZIP + 4 _____

NAME OF OWNER'S AGENT (IF ANY) AT THE SHOW	CODE #

I CERTIFY that I am the actual owner of the dog or that I am the duly authorized agent of the actual owner whose name I have entered above in consideration of the acceptance of this entry. I (we) agree to abide by the rules and regulations of the American Kennel Club in effect at the time of this show or obedience trial, and by any additional rules and regulations appearing in the premium list for this show or obedience trial or both, and further agree to be bound by the "Agreement" printed on the reverse side of this entry form. I (we) certify and represent that the dog entered is not a hazard to persons or other dogs. This entry is submitted for acceptance on the foregoing representation and agreement.

By signing the entry form we certify that the Junior Showman does not now, and will not at any time, act as an agent/handler for pay while continuing to compete in Junior Showmanship.

SIGNATURE of owner of his agent
Duly authorized to make this entry _____

Telephone (____) _____

Email Address: _____

Figure 19.1. The AKC entry form

Single copies of the latest editions of the "Rules Applying to Dog Shows" and "Obedience Regulations" may be obtained WITHOUT CHARGE from any Superintendent at any show where they are superintendent or from THE AMERICAN KENNEL CLUB, 5580 CENTERVIEW DR, RALEIGH NC 27606-3390

AGREEMENT

I (we) acknowledge that the "Rules Applying to Dog Shows" and, if this entry is for an obedience trial the "Obedience Regulations." Have been made available to me (us), and that I am (we are) familiar with their contents. (I (we) waive any and all claims, causes of action, I (we) might otherwise have against the AKC and any AKC approved judge. Judging at this show, under AKC Rules, Regulations, and Guidelines. I (we) agree that the club holding this show or obedience trail has the right to refuse this entry for cause which the club shall deem to be sufficient in consideration of the acceptance of this entry and of the holding of the show or obedience trial and of the opportunity to have the dog judged and to win prize, money, ribbons, or trophies, I (we) agree to hold this club, its members, directors, governors, officers, agents, superintendents or show secretary and the owner or lessor of te premises and any employees of the aforementioned parties harmless from any claim for loss or injury which may be alleged to have been caused directly or indirectly to any person or thing by the act of this dog while in or upon the show or obedience trial premises or grounds or near any entrance thereto, and I (we) personally assume all responsibility and the liability for any such claim and I (we) further agree to hold the aforementioned parties harmless from any claim for loss of this dog by disappearance , theft, death, or otherwise, and from any claim for damage or injury to the dog, whether such loss, disappearance, theft, damage or injury, be caused or alleged to be caused by te negligence of the club or any of the parties aforementioned, or by the negligence of any other person, or any other cause or causes.
I (we) hereby assume the sole responsibility for and agree to indemnify and save the aforementioned parties harmless from any and all loss and expense (including legal fees) by reason of the liability imposed by law upon any of the aforementioned parties for damage because of bodily injuries, including death at any time, resulting from, sustained by any person or persons, including myself (ourselves) or on account of damage to property, arising out of or in consequence of my (our) participation in this show or obedience trial, howsoever such injuries, death or damage to property may be caused, and whether to nor the same may have been caused or may be alleged to have been caused by negligence of the aforementioned parties or any of their employees or agents, or any other persons.

INSTRUCTIONS

1. (Variety) If you are entering a dog of a breed in which there are varieties for show purposes, please designate the particular variety you are entering, i.e., Cocker Spanierl (Solid color black, ASCOB, parti-color). Beagles (not exceeding 13 in. over 13 in. but not exceeding 15 in.) Dachshunds (longhaired, smooth, wirehaired), Bull Terriers (colored, white), Manchester Terriers (standard, toy). Chihuahuas (smooth coat, long coat), English Toy Spaniers (King Charles and Ruby, Blenheim and Prince Charles), Poodles (toy, miniature, standard) Collies (rough, smooth)
2. The following categories of dogs may be entered and shown in Best of Breed competitions: Dog that are Champions of Record and dogs which according to their owners records have completed the requirements for a championship, but whose championships are unconfirmed. The showing of the unconfirmed Champions in Best of Breed competition is limited to a period of 90 days from the date of the show where the dog completed the requirements for championship.
3. (Dog Show Class) Consult the classification in this premium list. If the dog show class in which you are entering you dog is divided, then, in addition to designating the class, specify the particular division of the class in which you are entering your dog, i.e., age division, color division, weight division.
4. A dog must be entered in the name of the person who actually owned it at the time entries for a show closed. If a registered dog has been acquired by a new owner, it must be entered in the name of its new owner in any show for which entries closed after the date of acquirement, regardless of whether the new owner has received the registration certificate indicating that the dog is recorded in his name. State on the entry form whether transfer application has been mailed to A.K.C. (For complete rules refer to Chapter 11, Section 3).

JUNIOR SHOWMANSHIP. If this entry is for Jr. Showmanship, please give the following information:

    ACK JR HANDLER #   JR.'S DATE OF BIRTH
    □□□□□□□□   □□ □□ □□

NAME OF JUNIOR HANDLER: _____

ADDRESS: _____

CITY: _____ State: _____ ZIP + 4: _____

If Jr. Handler is not the owner of the dog
Identified on the face of this form, what is the
relationship of the Jr. Handler to the owner? _____

Figure 19.1. The AKC entry form (continued)

2. *Entry fees.* Refer to the premium list for prices. Each show can be different. There may be a lower price for certain classes (often the Puppy classes and sometimes Bred-by Exhibitor), and if you enter more than one class the additional classes are usually less expensive than the first. (Be careful not to enter more than one regular conformation class—you can't enter the same dog in Bred-By and Open at the same show, for example.) Add up the entry fees for a single dog (remember, one entry form for one dog) and write down the total.

3. *Breed.* Of course, only AKC- (or SKC or CKC) recognized breeds can be entered. Some shows can have limitations on which breeds are being judged. Check the premium list for notices such as

There will be no classes for Welsh Terriers at this event.

This usually means there is a Specialty going on for that breed somewhere nearby on the same date. The AKC does not allow more than one club to sponsor an overlapping event within 200 miles.

4. *Variety.* If your breed does not have a recognized variety (see appendix B if you aren't sure), leave this field blank. If you re showing a Cocker Spaniel, this will be where you enter the color variety. For a Beagle, you would enter the size division, and so on.

5. *Sex.* Enter "Male" or "Dog" for males, "Female" or "Bitch" for females.

6. *Dog Show Class.* You may think it's been pretty easy up till now and are wondering what all the fuss is about. But this is the $64,000 question, and a lot of people get the answer wrong.

The "regular classes," offered at all AKC dog shows, are

- Puppy (can be divided into 6–9 months, 9–12 months)
- 12–18 Months
- Novice

 Talking Dog

Although your parents may have taught you that *bitch* is a dirty word, not so in the world of dog showing. It simply means a female dog, with no other connotation. In fact, you'll know you're on your way to being an old-timer when you discuss your bitch's heat cycles over lunch at a show.

- Bred-by Exhibitor
- American-Bred
- Open
- Best of Breed or Variety

There may be additional, "nonregular" classes, such as Veteran Dog/Bitch, Stud Dog, Brood Bitch, Brace, or breed-specific classes, such as Hunting Retrievers (meaning dogs with a hunting title to their credit). You can enter as many nonregular classes as apply to your dog, but championship points come only from the regular classes, and you may only enter one of those. We hope to help you choose wisely.

Following is a description of each of the regular classes. Read them all before you decide which to enter.

Puppy Class   This class is for dogs at least 6 months old (no dog may compete in an AKC show before 6 months of age), but less than 12 months old. It is usually divided into

- Puppy 6–9 months (6–8 months, or up to 9 months)
- Puppy 9–12 months (9–11 months, or up to 12 months)

Should you decide that this is the class for you, indicate the applicable subdivision on your entry. Note that Champions cannot be entered in the Puppy class (yes, dogs do become AKC Champions at under 1 year of age).

A dog's age is calculated from birth to the first day of whatever show you are entering. The first day of show is the first day of regular conformation competition. Specialty shows often include other events, such as obedience, tracking, herding, or hunting tests, sometimes scheduled a day or two prior to conformation judging. These associated competitions are not considered in determining the first day of a show.

So a dog born on July 15 may begin competing at any show starting on January 15 or later the next year (having attained the age of 6 months). You could enter Puppy 6–9 months until April 15 of that year. From April 15 to July 15, you could enter Puppy 9–12 months.

12–18 Months Class   This is the next age class after Puppy, for dogs 12–17 months, or up to 18 months. Age is determined the same as for Puppy class (so our mythical puppy could enter from July 15 to January 15). Note that the SKC calls this class "Young Adults."

Novice Class Only dogs born in the United States, Canada, or Mexico who have not won three first places in Novice or a single first place in Bred-by Exhibitor, American-bred, or Open may enter here. A win in a Puppy class will also exclude you if it meant your puppy was awarded any championship points.

Bred-by Exhibitor Class This class is a family affair. You or your spouse must be the breeder and owner of the dog, and again the dog must have been born in the United States, Canada, or Mexico. A member of your immediate family (you, a spouse, a parent, a child, or a brother or sister) must show the dog. The SKC makes a slight variation, requiring that the dog be bred and handled, but not owned, by the same person.

> ### Fancy That!
>
> The tricky part of Novice class is that some people feel it signals to judges that your dog hasn't done any real winning. Competition in this class is generally less than the other classes, with people afraid to enter and brand their dogs as "losers." It's true that Winners don't often come from the Novice class, but this may be simply because of inexperienced handlers and dogs.

American-Bred Class Often referred to as "Am-Bred," this is a true blue class for dogs born in the United States as the result of a breeding that also occurred in the United States. There are often as many dogs here as in the Open class.

Open Class The catchall class, open to any dog registered with the AKC who is not already a champion. This is generally the biggest, most competitive class at a show.

WHICH CLASS TO ENTER?

First, does your dog qualify for any of the age-specific classes (Puppy 6–9, Puppy 9–12, or 12–18 month)? If the answer is yes, your choice is easy: Just enter the age-appropriate class.

If you are the breeder/owner and either you or a family member can take the dog into the ring, enter Bred-by Exhibitor.

If neither of these applies to your dog, you have only Novice, Am-Bred, and Open to choose among. Although many people will tell you that champions don't come out of the Novice or Am-Bred classes and you should avoid them at all costs, it is much more fun to win a ribbon in either of these classes than to be ignored in Open. If you and your dog are both new to the dog show game, better to gain some experience and risk the stigma, real or imagined, of these classes than to make fools of yourselves in Open, where the hottest competition and professional handlers make for an intense experience. At a smaller show, you may prefer to try Am-Bred if your dog qualifies. At large shows, you may prefer the smaller Novice class. Wait until you have some experience and more settled nerves to venture into Open.

Now back to our line-by-line look at the entry form.

7. *Class Division.* This is usually left blank. But some premium lists may note something special, such as

Labrador Retrievers will be judged in Black, Yellow, and Chocolate classes.

If there is a note such as this pertaining to your breed, fill in the appropriate information here.

8. *Additional Classes.* This is for any additional classes you are entering for the same dog. Remember, an entry form applies to only one dog. Don't use this space to enter a second dog. You must use a separate entry form for that. If you were going to enter a regular class and perhaps Brace, you would write "Brace" here.

9. *Obedience Trial Class.* Some shows will also offer an obedience trial. If there is one, and you are entering your dog, write the class here.

10–13. *Junior Showmanship.* Many shows offer a special class for handlers at least 10 years old but less than 18. In the Junior Showmanship class,

Watch Your Step

Be careful to enter your dog in a class for which it is qualified. If you enter 12–18 months, win your class, and go on to be Winners Dog when your pup is actually a week past the age cutoff, the error will be caught when the results are sent to the AKC. You will have to return any awards, and you will not receive any championship points.

judging is on how well the handlers present their dogs rather than the merits of the dogs. (In fact, UKC allows Junior handlers to handle mixed breeds!) If you are interested in Junior Showmanship, see chapter 12.

14. *Full Name of Dog.* Use the full registered name of your dog as it appears on your AKC registration form. Don't abbreviate. Include any titles your dog has earned that are recognized by the AKC, such as a CD (an obedience title), TD (a tracking title), or CH (champion, the conformation title). Do not include titles awarded by any organization other than the AKC.

15. *AKC Reg. No.* Your dog's AKC registration number goes here. Print carefully! This number and your dog's registered name are all that identify the dog in case any championship points are won. If these items are incorrect, incomplete, or illegible, the points might never be credited to your dog.

16. *Date of Birth.* Enter your dog's month, day, and year of birth.

17. *Place of Birth.* Check off either USA, Canada, or Foreign.

18. *Breeder.* If you were the breeder, you can write "Owner." Otherwise, fill in the full name of your dog's breeder, as shown on the registration certificate.

19. *Sire.* Write in the full registered name of the sire of your dog, as shown on the registration certificate.

20. *Dam.* Write in the full registered name of the dam of your dog, as shown on the registration certificate.

21. *Actual Owner(s) Name.* Enter the owner of the dog, presumably yourself. If the dog is co-owned, you *must* include the other owner name(s) as well. All names must be exactly as they appear on the registration.

22. *Owner's Address.* Enter the owner's address, and phone, fax, e-mail information.

Talking Dog

The *sire* is the father of your dog, the *dam* is the mother. *Get* refers to a dog's puppies, as in "My bitch's get are always vigorous and healthy."

23. *Name of Owner's Agent at Show.* If you are taking your dog to a show, just leave this line blank. But if you are sending your dog off to a show with someone else, put that person's name here. If you will be showing someone else's dog, perhaps to gain some experience in the ring, then put yourself down as agent.

24. *Signature.* Sign here. If more than one person co-own the dog, only one needs to sign. An agent listed on line 23 may also sign. But some authorized person *must* sign. An entry form without a valid signature will not be accepted.

25. *Waiver.* When you sign here, you affirm that you have read and understand all show regulations, agree with them, and will abide by them. There may also be information on refund policies here, as well as a statement of how errors on entry blanks will be handled.

Check the front and back of the form to be sure you have filled out everything!

THE UKC ENTRY FORM

The United Kennel Club makes choosing a class and filling out the entry form much simpler. There are only four classes to choose among (aside from classes for Champions, discussed in chapter 26). All are based on age, as follows:

- *Puppy Class*—at least 6 months to under 1 year
- *Junior Class*—at least 1 year to under 2 years
- *Senior Class*—at least 2 years to under 3 years
- *Veteran Class*—3 years and over

The entry form, included in the "Rules Special Issue" (which also includes all the regulations for showing in UKC Conformation, Obedience, and Agility), is very simple and easy to understand (see figure 19.2).

The UKC makes matters simple, allowing you to simply check off the classes you

Fancy That!

Clubs sponsoring UKC shows are permitted to allow "day of" entries. The time that day-of-event entries will be accepted can be found in the premium list or in the show's listing in the UKC magazine *Bloodlines.*

are entering. Remember to fill in the name of the show-giving club and the date(s) of the show(s) at the top. You can even use one form for a multiple-day show if you are planning to enter the same classes each day.

When you submit your day-of-event entry, or when you check in if you pre-entered, you will receive your armband number.

The ARBA Entry Form

You can enter an ARBA show online, filling out the form shown in figure 19.3. The classes are close to the AKC's—the puppy classes are 6–9 Months and 9–15 Months. Novice is an optional class and may or may not be offered. Bred-by Exhibitor, American-Bred, and Open are always offered.

The qualifications for Novice are that the dog is at least 6 months old and has not won a single first prize in Bred-by, Am-Bred, or Open, or two first prizes in Novice. The dog cannot have received any CAC-US cards toward the championship.

Bred-by dogs must be handled by their breeder or co-breeder. Am-Bred must only have been whelped (not necessarily conceived) in the United States.

The nonregular classes that could be offered include Junior Puppy (3–6 months), Veterans (7 years or older), Brace, Stud Dog, Brood Bitch, and Junior Showmanship.

Mailing Entries in on Time

Once you have an entry form completely and correctly filled out, make out a check for the total entry fee to the show superintendent or the sponsoring club. If you are using the U.S. mails, put the entry form and check into an envelope and post it, allowing plenty of time for it to reach its destination.

For shows with close deadlines, or big important shows that fill almost immediately, some people use overnight delivery services. They are certainly more expensive than regular mail, but show entries are not cheap themselves, and if you want to ensure the safe arrival of your entry, you may consider the extra delivery fee worth your while.

Some shows can also now be entered online. Check the Web sites included in appendix A. Infodog (www.infodog.com) is allied with MB-F show superintendents, and they will accept entries for these shows until

United Kennel Club, Inc. Entry Form

Please print or type all information.

FOR CLUB USE ONLY

Armband# _____

Height of Dog _____

Weight of Dog _____

Host Club _____

Breed of Dog _____ **Variety** _____

(if applicable)

Registered/Listed Name of Dog _____

U.K.C. Registration/Listing Number _____ **Date of Birth** _____ **Sex** _____

☐ Permanent Reg.   ☐ Limited Privilege   ☐ Temp. List.

Sire (*optional*) _____

Dam (*optional*) _____

Breeder (*optional*) _____

CLASSES ENTERED

Conformation Class
- ☐ Puppy
- ☐ Junior
- ☐ Senior
- ☐ Veteran
- ☐ Champion of Champion
- ☐ Grand Champion

Obedience Class(es)
- ☐ Novice A
- ☐ Novice B
- ☐ Novice C
- ☐ Open A
- ☐ Open B
- ☐ Utility A
- ☐ Utility B

Agility Class(es)
- ☐ Agility I
- ☐ Agility II
- ☐ Agility III

Agility Division
- ☐ Division 1
- ☐ Division 2
- ☐ Division 3

Obed./Agility: Include Height of Dog _____

Non-Licensed Class(es) _____

Junior Showmanship Class _____

Junior's Birthdate _____

Name of Junior _____

• If entry form is not filled in correctly, or signed, championship points may be withheld. • U.K.C. and the host club are not responsible for loss, accidents or theft. • Absolutely no alcoholic beverages or unprescribed drugs will be allowed on the grounds or during a U.K.C. licensed event. • U.K.C. and the host club assume no responsibility for any damage or injury sustained by the exhibitors, handlers, or to any of their dogs or property, and further assume no responsibility for injury to children not under the control of their parents or guardians. • My signature indicates that I understand and agree to abide by all of the current U.K.C. Rules & Regulations.

Owners name(s) _____

Address _____

City _____ **State** _____ **Zip Code** _____

Telephone: Days _____

Handler's name (if different) _____

I swear that this dog is not being handled by a professional handler.

Signature of owner/handler _____ **Date** _____

Total entry fee $ _____

Rev. 11-97/fo1fbl

Figure 19.2. The UKC entry form (continued)

Official U.K.C. Entry Form

EXHIBITOR INSTRUCTIONS
for completing this form

- Use one entry form for each dog you are entering.

- One form may be used for multiple-day entries of the same dog.

- Please fill in:
1) The name of the host club.
2) The date(s) you are entering.
3) The breed of the dog you are entering.
4) The breed variety, if applicable.
5) U.K.C. registered/listed name of the dog. Include only U.K.C. titles on this form. Please check the box that pertains to your dog (*Permanent Reg., Limited Privilege, Temp. List*).
6) The dog's U.K.C. registration/listed number, date of birth, and sex.
7) The class(es) entered. Check the appropriate box for regular Conformation, Obedience, and/or Agility classes and divisions entered. Fill in the name of any Non-Licensed (Obedience or Conformation), and Junior Showmanship classes entered.

- Sign the Owner/Handler statement.

As per the Official U.K.C. Rules & Regulations ...

- Registered Owners/Designated Handlers are advised to double check that all information on the submitted Entry Form is correct and that the Entry Form is signed. It is not the responsibility of the entry taker to determine or verify that the information on the submitted form is accurate.

- If a dog is entered and/or shown in the wrong class or an incorrect Registration Number on the entry Form by the owner/handler, no championship points will be awarded. It is the responsibility of the owner/handler to see that their dog has been entered and is shown in the correct class.

Official U.K.C. Conformation Classes
- Puppy (6 months of age and under 1 year)
- Junior (1 year of age and under 2 years)
- Senior (2 years of age and under 3 years)
- Veteran (3 years of age and older)
- Champion of Champions (Open to all dogs that have earned the Champion of Champions title)
- Grand Champions (Open to all dogs that have earned the Grand Champion Title)

ENTRY TAKER Instructions
- Accept only completed Entry Forms.
- Entry form must be signed.
- Include the armband number assigned to the dog in the area indicated.
- If necessary, include the height/weight of the dog in the area indicated.
- For Toy Fox Terriers, include the weight of the dog in the area indicated.
- *The Entry Form for each winner must be included with the applicable Event Report Form.* Note: If a dog is entered, and wins, more than one day, attach the Entry Form to the sheet for the first day the dog won, with a note on the other Event Reports stating where the Entry Form may be found.

Figure 19.2. The UKC entry form

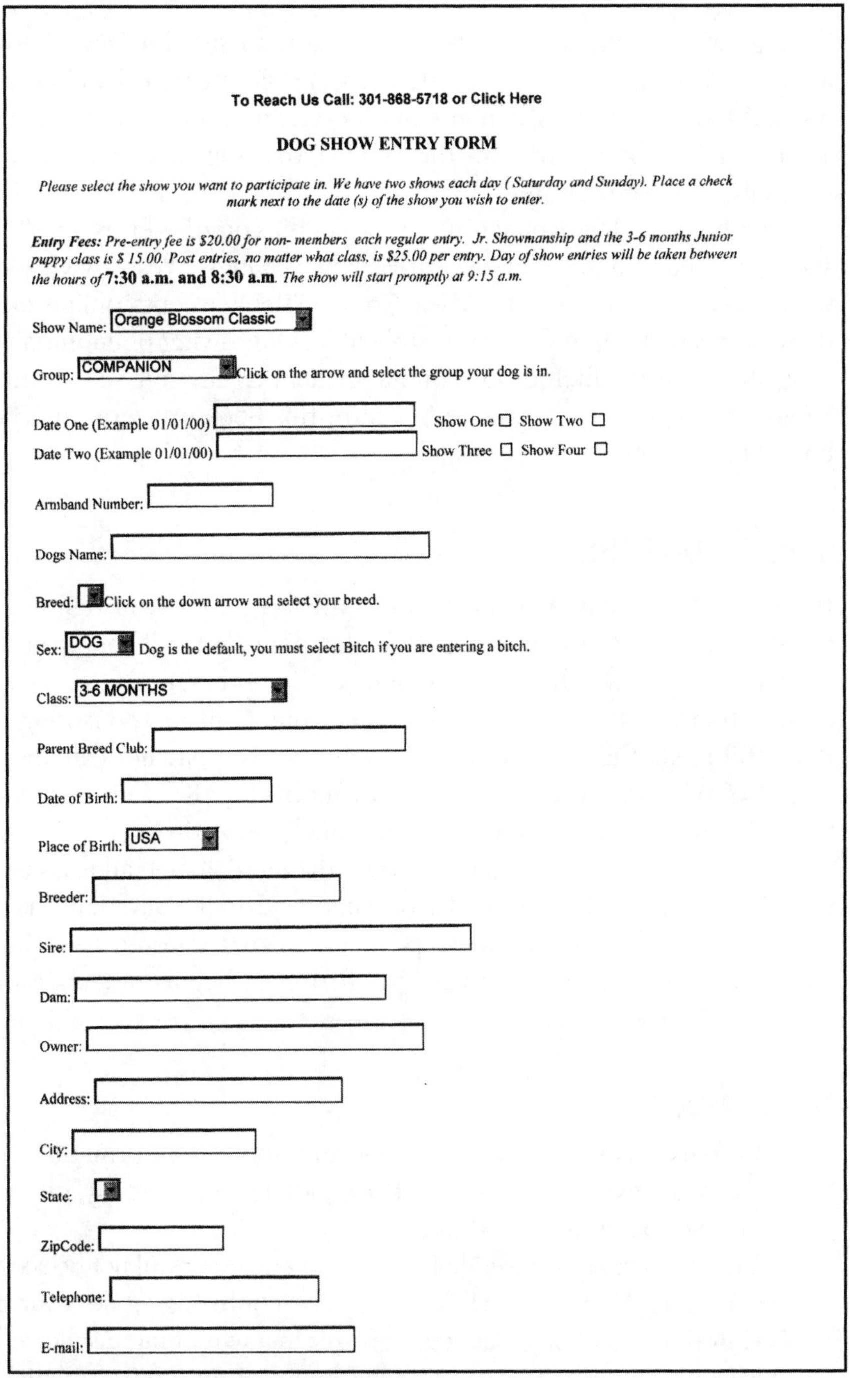

To Reach Us Call: 301-868-5718 or Click Here

DOG SHOW ENTRY FORM

Please select the show you want to participate in. We have two shows each day (Saturday and Sunday). Place a check mark next to the date (s) of the show you wish to enter.

Entry Fees: *Pre-entry fee is $20.00 for non- members each regular entry. Jr. Showmanship and the 3-6 months Junior puppy class is $ 15.00. Post entries, no matter what class, is $25.00 per entry. Day of show entries will be taken between the hours of* **7:30 a.m. and 8:30 a.m**. *The show will start promptly at 9:15 a.m.*

Show Name: `Orange Blossom Classic`

Group: `COMPANION`   Click on the arrow and select the group your dog is in.

Date One (Example 01/01/00) [   ]   Show One ☐ Show Two ☐
Date Two (Example 01/01/00) [   ]   Show Three ☐ Show Four ☐

Armband Number: [   ]

Dogs Name: [   ]

Breed: [▪]Click on the down arrow and select your breed.

Sex: `DOG`   Dog is the default, you must select Bitch if you are entering a bitch.

Class: `3-6 MONTHS`

Parent Breed Club: [   ]

Date of Birth: [   ]

Place of Birth: `USA`

Breeder: [   ]

Sire: [   ]

Dam: [   ]

Owner: [   ]

Address: [   ]

City: [   ]

State: [▪]

ZipCode: [   ]

Telephone: [   ]

E-mail: [   ]

Figure 19.3. The ARBA online entry form

closing. Other events can also be entered at their site, but have cutoff dates a day or two earlier than the stated closing. Entries are batched and forwarded to show superintendents or show secretaries via Federal Express. There is a handling charge for this service, but there's no worry about mail not being delivered in time.

Another site, The Entry Line (www.dogbiz.com/the-entry-line/) handles shows in the Ontario/Quebec area. Show Dogs West (www.showdogs west.com) says it covers the West Coast. ARBA accepts online entries at their Web site. Online show info and entry is a growing phenomenon. Type "dog show entry" (include the quotation marks) in your search engine of choice to find sites that came online after this book was written. There are bound to be some.

MAKING CHANGES

If you want to make changes in your entry—perhaps you realize you entered the wrong class—or if something happens that will keep you from attending the show, the AKC requires that you send the change or cancellation in writing to the Show Superintendent or sponsoring club. It must still reach them before close of entries. You may *not* call and ask for your dog to be moved from one class to another—AKC requires that all information pertaining to show entries be made in writing.

Once the close of entries has passed, the *only* change allowed is a move up to the Best of Breed class (see chapter 26) if your dog has earned enough points for a championship since you first entered the show. This change only can be made up until the first class begins judging on the actual date of the show.

Remember

○ Premium lists contain lots and lots of important information.
○ Entry forms must be filled out completely and correctly, or your dog may not be entered in the show.
○ Entries must be received before close of entries or will not be accepted.
○ Choosing the correct AKC class can be confusing—take your time.
○ Entering the wrong class could result in a win being disallowed.
○ Making changes after an entry has been submitted is difficult—get it right the first time.

20

Double-Check and Dress for Success

In This Chapter

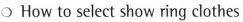

- How to select show ring clothes
- That all-important footwear
- Confirmation of entry
- The judging schedule

Once you have sent in your entry, you're on your way into an actual show ring. Now is the time you should definitely have an "exhibition outfit" picked out and ready to go.

Dressing for a dog show presents interesting, often contradictory, choices. You want to be well groomed and attractive, but able to move vigorously around the ring, bend over, crouch, or kneel down. Not-fully-considered clothing choices, especially for women, have resulted in unexpected (and embarrassing) exposure. Men have suffered similar embarrassment when seams did not prove strong enough. And, of course, there is comfort to consider.

As the show date approaches, you will receive some additional paperwork. This will let you know your entry has been received and give you an idea of when the class you have entered will be judged. In the meantime, keep practicing, perhaps take in a fun match or two if some are available, and try out your exhibition outfit.

HOW TO SELECT SHOW RING CLOTHES

With some experience behind you, you will actually be able to gauge the importance of a show by how the exhibitors are dressed. Although it is the dogs that are the center of attention, the exhibitor is part of the visual package. It's worth your while to present the picture expected of you.

Men generally appear in sports jackets or suits, occasionally even with cummerbunds and bow ties for really prestigious shows. Women have a choice of pantsuits, skirt suits, or dresses. The more prestigious the show, the more formal the clothing. As a novice, you will probably be showing on your local circuit and skipping the really big shows, if there are any in your vicinity, so don't worry about any evening wear just yet.

There is plenty to consider. The color of your clothing should be chosen with the dog in mind. You want to complement your dog's coat but provide a good contrast. The judge needs to see your dog clearly when it is standing in front of you. If you were showing a Soft-Coated Wheaten Terrier and chose a tan ensemble to wear, the dog would blend into your clothes. Don't make the judge's job harder.

Try on different outfits you are considering. With each one, stack the dog in front of a mirror. Which colors set off your dog well? If several seem to work well, then you can consider which best suits you.

If you are really unsure, and have enough time before a show, enlist a friend or relative to take photographs of you in your various outfits under consideration, with your dog stacked before you. Sometimes it's easier to

Tips from the Pros

Be conscious of the color of dog you're showing. Nothing too dark with a dark dog. Remember that in a black-and-white photograph, red prints as black. When showing a small dog, don't have your skirt a length that's going to hit the dog in the face when you move. Definitely something with pockets. Nothing tight, but not billowing out and smothering the dog or something the wind can catch and do a Marilyn Monroe on the wrong side of the tracks.

—Taffe McFadden, AKC professional handler

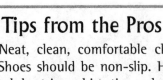

Tips from the Pros

Neat, clean, comfortable clothing is appropriate for this *sport.* Shoes should be non-slip. Heels are definitely out of place. Men look best in a shirt, tie, and sport coat; but if the weather is warm and the judge has removed his jacket, you can certainly take yours off. Worn-out jeans are inappropriate, as are shorts. Women should remember that showing a dog can mean bending over and sometimes squatting down. Choose a nice pants outfit or a skirt that is long enough to be discreet but not of a length to hit your dog in the face as you move. Outlandish garments are always out of place in the show ring. You are the background for your dog, so dress in a color that shows him to his best advantage. Don't wear bulky or jangling jewelry.

–Lilian S. Barber, AKC judge and exhibitor,
author of *The New Complete Italian Greyhound*

see how things really look in a photograph than it is looking at your own reflection.

For women choosing a skirt or a dress, the situation gets more complex. Check that the garment is long enough to spare you any embarrassment when you bend far enough over to reach your dog's outside foot. Also see that the hemline is not at a height that hits the dog right in the face when you are standing together. The skirt should be full enough to let you move freely and kneel down, without having it ride up. But too full a skirt can billow out and swallow up the dog, making it difficult for the judge to see, or even throwing the dog off stride. Wraparound skirts on a windy day have entertained many a dog show gallery and are best avoided (the skirts, not the windy days).

Men's jackets should remain buttoned. An open jacket flying around can be distracting to dogs in the class, or even hit your dog in the face. If the weather is warm, and you would really like to shed the jacket, look to the judge—your own, if male, other rings if not. If judges are wearing their jackets, keep yours on as well.

Men are notorious for having pockets full of change. Empty them before entering the ring so you don't "jingle" when you gait your dog.

Figure 20.1. There is plenty of kneeling or bending over involved in showing a dog. Make sure that your outfit does not impede or embarrass you.

Whatever clothes you choose, they should be washable. They will be susceptible to paw prints, dog hair, and probably drool. Having to dry-clean an outfit after each show will run you serious and unnecessary money.

Unless you will be concentrating on UKC shows (where bait and grooming tools are not allowed in the ring), show outfits should include pockets. Although some handlers stick combs in their armbands for easy access, bait—most often dried liver—is carried in pockets. Another reason you will want your clothes to be washable.

Watch Your Step

Jewelry can become quite a distraction for some dogs. It can either make strange noises while the handler is moving or flash light into a dog's eyes. You don't want to throw off your own dog's performances, and you won't gain any friends by distracting others.

Figure 20.2. The typical male show ring outfit—buttoned jacket, slacks, and tie.

Wearing your exhibition outfit to conformation class will let you see how it feels in action. You can even solicit the opinions of your instructor and classmates.

As far as accessories go, most handlers avoid jewelry and scarves and such. Necklaces and scarves can dangle and interfere with your handling when trying to stack the dog. Bracelets and rings can get caught up in leads. A tie tack or pin is about as much as you will see on experienced handlers.

LOOKING GOOD IN THE RING

Exhibitors debate whether show clothes should be worn to an event or carried along to be changed into. It all depends on circumstances and personal preference.

Talking Dog

An armband holder, though not strictly clothing, may be a welcome accessory. This is a plastic sleeve with elasticized straps and Velcro. Your entry number fits into the sleeve section. It's certainly not mandatory, but it could be more comfortable than the often-used alternative of a rubber band.

If you are attending a show only a short distance from your home, or are comfortably ensconced in a motel or RV for a more distant show, and your class is in the morning, you may want to arrive dressed in your show clothes and ready to go. If instead you are driving a considerable distance, with a class later in the day, you may want to save your show clothes until after the drive and setup and maybe even after grooming your dog. It's up to you.

In case you will be wearing your show clothes throughout the day, you may want to include an apron or beautician's cape in your supplies. You certainly don't want to get any grooming sprays on your outfit. You can even wear your apron or cape while eating lunch, if you are the type who can eat before showing.

An additional consideration for your ring presentation is your own hair. You will spend at least part of your time bending over or looking down. You don't want to be struggling to keep your hair out of your eyes while you're trying to see if your dog is presented well.

Tips from the Pros

Gentlemen wear jackets and ties with slacks—no blue jeans. A gentleman may take off his jacket if the male judge in his ring has removed his—otherwise he must suffer! Ladies should wear skirts and blouses or dresses. If a lady bends over to set up her dog, she should have a skirt or dress long enough so as not to show her undergarments. A lady never wears a low-cut dress or blouse that reveals too much. Dresses and skirts shouldn't billow out in a breeze. A well-known professional handler used to weight down her skirt with drapery weights.

—Sharon Irons Strempski, AKC exhibitor and
breeder of Affenpinschers

Figure 20.3. In many European shows, handlers wear native costume at least for some special classes. (Photo courtesy of Dr. Bernd Guenter)

Of course you want to look good, but comfort is essential. Always keep that in mind when assembling an outfit.

THAT ALL-IMPORTANT FOOTWEAR

Fortunately for dog show exhibitors, there are plenty of good walking shoes being provided by manufacturers. The time when it seemed like the only choices were high heels or sneakers is blessedly behind us.

Tips from the Pros

Shoes should have good traction indoors on slick floors and be a conservative height. Nothing that makes much noise when you move on a hard floor, no hard heels. Bring along duck boots or some other low boots in case of bad weather.

—Taffe McFadden, AKC professional handler

By all means, choose a good walking shoe as part of your show ring ensemble. If you are showing a large breed, you will be trotting or running around the ring. Even with a smaller breed, you want sure footing to avoid any slips. Wear shoes with nonskid soles, either flats or a short stacked heel. Anything higher has no place in the show ring. Even if you didn't end up face down on the ground, imagine what could happen if you stepped on your dog's foot with one of those spikes!

Include an extra pair of workable shoes in your show kit, and extra socks or pantyhose as well. Wet grass can soak through both shoes and socks very quickly and make for very uncomfortable feet. You will really appreciate something dry to change into. Shoes can also break in an astonishing number of ways. So even though an extra pair of shoes may seem like a huge waste of space, it's better than trying to show in that old broken-down pair of sneakers you keep in the car, or even in borrowed shoes in someone else's size!

CONFIRMATION OF ENTRY

Yes, the "i" in confirmation is correct. This conf**I**rms your entry in a conf**O**rmation show.

Tips from the Pros

In the UKC, you don't have to dress up in your best outfit. In almost all cases, if you do you will feel a bit out of place.

—Pamela Kernan, UKC exhibitor

About one week before the show date, you should receive by mail your confirmation of entry and judging schedule. If you have not received confirmation by five days prior to the show, call the show superintendent or show chairman listed in the premium list. Ask this person to check and see if your entry was received. There's no point driving to a show if your entry somehow went astray. If the entry was received, ask the person on the phone to confirm your information to be sure that everything is correct.

The confirmation you receive by mail will state your dog's name, registration number, sex, breed, and classes entered. It may even be an actual copy of your original entry form. Check to see that all the information is correct, and note the armband number assigned to your dog.

If you notice any wrong information in the confirmation, call the show superintendent or show secretary immediately. Mistakes made by the club sponsoring the show can often be straightened out over the phone. If you have made a mistake and entered the wrong class, all you can do is skip the show and try to get it right the next time. Once the close of entries date has passed, no changes can be made to your entry. The only exception is if your dog attains a championship and needs to move up to Best of Breed (AKC) or Champion of Champions (UKC) class. This change can be made only up until the first class begins judging on the actual day of the show.

> ## Fancy That!
>
> Your armband is probably the most essential piece of paper on the show grounds. This number is what is written into the judge's book for awards. If it is not correctly associated with your dog's name and registration number, the award cannot be credited to you by the kennel club.

THE JUDGING SCHEDULE

Along with your confirmation of entry comes a judging schedule, which lists the total number of dogs entered in a show, which ring each breed will be shown in, and what time your breed will start (see figure 20.4). The judge may not start judging any breed earlier than the time given in the judging schedule. But it is entirely your responsibility to be at the ring on time—no one is going to hold up judging waiting for your entry.

JUDGING SCHEDULE – SATURDAY – AUG. 29, 1998

Ring NO. 1
JUDGE: Helen Miller Fisher
Total Dogs: 109

9:00 a.m.
2	BULL TERRIERS (Colored)	1-1-0
17	CAIRN TERRIERS	5-11-1D
5	AUSTRALIAN TERRIERS	1-4-0
1	BULL TERRIERS (White)	1-0-0

10:00 a.m.
38	GERMAN SHEPHERD DOGS	18-18-1D/1B
1	IRISH TERRIERS	1-0-0
1	BEDLINGTON TERRIERS	0-0-1B

11:30 a.m.
12	SCOTTISH TERRIERS	6-5-1D

12:45 p.m.
5	AMERICAN STAFFORDSHIRE TERRIERS	1-4-0
4	BORDER TERRIERS	2-1-1D
1	DANDIE DINMONT TERRIERS	1-0-0
4	FOX TERRIERS (Smooth)	2-2-0
1	KERRY BLUE TERRIERS	0-0-1D
2	MANCHESTER TERRIERS (Standard)	0-1-1B
3	MINIATURE SCHNAUZERS	1-2-0
4	NORWICH TERRIERS	0-3-1D
5	STAFFORDSHIRE BULL TERRIERS	2-1-2B
3	WEST HIGHLAND WHITE TERRIERS	1-1-1D

Ring NO. 2
JUDGE: Frank T. Sabella
Total Dogs: 99

9:00 a.m.
14	PUGS	6-6-1D/1B
2	MINIATURE PINSCHERS	0-1-1D
4	MANCHESTER TERRIERS (Toy)	1-1-1D/1B
5	ITALIAN GREYHOUNDS	2-1-2B

10:00 a.m.
11	PEKINGESE	6-3-2D
2	SHIH TZU	2-0-0
8	PAPILLONS	2-4-1D/1B
5	CHIHUAHUAS (Longcoat)	3-2-0

11:00 a.m.
6	YORKSHIRE TERRIERS	2-2-1D/1B
5	CAVALIER KING CHARLES SPANIELS	3-2-0
1	SILKY TERRIERS	0-0-1D
14	POMERANIANS	7-5-2D

12:45 p.m.
7	POODLES (Toy)	2-4-1B
7	BRUSSELS GRIFFONS	0-3-2D/2B
1	ENGLISH TOY SPANIELS (Blen & Pr Chas)	0-0-1D
7	CHIHUAHUAS (Smoothcoat)	1-4-1D/1B

Ring NO. 3
JUDGE: Stephen J. Hubbell
Total Dogs: 123

9:00 a.m.
13	AKITAS	3-8-2D
9	BULLMASTIFFS	3-4-2D
4	GIANT SCHNAUZERS	2-1-1D

10:00 a.m.
13	GREAT DANES	4-7-2B
10	BERNESE MOUNTAIN DOGS	3-4-3D
1	COLLIES (Smooth)	0-0-1B
1	GREAT PYRENEES	1-0-0

11:00 a.m.
15	DOBERMAN PINSCHERS	5-9-1D
9	COLLIES (Rough)	3-5-1D
1	KOMONDOROK	0-0-1D

12:45 p.m.
19	ALASKAN MALAMUTES	8-7-4D
4	SHETLAND SHEEPDOGS	2-2-0
12	WELSH CORGIS (Pembroke)	6-6-0
6	OLD ENGLISH SHEEPDOGS	2-3-1D
6	WELSH CORGIS (Cardigan)	2-3-1B

Ring NO. 4
JUDGE: Dany Canino
Total Dogs: 111

9:00 a.m.
9	MASTIFFS	4-3-1D/1B
4	NEWFOUNDLANDS	3-1-0
6	SIBERIAN HUSKIES	3-2-1D
30	ROTTWEILERS	8-18-2D/2B

11:00 a.m.
4	PORTUGUESE WATER DOGS	1-1-2D
21	BOXERS	8-11-2D

12:45 p.m.
10	SAINT BERNARDS	3-5-2D
4	SAMOYEDS	1-2-1D

1:15 p.m.
5	NOVICE JUNIOR	5-0-0
5	NOVICE SENIOR	5-0-0
2	OPEN JUNIOR	2-0-0
11	OPEN SENIOR	11-0-0

Ring NO. 5
JUDGE: Christina Hubbell
Total Dogs: 80

9:00 a.m.
8	BRITTANYS	3-4-1B
5	POINTERS (German Shorthaired)	3-1-1B
1	POINTERS	0-0-1D
35	RETRIEVERS (Golden)	13-17-2D/3B

11:00 a.m.
1	SETTERS (Gordon)	0-0-1D
3	RETRIEVERS (Chesapeake Bay)	0-0-2D/1B
3	RETRIEVERS (Flat-Coated)	0-1-2D
7	SETTERS (Irish)	3-2-1D/1B
12	RETRIEVERS (Labrador)	6-5-1D
5	SETTERS (English)	1-3-1D

HURRICANE RIDGE KENNEL CLUB   **AUGUST 1998**

Figure 20.4. Sample AKC judging schedule

The numbers following the breeds in figure 20.4 refer, in this order, to the number of dogs entered in the regular classes, number of bitches entered in the regular classes, number of champion dogs entered, and number of champion bitches entered. So for Pugs, there are six dogs in the regular classes, six bitches in the regular classes, one champion dog, and one champion bitch.

Be sure to take the judging schedule with you to the show as a reminder of your ring number and starting time. Some judging schedules even contain a map of the show grounds, helping you find your way to your ring.

Along with the confirmation and judging schedule may come an entry pass or ticket to get into the show. Don't forget that, or you may have to pay admission at the gate to get onto the show grounds.

Remember

○ The formality of show clothes should match the prestige of a show.
○ Clothes must complement the dog and provide comfort and freedom of movement for the handler.
○ Hairstyles should stay clear of your face.
○ Shoes must be comfortable and nonskid.
○ Confirmation of entry must be carefully checked for any problems.
○ Judging schedules will give you an idea of the time your class will occur.

21

Packing It In

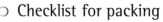
As with most other hobbies and avocations, dog showing can start out with a few simple pieces of equipment and quickly grow into a gotta-have-it paraphernalia obsession. Many long-time exhibitors derive great glee from MacGyver-ing ordinary objects into makeshift grooming, showing, and traveling equipment. An entire book could be written on the conformation uses of Rubbermaid and Tupperware products!

Part of your early training and practice should be to find what works best for your dog. A good class may let you try different grooming tools, collars and leashes, etc., without having to buy each variety from the pet supply store. Or you may be able to conduct brief in-store trials with equipment. It's good to experiment, and especially to find what best suits your dog, but don't fall into the trap of thinking "if only I'd had that (fill in the blank), we would have won that class."

CHECKLIST FOR PACKING

As a beginner in dog showing, you may still be acquiring the basics. This list will doubtlessly grow and change as your career progresses, but there are roughly two dozen items generally considered essential. Copy this list, amend it as you wish, and check each item off as you pack it in your transport. You'll have one (or two dozen) less thing to worry about.

❑ Clean, well-groomed dog
❑ Tack box or bag with grooming equipment
❑ Grooming table
❑ Regular collar and lead
❑ Show collar and lead
❑ Water bowl, bucket, or cup
❑ Water from home
❑ Bait (food or toy or both)
❑ Crate and/or exercise pen
❑ Grass mat, blanket, or dog bed
❑ Towels
❑ Equipment dolly
❑ Sandwich bags or other impromptu pooper-scooper
❑ Confirmation of entry and parking pass
❑ Show clothes and/or apron
❑ Extra shoes and socks
❑ Chair
❑ Shade (tarp, canopy, umbrella, ex-pen cover)
❑ Armband holder or pin or rubber band
❑ Sunscreen
❑ Ice chest and/or thermos with drinks
❑ Lunch
❑ Video camera, if you have one, and someone to tape your performance

For some breeds, owners may consider it essential to have drool rags, coat wraps, snoods to keep ears out of drinking water, or hair clips.

YOUR TACK BOX

Your well-equipped tack box or bag is of course essential. But exactly what goes into that tack box will vary greatly, depending on the breed of your

Tips from the Pros

Take an extra leash and collar with you, towel, something to clean your dog if it gets unexpectedly dirty. To prepare myself, I make a list of the things I need to take to the show the next day. I check the list before leaving for the show. This is the only way I have found so I don't leave anything important behind.

—Karen A. Brancheau, UKC exhibitor and judge,
owner of StoneFox Kennels and StoneFox Grooming and Pet Supplies

dog and your personal preferences. Chapter 13, "Grooming for Success," delves into how to groom your dog and what you need to accomplish it. Use your experience to make your own separate tack box checklist. And get into the habit of returning items to the tack box after you have used them, or replacing them if you use them up. That way the box will always be ready to go. The salespeople in the booths at shows may love you if you're constantly forgetting pieces of equipment and having to buy them on site, but that's just wasting money you could be using for entry fees!

You will undoubtedly include at least a couple of combs and brushes. Unless you break one (teeth do fall out and handles break) or change your choices, they should always be readily available. Scissors are also considered essential. Make sure they are sharp so they don't pull hair when you clip.

A spray bottle or two is always a good idea. One bottle should contain water from home. On hot days, a spray of cool water into your dog's mouth or under the tummy and on the pads can help keep a dog refreshed. Or if the site is muddy, a water spray bottle and a towel can quickly clean off feet. A second spray bottle might contain coat dressings or grooming sprays.

For indoor shows, many competitors carry a product called Tacky Foot. It's put on the dog's pads to improve traction on slippery surfaces, such as ring mats or even wet grass. But some feel that this is a hazard to the dog's health, should he or she lick the stuff off the paws.

Among AKC exhibitors, you may see a variety of chalks and colorings and hairsprays. Even though the official regulations proclaim that no foreign substance may remain in the coat when the dog is brought into the ring, this is often ignored. Exhibitors commonly use chalk, powder, or cornstarch to make white coats appear whiter. Poodle handlers traditionally

Tips from the Pros

I enjoy UKC because there are less politics, less chalking, dying, and all the other things that people do to their dogs to make this just a beauty contest instead of a dog show. Winning at any cost just doesn't cut it because what you hide from people today will present itself in the next generation.

—Karen A. Brancheau, StoneFox Kennels

use hairspray to achieve the massive bouffant headdress. Some even use felt tip pens to blacken noses. Any artificial substance that changes the appearance of the dog is against the rules! As the saying goes, do not try this at home!

To go along with your well-equipped tack box, you may want a grooming table. Some people simply use the top of a plastic crate, or just groom the dog on the ground, but many showing long-coated breeds consider a grooming table indispensable. With small breeds, a grooming table not only saves your back, but also gives the dog more experience on a table, where it will be shown in the ring. Remember to make it as pleasant as possible. Should you be handling a Dalmatian, Foxhound, or other smooth-coated breed, you may not consider a table essential.

OTHER EQUIPMENT

The first item on the checklist is pretty self-evident: It's hard to do well if you leave the dog at home. And few things annoy a judge more than bringing a dirty or ungroomed dog into the ring.

Many exhibitors use the dog's regular leash and collar to walk the dog onto the show grounds and to exercise the dog. The much flimsier show lead is only used for the actual trip to the ring. Leashes do break, and there's no point in putting yourself at higher risk when it's not necessary. Bringing a spare show lead in case yours does snap is not a bad idea, though you could buy one at nearly any show.

A water receptacle of some sort is, of course, essential. Many also advocate carrying water from home, even if you know water will be available at the show site. This does ensure that you will have water available directly upon your arrival, without having to run around looking for it. Some say it also ensures that your dog will not suffer a digestive upset from drinking "foreign" water.

If you use cooked liver or hot dogs as bait, you will need room in your cooler for them, as both are highly perishable. If you use freeze-dried liver or some other nonperishable choice, then the cooler isn't necessary. Don't forget that extra-special in-the-ring-only squeak toy if you use one. Squeakers are sometimes allowed in UKC show rings—bait never is.

Either a crate or exercise pen is a must. As we explained in chapter 7, you will spend a lot of time at a show simply waiting around. Having a secure place to put your dog will allow both you and your dog to relax and enjoy the event more. Whether you prefer a crate or an exercise pen is a matter of personal choice. For a crate, you have a choice of collapsible wire, foldable mesh fabric, rigid airline, and maybe some others by the time you read this. Whatever style you choose, you will want some sort of pad or mat to offer your dog some cushioning. With an exercise pen, you'll want a grass mat or blanket to keep your dog off the ground. You certainly don't want your immaculately groomed dog rolling around in the dirt minutes before you're going into the ring. Grass mats are particularly nice, made in dimensions that extend beyond the exercise pen to give you a clean place to sit at ground level if you wish, or to deposit all your other paraphernalia.

Towels have many uses at dog shows, and you will want one or more as part of your equipment. We've already explained that a spray bottle of water and a towel can salvage your dog if he or she somehow manages to get dirty before you have made your ring appearance. Exhibitors showing loose-lipped breeds, such as St. Bernards and Newfoundlands, often carry smaller towels, even in the ring, to wipe away the drool. Towels can even be wet down with cold water then wrung out and laid over the dog's back as a cooling device. You will find plenty to do with towels—include them in your equipment.

With an ever-growing mound of paraphernalia, one item you will certainly appreciate is an equipment dolly. This is a flat metal platform on wheels, with a handle to pull it by. It can hold all your other equipment, including a crated dog. When the parking lot is a quarter mile from the rings, with a huge hill in between, shifting everything in one trip with a loaded dolly will be a godsend. I went a step further by putting my dog in a harness and having *him* pull the equipment dolly. It not only moved the equipment, but it also proved to be excellent conditioning for the dog and a great source of show-ground amusement when we started offering rides on the cart to other exhibitors.

On most show grounds, there will be a designated exercise area where dogs may relieve themselves. At particularly well-organized shows, there will be pooper-scoopers and trash cans scattered about the grounds, and maybe even a squad of young people patrolling for pickup. You should still have some means of picking up after your own dog. You might be walking away from the heart of the show area, taking a break in a park, or staying at a motel. You should *always* be ready to clean up. Host clubs have an increasingly hard time finding show sites and lodgings that allow dogs because less-than-conscientious owners leave a mess behind. Sandwich bags or produce bags are easy to stuff in a pocket. Slipped over your hand like a mitten, they can be used to pick up any mess and disposed of in the appropriate receptacle. Always make sure you have some plastic bags in your show kit.

> ## Fancy That!
>
> My dog, in fact, progressed from pulling show equipment on a dolly to pulling a sulky cart with people aboard. He was the hit of dog sports demonstrations, giving rides to all the children in attendance. If you have a draft breed, even a children's wagon can be adapted to a dog cart.

Remember the confirmation of entry. It can help you find your way to the show site and the correct ring. Don't forget the admission ticket if one was included with the confirmation.

If you are wearing your show clothes to the event, bring an apron or beautician's cape to protect your outfit while you are grooming the dog (and eating lunch). Otherwise, carry your show outfit to change into. Always bring an extra pair of shoes and socks to avoid wet feet or the extreme stress of having to borrow shoes from someone if yours happen to break.

You may or may not consider a chair essential. If you don't change into your show clothes until the last minute, you may not mind sitting on the ground. Just keep in mind that it can be a long day if you have nowhere to sit.

At outdoor shows, reliable shade or protection from the weather for your dog (and secondarily yourself) is necessary. This could be as elaborate as a collapsible canopy—used by many who show more than one dog because it provides 40 square feet or more of protection—or as simple as a beach umbrella or a tarp over an exercise pen. Whatever you are using, remember that shade travels as the sun moves overhead. Check often to see that your dog is still protected.

Shows generally have rubber bands for exhibitors to use with their armbands. But they might run out. Bring your armband holder if you have one, or a safety pin or rubber band, just to be sure.

Fancy That!

Dog show exhibitors who often show together sometimes share one of the large portable canopies, creating their own little shady campground. Maybe someone who used to bring a lot of dogs has cut back and now has room under the canopy for you!

If your show is outdoors, you will be spending much of your time in the sun. We are all now well advised to use sunscreen to protect against skin cancer. Hats or visors are not recommended for the ring. They may fall off when you bend over, obstruct your vision, or upset your dog.

Food and drink may or may not be available or to your liking. If you want to be sure, bring your own beverages and your lunch. Many coolers can also be used as seats, so they can serve two purposes.

If you have a video camera and someone to operate it while you're in the ring, by all means take advantage of the opportunity to later see yourself in action. You often will find it hard to believe some of the things you did.

Whatever you decide is essential for you to have, pack it the night before the show. You still have time to replace anything you may be missing, and it leaves less to do in the morning. Departures for shows are often quite early, and your thinking may be as dim as the dawning light.

YOUR ROAD KENNEL

Like most people, you'll probably start off using the family car to go to dog shows. If you have a compact, you might find it difficult to fit even the basic equipment into the car. There are carriers you can attach to the front bumper to hold at least an exercise pen and equipment dolly. You can become quite expert at fitting everything into your vehicle.

Now, we're certainly not saying that you have to run out and buy another vehicle to be successful at dog showing. But you will quickly notice

Talking Dog

"Going to the dogs" has a whole different meaning among dog show aficionados. Some might consider buying a new vehicle for the comfort of your dog as a downward slide, but not fanciers! Conversations ringside are as likely to be about the latest in transport as they are to be about the dogs in the ring.

that nearly everyone else is driving a van, an SUV, or a motor home. It seems to be a progression that creeps up on exhibitors without them realizing it: "I really should have a crate *and* an exercise pen . . . and I'm going to all these shows anyway, so if I had a second dog to show I'd double my ring time with only another entry fee . . . but boy, that car is crowded, and think how much nicer a van would be!" So you start pricing vans.

There's no question that vans are nice vehicles for showing dogs. With their removable or fold-down seats, they offer a lot of floor space for dogs and equipment. But don't run out and throw yourself into debt just because "everybody else" drives a van to the shows. Even a compact station wagon can fit two size-400 Vari-kennels, and a bumper bracket or roof rack for holding other large equipment is way cheaper than a new van.

Besides, the real professionals all bypass vans for motor homes. A lot of your fellow exhibitors may be driving them, too. And while it's true that a motor home or even a van can serve as your home on wheels and save you from having to find and pay for motel rooms, in many parts of the country you could buy an actual *home* for the cost of a motor home. And that's before filling up at the gas station.

Remember

- ○ Pack your car and check your checklist the night before a show.
- ○ Always return items to your tack box after using them.
- ○ Don't use artificial substances such as chalk or hairspray on your dog, even though you may see others doing it.
- ○ Always present a clean, well-groomed dog to the judge.
- ○ Always be ready to clean up after your dog.
- ○ Change your checklist as you change your "essential" equipment.

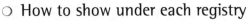
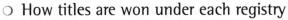

22

A Special Look at the UKC, ARBA, CKC, and FCI

Although the vast majority of dog showing in the United States takes place under the auspices of the AKC, other options are available both inside and outside the country. We have been noting the differences between the AKC and other registries throughout the book, but all the basic information is collected here for the benefit of those interested in alternatives to the AKC.

The activities conducted by these registries can be somewhat regional. Obviously the Canadian Kennel Club (CKC) operates in Canada, so those fanciers living on the northern border of the United States or willing to travel (or of course those residing in Canada!) will be most interested in notes on the CKC.

The United Kennel Club (UKC) is headquartered in Michigan. The UKC is a national organization; however, there are areas with no local UKC clubs and hence no events. UKC aficionados in an area can band together to form a local club and gain permission to hold events. It only takes about a dozen dedicated people.

The Federation Cynologique Internationale (FCI) is a worldwide organization, but one that presents some problems in the United States. The AKC is the recognized U.S. kennel club, but the AKC does not recognize many of the breeds recognized by the FCI, making dogs of these breeds born in the United States ineligible for competition. To further complicate matters, the United States is not a formal member country of the FCI.

Read the section for any kennel club that interests you. But be sure to contact the organization for their latest set of rules, as details do change from time to time. Certainly the breeds recognized by any particular kennel club may be updated often.

UNITED KENNEL CLUB

Several of the UKC's basic differences from the AKC are meant to keep UKC shows more friendly and family oriented.

No professional handlers are allowed. This means people generally show their own dogs, though friends may help each other out, too. Novices will still have much to learn about showing, but they can be comforted that no one in the ring with them is making a living by showing dogs.

At the Show

Most shows accept day-of-event entries. In fact, show-sponsoring clubs have to make a special request to demand pre-entries only. Day-of-show entries will be accepted until a time specified in the event flier, premium list, and show listing in *Bloodlines* magazine. This allows more flexibility in your plans.

Armbands are picked up at the check-in table. Because all exhibitors will converge on the same location, there may be a substantial line.

All dogs are shown on the ground unless a judge requests use of a table or bench. Beagles and the six breeds of Coonhounds recognized by the UKC operate under special rules based on their hunting heritage. You can receive

Tips from the Pros

The UKC definition of a professional handler is very broad. They consider their prohibition against professionals "one of the cornerstones of U.K.C. philosophy." Here is the official UKC definition:

A Professional Handler is a person who exhibits dogs in Conformation, Obedience, or Agility for compensation. This category includes any person who accepts any pay, gift, or remuneration of any sort in return for exhibiting a dog. Remuneration includes, but is not limited to:

1. Payment for exhibiting a dog in a U.K.C.-licensed event;

2. Reimbursement for lodging, mileage, travel, meals, other travel expenses, or any other expenses incurred at or traveling to or from a U.K.C.-licensed event;

3. Payment of entry fees by another exhibitor for dogs owned by the Professional Handler in return for handling services.

Among the factors that may be considered in determining whether a handler is a Professional Handler are:

1. Business cards indicating that the person in question is a Professional Handler;

2. Advertising Professional Handling services on a vehicle, in a publication, or in any other dog-related venue;

3. Offering Professional Handling services through a training facility;

4. Acting as a Professional Handler at events offered by other organizations;

5. Exhibiting multiple dogs, particularly those that the handler neither owns nor co-owns;

6. Exhibiting multiple breeds of dogs, particularly those that the handler neither owns nor co-owns.

An individual may be a Professional Handler even regardless of whether or not handling dogs is his/her primary source of income.

—From the Official UKC Rules & Regulations

detailed rules by contacting the UKC. The four varieties of Belgian Shepherd Dogs also have special rules, amounting to three choices in how they are judged, but these are included in the Official UKC Rules & Regulations.

In grooming for the UKC ring, only minimal trimming, to reflect the "natural" trimming that would result if the dog were performing its function, is allowed. Thorough brushing, nail trimming, ear cleaning, trimming of excess hair from the pads, and trimming for sanitary purposes is expected. In appropriate breeds, stripping is required. After saying all of this, UKC notes that "There are certain breeds for which traditional show clips have evolved from functional trimmings (for example, Poodles, Schnauzers and Wirehaired Fox Terriers). These functional trims were adopted for practical purpose."

No grooming or grooming tools are permitted in the ring.

No food is allowed in the ring either. Dogs are not baited with dried liver or any other tasty morsels in the UKC ring. Squeaky toys may sometimes be used, at the judge's discretion.

UKC prohibits drinking and taking of nonprescribed drugs on its show grounds. This applies to spectators as well as exhibitors and judges.

> **Fancy That!**
>
> UKC's emphasis on dog showing as a family event also results in less emphasis on the handler's wardrobe. Though you should still be clean and presentable, you probably won't be out of place in jeans.

Classes and Titles

UKC sanctions Single Breed Shows (only one breed being judged), Multibreed Shows (more than one breed, with special additional classes if at least ten breeds are judged), and All-Breed Shows (all breeds recognized by the UKC).

Beyond the title of Champion, the UKC offers a Grand Champion and National Grand Champion. Dogs that have attained their championship compete against one another in the Champion of Champions class. At least three dogs must be competing for a win to count toward the five wins necessary to earn the title of Grand Champion (GR CH). The National Grand Champion class may be held for only those breeds with a set number of Grand Champions. At this time, American Eskimo, Toy Fox Terrier, and American Pit Bull Terrier parent clubs hold the National Grand Champion class at their fall national shows. If at least five dogs compete, the winner is entitled to the abbreviation NTL GR CH.

UKC clubs may also hold nonlicensed classes, some of them similar to those offered by the AKC, and some quite different. A 3–6 month Puppy Class may be held, followed by Best Puppy. Stud Dog and Brood Bitch, with a stud and two to four of his progeny or a bitch and two to four of her progeny shown as a group, are much like AKC. So is Brace, with two similar dogs of the same breed shown together by a single handler. State Bred, for dogs bred in the state of the show location and owned by residents of the state, is different. Seasoned class is for dogs age 7 or older, to "show specimens of the breed that are considered 'senior citizens' but are still in good condition. This is the only time many people, especially newcomers, have the opportunity to see these dogs. Spayed or neutered dogs are allowed to be entered." The UKC agrees with the AKC in allowing a Parade of Titleholders, with dogs spotlighted one at a time while a commentator reads out their accomplishments.

The new Altered Champion class, to be put into effect in late 2001 or 2002, will allow a whole new set of dogs into the ring. Purebreds who have been spayed or neutered will compete for championship points in a class of their own, conducted the same as all the other classes. While these dogs will never be bred, they are still examples of what has been produced by the mating of their dam and sire, and many are fine specimens of their breed. The Australian Shepherd Club of America is already conducting a two-year trial of altered champion classes.

In Junior Showmanship, UKC believes in starting them young. They also believe in letting the juniors show *any* UKC-registered dog, including mixed breeds. This is supposed to be judged on the handling talents of the Junior, after all. There are four divisions of Junior Showmanship:

> *Pee-Wee* for children 2 or 3 years old. Parents may accompany them to be sure the dog is under control.
> *Sub-Junior* for children 4 years old up to, but not including, 8 years old. They may also be accompanied by a parent.
> *Junior* for children 8 through 12 years old.
> *Senior* for those 13 through 17 years of age.

Finally, UKC offers the Total Dog award, in support of their emphasis on performance events. This title goes only to a dog that wins in the conformation ring (Best Male or Female of Variety, Best Male or Female, Champion of Champions, Grand Champion, or Best of Breed) *and* achieves a qualifying score in Obedience or Agility at the same event. UKC conformation shows are likely to include one or the other, or both, of these performance sports.

UKC also keeps track of the Top Ten Show Dogs (based on the number of dogs they have defeated in the show ring) for three dozen of the breeds they register:

Afghan Hound	Chinese Shar-Pei	Louisiana Catahoula
American Black &	Chinook	Leopard Dog
Tan Coonhound	Cocker Spaniel	Manchester Terrier
American Eskimo	Dachshund	Plott Hound
American Pit Bull	Dalmatian	Redbone Coonhound
Terrier	Doberman Pinscher	Rottweiler
Anatolian Shepherd	English Coonhound	Samoyed
Beagle	German Pinscher	Shetland Sheepdog
Belgian Shepherd	German Shepherd Dog	Toy Fox Terrier
Dog	Golden Retriever	Treeing Walker
Bluetick Coonhound	Havanese	Coonhound
Boston Terrier	Irish Setter	Yorkshire Terrier
Bouvier des Flandres	Jack Russell Terrier	

Class Divisions

UKC offers only a few variety divisions:

Alaskan Klee Kai—Toy, Miniature, Standard
American Eskimo—Miniature, Standard
Belgian Shepherd Dog—Groenendael, Laekenois, Malinois, Tervueren
Berger de Pyrenees—Rough-Faced, Smooth-Faced
Collie—Rough, Smooth
Dachshund—Miniature, Standard (no division by coat types)
Fox Terrier—Smooth, Wire Haired
Jack Russell Terrier—10 inches–12$\frac{1}{2}$ inches, over 12$\frac{1}{2}$ inches–15 inches

Talking Dog

"Ratings systems" for AKC dogs are not run by the AKC. And there is some controversy about them. But UKC runs its own rating system directly from its own records.

Manchester Terrier—Standard, Toy
Xoloitzcuintli—Toy, Miniature, Standard

For Toy Fox Terriers only, each dog is weighed at the check-in table. This is part of the breed's parent club regulations.

ARBA

Obviously, ARBA mostly recognizes breeds outside the purview of the AKC. That is its main reason for existence. It has more in common with the UKC on this point.

ARBA's regular classes, divided by sex, are

6–9 Months
9–15 Months
Novice (optional)
Bred-by Exhibitor
American Bred
Open
Winners Competition

There are also a couple of regular ARBA classes in which dogs and bitches compete together:

Breed Club Class
Certificate of Aptitude for Championship in the United States

The Breed Club Class is only open to dogs that have been awarded a championship by their parent breed club (dogs must be registered with some other kennel club to be registered with ARBA, and it is this other kennel club that is referred to here). One dog and one bitch are selected.

CAC-US competition is open to the Breed Club Class Winners Dog and Winners Bitch, and the Winners Dog and Winners Bitch from the other classes. A CAC-US is given to one dog and one bitch. A dog must receive a rating of "Excellent," the same as in the FCI, to receive a CAC-US.

A dog can earn a Junior Championship of Beauty by receiving four Certificates of Aptitude for Championships in the United States from four different judges. The full Championship of Beauty requires nine CAC-US from at least six judges. A dog that also obtains the title of Working or Field

Champion is designated a Grand Champion. If the dog also earns an Obedience Trial Championship, the title is then Supreme Grand Champion.

ARBA also has its own ranking system, published in its quarterly magazine *Rarity:*

> Highest scoring, top 10 all-breed winners
> Highest scoring, top 5 in each group
> Highest scoring, top 3 in each breed

The preferred gaiting pattern at ARBA shows is the "L," so practice it.

CANADIAN KENNEL CLUB

In 1992, Canada made it easier for U.S. dogs to compete in Canadian events. Prior to that date, U.S. dogs had to be registered with the CKC. This required that the *original* AKC certificate of registration and AKC certified pedigree be sent to Canada, and that the dog be tattooed or microchipped for identification. Sending the originals of these documents was always a worrying proposition. Getting the signature of the original tattooer also created problems.

Now U.S. dogs need only an Event Registration Number (ERN) to compete in CKC events and earn titles. This does *not* register a dog with the CKC for breeding purposes—only for competition.

The ERN requires only a photocopy of the dog's registration certificate, along with a written request for an ERN, a full return address, and a check or money order for $53.50 Canadian, payable to the Canadian Kennel Club. You can even fax your request if you include a Visa or MasterCard number, expiration date, and name and signature of the cardholder.

Send or fax your request to

The Canadian Kennel Club
Shows & Trials Division
100-89 Skyway Avenue
Etobicoke, Ontario
M9W 6R4 Canada
Fax: 416-675-6506

Fancy That!

Canadian dogs, and U.S. dogs fully registered with the CKC, are required to have a permanent form of positive identification, either microchip or tattoo.

Dogs may be entered in CKC shows before applying for an ERN, but you must apply within 30 days of the event or forfeit any points awarded.

Contact the CKC (or any other registry you plan to show under) for its latest rules and regulations. They are quite similar to those of the AKC, though professional handlers are much less common.

FEDERATION CYNOLOGIQUE INTERNATIONALE (FCI)

If you truly want to fly to the heights of dogdom, then seek the Certificat d'Aptitude au Championat International de Beauté (CACIB), or International Champion, awarded by the FCI. This is like no other title except perhaps the national championship offered by some of the European countries through earning of the Certificat d'Aptitude au Championat (CAC).

Consider the hundreds of AKC shows offered each year and that multiple dogs can earn championship points at each of the shows. Now consider a championship show for Bernese Mountain Dogs in, say, Switzerland. Only three or four of these shows are offered each year. At each of those shows, only one male and one female can receive the CAC. The dog must first receive a rating of Excellent from the judge, the highest rating available, in the usually enormous Open class. The dog must then win the class and go on to beat the winner of the Champions class of his gender (if there are any entered). To be Swiss Champion, a dog must accomplish this three times, two of these at international shows. Each breed club decides if a

Tips from the Pros

I think that currently, as at any time, there are only three or four German, one or two Swiss, and worldwide about a half-dozen International Champions alive. Of course, we all know one another, and since each of us knows the ordeal of becoming a champion, we also respect one another. Also, we are proud that—just as the champions of the previous generations served as models for us—today we are the models.

—Int CH Berri Max v.d. Horlache, owned by Bernd Guenter, originally published in *Bernese Mountain Dog Club of Great Britain Magazine*, May 1994.

working title (where the dog has to perform its historic function) will also be required. It's not surprising that any breed usually only has one or two Swiss Champions alive at any one time.

The story is similar in Germany. Even though there are more shows held each year, it takes four CACs to earn the title German Champion. In either country (as in all FCI countries), and for the International Championship as well, at least a year must elapse between earning the first CAC or CACIB and the last. Because a dog has to be at least 15 months old to enter the Open class, no certificates can be won at a younger age.

Figure 22.1. "Max," the only Int CH entered at the 1993 show in Bern, Switzerland. (Photo courtesy of Dr. Bernd Guenter)

The order of the classes can vary from country to country. In Austria, the order is similar to that seen in the United States: Minor Puppy (6–9 months), Junior (9–15 months), Intermediate (15–24 months), Open (15 months plus), Working (15 months plus, with a working certificate), Champion, Veteran (7 or 8 years plus). In Germany, Open class is moved to the final position. Many countries now offer "Junior Champion" titles for dogs that win Best Junior three times. But this does not qualify the pup for the Champion class.

For the International Championship, a dog must earn four CACIBs, with the added requirement that they are achieved in at least three different countries. One must be the breed's country of origin or the owner's country of residence.

The United States is not a member country of the FCI. AKC registration is recognized, and an AKC-registered dog can be shown. However, for a U.S. dog to win a CACIB, the dog must rely on an unwritten gentleman's agreement and the willingness of the FCI member country where the dog is being shown—Puerto Rico and Mexico are the closest—to submit the paperwork.

FCI shows differ in many ways from the AKC. Professional handlers are present, but not in great numbers. Bait is now allowed in the ring, but some judges frown on its use. Double handling is supposedly illegal, but still widely employed, especially in such breeds as German Shepherds, Doberman Pinschers, and Rottweilers. Males and females are shown simultaneously in separate rings. The dogs are not formally stacked. They are first walked around the ring as a group. Then each dog is brought to the center of the ring alone and gone over by the judge for as long as 10 minutes. After that, the dog is gaited, and the judge dictates his or her critique of the dog. Each handler receives a written copy of the critique.

Watch Your Step

It's unclear why the United States is unwilling to become a member country of the FCI. As an active country in the world of dog showing, it's unseemly for U.S. dogs to have to sneak through the back door to an International Championship.

Tips from the Pros

Even at big events, only very few, if any, titleholders are present. Thus, in the 1991 World Dog Show in Dortmund, Germany, which drew a total entry of 143 BMDs [Bernese Mountain Dogs] from all over Europe, there were only five Int CHs (two each from Germany and the Netherlands, one from Italy). The 1993 CACIB show in Bern, Switzerland, saw 97 BMDs (among them 26 Open dogs and 31 Open bitches), but none at all in the Champion class. Only one Int CH from Germany (10.5-year-old Berri Max v.d. Horlache) was entered in the Veteran class.

—From "International Champion—A Myth Explained"
by Bernd Guenter, originally published in *The Alpenhorn*,
Official Magazine of the Bernese Mountain Dog Club of America, April 1994.

Each dog receives a rating of Excellent (*vorzüglich*, or V), Very Good (*sehr gut*, SG), Good (*gut*, G), Acceptable (*genugend*, Gen), or Not Acceptable (*nicht genugend*, Nggd). Only those dogs receiving the highest rating in the class remain in the ring after all have been judged. These dogs are gaited as a group, and dogs are removed until only four remain. These four are placed first through fourth, and the judge explains to the crowd what he or she liked about each dog.

Even for a dog that wins the Open class and goes on to defeat the winner of the Champions class, the CACIB is not assured. It is awarded at the discretion of the judge, though the competition is so extensive that it is unlikely that a dog not deserving of the CACIB would rise to the top.

Remember

○ UKC show rules differ markedly from the AKC.
○ No professional handlers or bait or grooming tools are allowed in UKC show rings.
○ ARBA uses a system of earning titles similar to the FCI.
○ The CKC allows U.S. dogs to show and earn titles without registering. Instead, they apply for an Event Registration Number.
○ The FCI awards the International Champion title.
○ The United States is not a member country of the FCI.

Part V

Show Time

Photo courtesy of Dr. Bernd Guenter

There are people involved in this sport as well as dogs. The all-important figure, as far as exhibitors are concerned, is the judge. It's the judge's opinion you are paying for when you send in your entry. Judges have experience as breeders and handlers and a fierce dedication to this sport of dogs. They are assisted by ring stewards, who check in entrants and herd classes in and out of the ring. And for the winners, there's a show photographer to memorialize the event.

Finally, to keep more advanced competitors involved, there are chapters on the higher echelons of showing—specialing, advertising, and the various ratings systems—and what to consider before breeding your show dog.

We wish you success in the ring, but more than that, we wish you a long and happy life in the company of dogs.

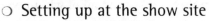

23

Setting Up Camp

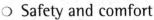

In This Chapter

- ○ Setting up at the show site
- ○ Safety and comfort
- ○ Studying the catalog

If you're a normal novice exhibitor, you probably left home in the dark, possibly got lost before finding the show site, and just maybe left some piece of equipment behind. Never fear—you're not alone. This experience is shared by most new (and some not-so-new) conformation competitors. As long as you find your way to your destination in time to check in and settle your jangling nerves, all will be fine.

If you find that you did forget something, you'll still be all right—as long as the something isn't your dog. There are all sorts of sales booths at nearly every show, and you can buy whatever it is you left behind. Or, if you have forged some friendships, as we've advised, you can borrow.

Don't dwell on your morning's hardships. Settle down and get on with it; follow a setup routine. Dogs value a routine, and it will help settle your nerves as well.

SETTING UP AT THE SHOW SITE

Some people arrive the night before a show. If you are planning on staying in a motel or hotel, have a confirmed reservation and confirmation that your dog will be welcome. All dog-friendly housing in the vicinity of a show fills up quickly.

Many shows have some sort of camping facilities available. Shows at fairgrounds often have actual campgrounds, with grassy or wooded campsites. If you have tenting equipment, you could use it here. Other shows simply let exhibitors into the parking area the day before a show and have restroom facilities available. People (and their dogs) sleep in their station wagons, vans, SUVs, capped pickups, and motor homes. It may not be tops in comfort, but it is cheap. If you decide to try this, park away from the behemoth motor homes. They will likely run noisy generators, spew exhaust fumes, and contain multiple dogs, not all of whom will be quiet.

Whether you are staying at home for an early departure, renting a room at a motel, or roughing it in a parking lot, as a novice exhibitor you will probably find it difficult to sleep. Do your best to get some rest. Play a radio quietly or listen to a relaxation tape, and try to zone out.

In the morning, you will set up your little show encampment.

Most of the shows you attend will be unbenched. At these shows, there will either be a large general area set aside to contain all exhibitors, or you may be completely left to your own to find a patch on the show grounds to stake out as your own.

It will help to know what you want your particular little setup area to provide. Don't plan on finding shade. Some show grounds don't have any to offer, and any there will quickly be filled. But do look for a level piece of

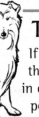

Tips from the Pros

If you're outdoors under tents, make sure you know which way the shade is going. You don't want to get stuck with sun shining in on your dog. Try to stay away from people with large breeds and people spraying chalk all over the place.

—Sharon Irons Strempski, AKC exhibitor and
breeder of Affenpinschers

ground, especially if you use a crate rather than an exercise pen. You don't want your dog upset by an unstable, rocking crate.

Also consider your dog's temperament. If other dogs in close proximity get your dog worked up while crated or penned, you'll want to look for a place that offers some boundaries. Make your setup backed up against bushes with a tree on one side and your chair and/or grooming table blocking the other side. Or use building walls or windbreaks or whatever you can find. Also consider the likely traffic patterns of the show site. If you set up along the path to the restrooms (canine or human), the coffee wagon, or the superintendent's table, there will be a constant parade of exhibitors and their dogs passing by your crate or exercise pen.

Sometimes simply facing the open side of your ex-pen or crate away from the crowd, using a cloth cover to block the other sides, is enough to keep things calm. A dog certainly knows exactly what's around without having to see it, but out of sight does seem to lead to out of mind in this case.

If you are participating in one of the few remaining benched shows, you will have been assigned a space. Your space is a section of bench, generally with some sort of divider to keep the dogs separated, and space in front for your chair and other basic equipment. Your dog must be on the bench whenever you're not in the ring, the grooming area, or the exercise area. Do *not* bring an unsocialized dog to a benched show. The close proximity of other dogs and constant parade of spectators will soon have your dog a nervous wreck, could ruin his or her feelings toward shows, and in the worst case might result in a dog bite.

At indoor shows, you may find that your crate or pen will be outside, but your grooming table will be inside. Check out the setup the evening before if you're on the grounds, and see if you can stake out any territory.

Any time you are setting up outside, try to set up somewhere near your show ring. In case the weather turns bad—and do not think just because the day dawns bright and sunny that it will stay that way—you will not have to walk so far to the ring, and the judge may get to see you and your dog before you both resemble drowned rats. Also, you will be able to watch how the judge operates the ring while still keeping an eye on your dog and your possessions. Valuables have unfortunately been known to vanish from untended show setups. And if your dog is as new to this as you are, you don't want your extended absence to result in a panic attack.

Watch Your Step

Petty theft is as likely to occur on show grounds as anywhere else. Setting up with friends will increase the chance that one of you will be there keeping an eye on things. Though rumors of dogs being released from crates and pens by animal rights activists are almost entirely untrue, it's not a bad idea to have someone watching the dogs.

If you have more to move than you can handle at one time, leave the dog in the car while you set up. It's unlikely to be threateningly hot in the early hours of the morning. Get your ex-pen on its grass mat, with its cover in place, or be sure your crate is well leveled. Set up your chair. Then go back and get the dog and any smaller equipment still left behind.

Once you and your dog are set up on site, take your time and go through your equipment. Hang your show lead off the ex-pen or the back of your chair so it will be readily accessible when it's time to head for the ring and your case of nerves has rendered all your brain cells inoperative. Organize your grooming tools. Be sure you have your bait or your special ring-only squeaky toy. By checking all your equipment early, you will know if you have forgotten anything while there is still time to borrow or purchase a replacement.

SAFETY AND COMFORT

When you settle your dog in the crate or ex-pen, be sure that he or she is safe and secure before setting off to investigate the show grounds. Check that the crate door is completely latched. If you are using a Vari-Kennel or similar crate (the solid plastic airline-type crates), check the screws and plastic nuts that hold the upper and lower halves of the crate together. Vibrations from being in the car can loosen the nuts.

If you are using an exercise pen, be sure the two ends are secured together. (Most ex-pens come as four to ten metal panels clipped end to end—you bend the panels into a square or octagon or whatever shape you like. Use a metal rod slotted through hooks on the outer ends of the panels, or the metal clips used to attach a leash to a collar, to fasten the ends to-

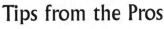

Tips from the Pros

Small dogs have been killed or injured at dog shows. This happens because dogs can't help being dogs. Sighthounds, for instance, were bred to hunt small animals on the move. It's not cruelty, it's genetics. If you're going to show your Toy, bring him to the ring in his crate if you can. The problem is that some dog clubs won't allow crates near the rings because they can block the aisles. . . . Toy exhibitors have made several suggestions to alleviate the problem. One is to set up a holding area for exhibitors and their small dogs who are going into a ring next, to keep the dogs out of the busy aisles where they could accidentally be stepped on.

—From Darlene Arden, *The Irrepressible Toy Dog*
(Howell Book House, 1998). Used with permission.

gether.) If the ex-pen has a door—some do and some don't—be sure that is latched, and use a metal clip to keep it from being jiggled open.

Many dogs have escaped from exercise pens by jumping up on the sides and knocking them over. A cover attached to all four sides helps, as it holds the pen in shape instead of letting it collapse. If you know your dog has a tendency to jump up on the panels, you may want to use tent stakes to anchor the bottom of the sides of the pen to the ground.

Whether you are using a crate or an ex-pen, make sure there is water in a cup or bowl for the dog. Then check that the dog is shaded, and will be for at least as long as you're planning to be away from your setup. Now you can go off and scope out the action with a clear mind. Always keep one ear cocked for your dog's bark—you should be able to recognize it anywhere. Return to check on things if you hear more than a bark or two.

Fancy That!

A pen cover is easy to put together, even for people who don't sew. If your ex-pen is 4 feet on each side, then 4 yards of material will run around three sides. Another $1\frac{1}{3}$ yards will cover the top. Pin or sew the side piece of cloth to three sides of the top piece. You even get to choose an appropriate fabric!

Now you can tend to your own needs. Locate the restrooms—being nervous will dictate that you will require them. If you are a coffee drinker and did not bring your own, this is one commodity available at nearly every show site. There may be food and soft drinks as well. Know your own temperament and whether you can afford to eat before you show.

ARMBANDS

Visit your ring and pick up your armband. (Note that at most UKC shows, you pick up your armband at the check-in table, not the ring.) If you brought your confirmation or remember your number, ask for your armband with your class and number, as

"Basenji puppy number 3, please."

If you have forgotten to bring your confirmation and all your brain cells have frozen and you can barely remember what breed your dog is, let alone what number, just say,

"Basenji puppy. I've forgotten my number."

The ring steward will look up your dog in the catalog, find the number, and give you your armband.

Many other exhibitors will be doing the same thing, so wait patiently for your turn. Also, never interrupt a steward when he or she is involved with the judge. Stewards need to receive their instructions on how the judge wants the ring to operate.

No one knows what dogs are actually present for competition until exhibitors pick up their armbands. Anxious handlers who need only a major to finish their dog's championship appreciate early check-ins. And remember, you must check in every day even if it's the same sponsoring club and show site.

If you are prone to putting things down and losing them, put your armband on your arm and keep it there until you are finished showing for the day. Slot it into your armband holder if you're using one. Otherwise, slide a rubber band up onto your left arm above the elbow—the ring stewards usually have a box of rubber bands right on the table. Tear little notches in the middle of the short ends of your armband and slip it under the rubber band, making sure the band catches in the notches to keep it from slipping out.

Figure 23.1. U.S. exhibitors think only of armbands, but there are other forms of ID, such as these bibs worn by European fanciers. (Photo courtesy of Dr. Bernd Guenter)

STUDYING THE CATALOG

Locate the superintendent's table. The show-sponsoring club will usually have a number of tables under a tent somewhere on the show grounds. The catalog sales table will probably be here as well. If you have any questions or problems, take them to the superintendent.

You will probably want to purchase a catalog for at least your first couple of shows. When you no longer need to bring a catalog home from every show, you can peruse a catalog at the superintendent's table. Be aware that at some shows, especially big prestigious ones or breed specialties, catalogs often sell out early in the morning.

Whether you purchase a catalog or not, check your dog's listing. If you should win, the information from the catalog will be used to list your win with the kennel club, so you want it to be correct.

The catalog lists all the dogs entered in the show. It also includes awards being offered and a variety of advertisements. The program of judging gives the ring number, the judge's name, the breeds being judged in that ring, the number of each breed entered, and a start time for at least the first breed in the ring in the morning and after lunch. Later breeds may or may not have starting times listed. If there is a start time, no judging can take place before that time. It may start later.

The class entries are broken down by group (except for the UKC), and the traditional order of groups for the AKC is Sporting, Hound, Working, Terrier, Toy, Non-Sporting, and Herding. Within each group, breeds are listed alphabetically. Remember that the AKC uses inverted breed names:

Retrievers (Golden)
Setters (English)
Spaniels (Welsh Springer)

Each dog will have its registered name, handler (often listed as "agent"), registration number, date of birth, breeder, parents, and owner listed. Once you have some experience under your belt, you can use this listing to prepare for your competition (knowing who you will face) and to look for friends on the show grounds.

There are places for you to "mark" your catalog—Best of Breed, Best of Opposite Sex, Awards of Merit for each breed, and Group placements. You may find it helpful to mark catalogs, at least for your breed, to keep track of who's beating who and which dogs different judges are placing first. (You could, of course, note the same information on a piece of paper without buying a catalog.)

POTTY BREAKS AND EXERCISE

Don't get so involved with wandering around the show grounds that you neglect your dog. The *dog* is why you're here, after all. After your initial tour of the grounds, go back, get your dog, and take him or her for a potty break. If your class is an early one, get yourselves ready for the ring—do any last-

Talking Dog

Remember, the dog's registered name is the long name on the pedigree. It may have no relation to the dog's call name, the short name used every day. My Keeshond's registered name was Kentucky's Boolah Boolah, but no one ever knew her as anything but Sundance.

Tips from the Pros

Remember that not all dogs are friendly with other dogs. Know where your dog is at all times and don't let it go up to strange dogs. The same goes for your children.

—Pamela Kernan, UKC exhibitor

minute grooming, get your dog either geared up or quieted down, whichever is right for your dog, and stand by near your ring. Either have your show lead on, or have it with you to change to just before you go in. If you have any friends at ringside, you can leave your regular lead with them. If not, you can leave it on the steward's table. Don't forget it when you leave the ring.

If you do not have an early class, take your dog with you to tour the merchandise booths. You may want to try on collars or backpacks, try out a new squeaky toy, or test a new treat as bait. A warning—you can easily spend *a lot* of money in the booths at a show. Buying your dog a new toy and yourself a new T-shirt at every show may not send you to the poorhouse, but it could have paid for an entry or two.

Remember to keep an eye on your ring and allow time to get ready to show, including potty breaks for both of you. (And always remember to pick up after your dog.)

Remember

- ○ Many shows offer camping facilities, or at least a parking lot, for overnight stays.
- ○ Set up your crate or exercise pen with your dog in mind—level, shaded, secluded if that helps your dog.
- ○ Set up near your ring.
- ○ Be sure your setup is secure.
- ○ Check that you haven't forgotten anything.
- ○ Locate the restrooms.
- ○ Pick up your armband.
- ○ Buy a catalog, or at least check your dog's entry in the copy on the superintendent's table to see that it is correct.
- ○ Mark your catalog to help you know which dogs are winning under which judges.

24

In the Ring

In This Chapter

❍ Steward's instructions
❍ Judge's instructions
❍ Etiquette
❍ Show photographers

It has happened many times that exhibitors, with only a few brain cells still functioning in their panicked state, have focused their remaining attention on the dog so completely that they did not hear the judge ask to "take 'em around" one more time or even missed the judge pointing to them for Winners! Such oblivion can result in all sorts of mayhem in the ring—being run over by (and earning the disdain of) other handlers, running over the exhibitor in front of you because everyone else has stopped, even losing consideration for a placement because of your nonperformance.

The moral is keep your wits about you. Easier said than done, of course, especially as a nervous novice. But before you start showing for real, you should be able to gait your dog while keeping one eye on the judge without falling over. Practice!

STEWARD'S INSTRUCTIONS

Before you actually begin your time in front of the judge, you are in the hands of a steward. You already picked up your armband from this person, and you should now be standing quietly outside the correct ring with your dog, waiting for your class to be called into the ring.

This person (or persons—sometimes two per ring are supplied) is a volunteer, often a member of the show-sponsoring club. Their duties are to hand out armbands to exhibitors; be sure that the judge has a judging book, pen, and any other necessary supplies; and get each class into and out of the ring. They also make sure all those pretty ribbons are ready to be handed out in each class.

While you are waiting, do not fuss over your dog and make both of you nervous. Definitely do not chat with the steward or judge. They have their own duties to perform, and others may make remarks about favoritism, though all you were doing was saying hello.

You have been wearing your armband all day. Glance at it now so that your number is fresh in your head. The steward will call you into the ring as a group or by your armband number.

If you are called in as a group, you will have your choice of where in line to place yourself and your dog. Head for somewhere near the back of the line so you will have plenty of opportunity to observe other exhibitors and how the judge is running the ring. Also try to place yourself near dogs that will work to your advantage. If your dog is just barely tall enough to conform to the standard, don't put yourself next to the biggest dog in the class and make yours look like a runt.

If you are called into the ring by number, you follow the exhibitor called immediately before you. You have no choice of where in line to be. So be alert so you will know where you should be in line.

JUDGE'S INSTRUCTIONS

Once you are in the ring, you are under the control of the judge. Nearly all exhibitors take their place in line and quickly stack their dog to give the best possible first impression. But if you have watched the judge conduct other classes, you will know if you should be ready to gather up your lead and go around as part of the group.

Tips from the Pros

I am constantly looking from the dog and the distance between the dog and myself, to the ground, to the judge. When I walk without a dog, I have to look at the ground so I don't trip, but when I'm moving with a dog I'm somehow able to keep looking at all these different things and it isn't a problem.

—Taffe McFadden, AKC professional handler

Judges are granted approval by the registry (the AKC, UKC, or other) to judge a specific breed, several breeds, the breeds in a group, or, at the very top, every single breed recognized by the registry. The AKC has approximately 3,000 approved judges. Only about two dozen are "all-rounders."

To become a judge, you must have a documented background in dogs. You don't have to be born "in" dogs (though it helps). But you do have to show a lot of interest. When applying for AKC approval, the prospect must show at least ten years of experience with a breed, including finishing at least two champions and breeding at least four litters. The prospective judge should steward and take assignments judging matches. There is a written test for AKC approval, then a review of all qualifications.

Fancy That!

How, you might ask, can someone be familiar with the standards for well over one hundred breeds? Well, of course the judge can review standards the night before a judging assignment. But think about how many baseball statistics or song lyrics some of your friends know. Judges just remember standards instead.

The UKC also tests a judging prospect in writing. If approved, the person becomes an apprentice judge and must apply to apprentice under three different senior UKC judges. At these events, the senior judge examines and gaits the dogs and decides on class placements. Then the apprentice judge does the same and gives the senior his or her assessment in private. Each senior judge must critique the performance of the apprentice. If all the critiques are satisfactory, the apprentice becomes a probationary judge. For the next year, the probationary judge can take judging assignments but cannot have anyone apprentice under them. Their events reports are monitored by the UKC. If no problems arise, the probation-

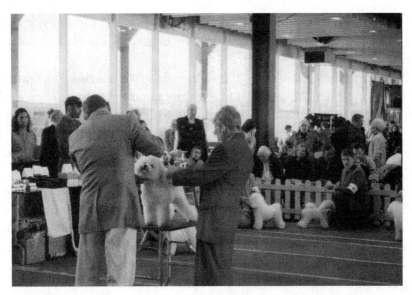

Figure 24.1. Judge Arlene Czech goes over one of the Bichons in the Puppy class. Note handler Bill McFadden keeping an eye on the judge from the back of the ring.

ary judge becomes a provisional judge for the next year, then passes a re-newal test to become a senior judge.

So be assured your judge has experience and knows your breed. But of course judges are human, with all the foibles that implies. See chapter 25 for more on this, and remember that you have paid for the judge's opinion of your dog on this day.

To develop that opinion, the judge will do a hands-on examination of each dog and gait each dog. Exactly how he or she accomplishes this is generally up to each judge, and why you should always have part of your

Tips from the Pros

Get the judge's pattern down—you don't want to disrupt the pat-tern—then play with the dog and relax. The best thing to do to get comfortable is to learn to play with your dog in the ring. The dog will relax and you'll relax too.

—Tom Glassford, former professional handler, AKC rep

attention directed toward the judge. Even if you have watched how previous classes were judged, an exceptionally large or small class might mean a difference in details.

Often the judge will send the entire class around the ring and back to their starting places to get an initial impression of the dogs. Then each dog will be examined and gaited individually, with the gaiting pattern generally an up and back or a triangle. But this isn't how it has to be. The judge might want to examine all the dogs first before moving any of them, and that is his or her prerogative.

How things happen once the judge has had a look at all the dogs can also vary greatly. In a small class, the judge may just put the dogs in their order of finish and hand out awards. Some judges place each dog in position as they see them after each examination, in which case you had better be especially alert in order to know where you are being directed. Some judges examine all the dogs in the class, then move their top four to the front of the line and send them all around the ring while they point to the winners. In really big classes or groups, the judge may "make a cut," pulling out only those dogs still in the running. The other dogs and handlers may be asked to stand back at the edges of the ring or dismissed from the ring entirely. The dogs still in contention are usually examined and gaited again before the placements are declared.

Always keep one eye on the judge any time the class is being sent around as a group after the individual examinations. It's embarrassing to be oblivious when the judge points to your dog as the Winner!

ETIQUETTE

Perhaps not exactly ring etiquette, but a point worth making, is how you feel toward your dog(s). While you may hear the opinion that you must acquire and dispose of dogs based on their performance (or lack of it) in the show ring, you won't hear that here. You should go into the ring with the conviction that your dog is a winner, and you should come out of the ring with that same conviction, whether or not you are carrying a ribbon. Such an air about you when entering the ring just might help propel you into the winner's circle. Such an attitude when exiting the ring will keep your head on straight and your relationship with your dog solid. You are only in the ring for a few minutes, after all, but you live full time with your dog. If you really get hooked on showing but your dog isn't the perfect specimen to take you where you want to go, then perhaps there's another dog in your future—but that doesn't mean this one gets left behind. Half of my dogs have been rescues without papers, never allowed to set paw in a show ring. But they were just as loving and devoted and fun as their pedigreed housemates—and even won just as many, or more, ribbons in other events.

Okay, down off the soapbox and back on the subject. Try to respond to the judge as a casual friendly acquaintance. Smile if you can. Judges don't like being glared at any more than any other person. But do not chat. The judge's mind should be on the business at hand—your dog—and you will only hurt your cause by doing something as gauche as mentioning your dog's latest win or excellent sire. Just show your dog as best you can and be alert for any instructions.

Accept with grace whatever placements are made. If it's a win for you, congratulations. But remember that others in the ring may be feeling crushed and discouraged, so don't do any dances of joy—at least not until you get back to the relative privacy of your car or motel room. If it's less than you expected, congratulate the winner and leave the ring with your head held high. Your dog is no less your wonderful dog just because you weren't awarded a piece of colored silk.

Don't indulge in gossip at ringside. You might listen, if you like, but don't take anything too seriously. Much of it is just blowing off steam, and some is downright vicious. As a novice, you will gain nothing by joining in the judge and competitor bashing. And you might make some lifelong (and inconvenient) enemies.

You can ask advice at a show, but there are right and wrong ways to do it. Specific questions are best—Am I trimming my dog's face correctly? Am I gaiting at the best speed? Could I get a better pose by using bait differently? Always ask first if the person has time to talk. People about to go

Talking Dog

Just as you shouldn't be kennel blind—oblivious to the conformation faults of your own dog—you shouldn't be *competition blind* either. This means focusing on the win only and forgetting to appreciate the wonderfulness of your dog.

Watch Your Step

Dog shows are a microcosm of society, and you will find plenty to like and dislike. Try to remember how it feels to be a novice so that you will help others once you become a seasoned veteran. It isn't any fun to be snubbed by cliques of exhibitors.

into the ring want to focus on their dog, not your questions. And some people show several dogs, even several breeds, and will be intent on getting the next dog ready and to the ring.

When someone does take the time to answer your questions, don't argue with him or her about the advice given. If you don't think it is correct, you don't have to follow it. But you don't have to insult the person either. Thank him or her for taking the time and go on about your business.

Don't ever ask for an opinion of your dog unless you really want one. And be careful whom you ask. Some malicious competitors may pile faults on your dog in the hopes of destroying your confidence. Even kind individuals might point out faults you'd rather not hear about. If you really have a question about some detail of your dog's conformation, better to wait and ask the judge. It's his or her opinion you've come for. (See "Judicious Judicial Conversations" in chapter 25.)

Finally, take a second to thank the judge and the stewards. Dog shows could not take place without the hours volunteered by these and many more people. Also support the sponsoring club's money-raising efforts—often a raffle—if you can, so they will have the funds to hold their event again the following year.

SHOW PHOTOGRAPHERS

If you've been attending shows, you may have noticed people in the ring with their dogs, the judge, and the rosette and/or trophy having their picture taken. There is almost always an official show photographer, except at matches. You too can have your winning photo snapped, but there is etiquette involved here too.

Because judges are included in photos, they must be taken when the judge is on a break—either before the next scheduled breed or in the lunch break or at the end of the day. Judges are busy people, sometimes running behind their schedule, so *don't* ask for a photo every time you win a ribbon. As a novice, you will probably be forgiven for wanting to memorialize your dog's first win, even if it is in the Puppy class over one other dog. But if you persist in taking everyone's time for photographs of such minor (at least in everyone else's eyes) events, you will quickly be seen as a nuisance. After your first thrilling win, try to resist asking for a photo every time. Your dog's win over a really competitive class, first major, first win over the "specials" or champions, Group placements, Best in Show—these are all deemed worthy of photography.

If you decide you want a picture, tell the steward as you exit the ring. He or she should be able to tell you when the next photo session will be. Be there with your dog and watch for the photographer to come into the ring and start setting up. There will probably be a few other exhibitors and their dogs. Don't shove them out of the way, but do be sure to get in there.

The photographers are professionals, and this is old hat to them. The judge will be standing there waiting, and there may be a signboard proclaiming the date, show-sponsoring club, and the win. Pose your dog—some let the dog sit facing the photographer, and some put the dog in a show stack. Look up at the photographer (who will be concentrating on the dog). Flash—it's over. Move aside and let someone else have a turn.

The photographer will know from your armband number (you are still wearing it, right?) who you are and your address. Two or three weeks later the photo—usually a color 8 × 10—will arrive in the mail. It will include a bill. You *can* return the photo without paying; however, you are expected to buy it . . . unless it's really awful. There will be an order form for additional prints, in case you just have to have a copy to send to Aunt Martha in Oshkosh.

Some people send a copy to the judge. Novices often think this is a gracious gesture. But judges generally have received so many of these photos that—unless it's a Group win at Westminster, say—it won't have any meaning for them. Save your money.

Some use these show photos to advertise wins. While you've probably already told everyone you know about your dog's win, you can let many more people know about it with an ad. As a novice, the appropriate place for you to advertise is in a magazine devoted only to your breed. The big, slick all-breed magazines are expensive, and your win is not likely to impress anyone. In your breed publication, others will get to know you and your dog, and you will help to preserve for posterity a record of the breed's individuals. Some think advertising plays a part in swaying judges to look more favorably upon a dog. This is unlikely, except for whatever effect familiarity may have on the subconscious. Advertise for your own satisfaction and to let others in the breed know about your dog.

Remember

- ○ Wait quietly for the steward to direct your class into the ring—enter in order if called that way.
- ○ Always be alert for any instructions from the judge.
- ○ Win or lose, always appreciate your dog.
- ○ Accept the judge's opinion of your dog, win or lose, with good grace.
- ○ Ask advice only at other people's convenience.
- ○ Ask for photographs only at significant wins.
- ○ Advertise wins in your breed magazine, if you wish.

25

Here Come da Judge

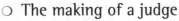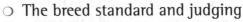

In This Chapter

- ○ The making of a judge
- ○ The breed standard and judging
- ○ Judicious judicial conversations
- ○ Judicial quirks
- ○ Protests

The judge is master of the ring. Some novices seem to view him or her as an ogre emerging from the shadows to terrorize them. But hold on a minute here! This is a person you have, in effect, hired to express an opinion of your dog. When you send in your entry form, you are reserving your time in the ring with the judge. So by all means be pleasant and polite, but do not cower in fear.

Judges vary widely in their backgrounds and expertise. Most have years of experience as either breeders or professional handlers. Generally, they take the step into judging in hopes of directing the future of their breed(s).

It may seem a glamorous sort of occupation. Flying off to judge in Hawaii or the Caribbean or even India *is* exotic. But these assignments are few and far between. Flying coach to Spokane, standing out in the rain all day, eating cold soggy sandwiches, and staying at the local TraveLodge is not the stuff of Hollywood, but it is the more typical judging weekend.

THE MAKING OF A JUDGE

Each registry has its own particular requirements for being approved to judge. You can't just wake up one morning and decide you'd like to be a judge. There are *years* of experience "in" dogs involved.

Registry Rules

For the AKC, it's at least ten years. That is, you have to be able to demonstrate at least a ten-year active history in the fancy. You must have shown at least two dogs of your own breeding to championships and bred at least four litters. Keeping detailed records of all your activities will prove invaluable if you ever do decide you want to be the one handing out the ribbons in the ring. Of course, you will probably track your dog's wins. Why not keep a dog diary, where you note each show entered and results, of course titles won, and your own involvement in the sport, maybe stewarding at shows, memberships in dog clubs, or even judging at fun matches? Even if you never decide to become a judge, it will be a nice book of memories.

There is an application to fill out. If your experience looks sufficient, there will be a written test and an interview by an AKC representative. Most breeders will apply for a single breed, their own. Some professional handlers might apply for an entire group, especially if they have been a "Terrier specialist" or otherwise known primarily for expertise with one of the groups.

Watch Your Step

In a minor vicious circle, new judges are unlikely to get many assignments because they do not attract exhibitors, and usually can only judge one breed. But they can't gain experience and a following of exhibitors without judging assignments.

If the test and interview go well, you will achieve the status of provisional judge. As a provisional, you must judge at least three assignments under the watchful eye of an AKC field representative. Getting those assignments can be a little tricky for a new judge. Being an active member of a kennel club will help. Once you make it through these, you must judge at least five more shows before you can apply for an additional breed.

The UKC requires prospective judges to submit the same sort of information for consideration:

- Dog experience, emphasizing UKC activities and the breed(s) for which the person is applying, including dogs owned and litters bred
- Showing experience, including shows attended annually, breeds exhibited, awards won
- Judging experience, whether another registry's shows or UKC matches, including club names and dates, breeds judged, and number of dogs exhibited
- General knowledge pertaining to breed(s) requested, including any seminars attended and any references

There are special additional rules to be approved to judge the American Eskimo, Toy Fox Terrier, or American Pit Bull Terrier. The UKC is the official parent club for these breeds and requires a more stringent process involving apprentice, probationary, and provisional status before becoming a full senior judge.

The American Rare Breed Association simply notes that any AKC- or CKC-licensed judge may judge any breeds at an ARBA show. Any FCI judge can judge the breeds he or she is licensed to judge by their own kennel club.

Experience and Expectations

Judges, especially new judges, can vary widely in their expertise. A breeder who has focused on a single breed for 20 years is going to know that breed intimately, more intimately than a handler who has shown the 20 or so breeds in one of the groups. Breeder/judges are often said to be the toughest judges, passionately striving for excellence in their breed. But of course some individuals will be decisive and self-assured, and others will be more uncertain and hence more likely to be influenced by the person holding the leash or all the ads featuring a dog's wins. Some breeder/judges can also become unhealthily obsessed with tiny details of the breed.

There are judges approved for only a single breed or two. Some may be old-timers content to confine their activities to their chosen breed, but many are newly approved judges. Most add breeds as they gain experience, because a multibreed judge allows a club to hire fewer judges for their shows. Many work through a group, adding breeds until they are approved to judge the entire group. And a few go on to become "all-rounders," able to pass judgment on every breed recognized by the registry. Obviously a person cannot have intimate experience with over one hundred breeds to the same degree as those one- or two-breed breeder/judges. But without the work and study of the all-rounders, there would be no Group Firsts or Best in Shows.

You may think the judge's job is simply to choose the best example of the breed in the ring. If that were so, a lot of classes could end immediately after the dogs walked into the ring, with the judge pointing to the winner. Choosing the "best" dog is only part of the job. Each exhibitor has paid an entry fee. For that fee, the exhibitor is due a thorough examination of his or her dog and the judge's opinion of the dog. No, not an actual expressed opinion—though in the FCI, exhibitors *do* receive an actual written critique—but further examination, indicating the dog is good enough to be considered for a placement or *making the cut*, an even stronger indication.

Tips from the Pros

Serious faults creep into a breed simply because the faults, instead of being penalized by judges, are ignored. In fact, almost by a wave of a hand type can be altered, so that judges can make or mar a breed. It might even be said that it is really the judges who are ultimately responsible for the many serious faults which are seen in far too many pedigree dogs today. . . . If judges were really sincere and absolutely adamant regarding soundness, then we should not see so many unsound dogs in the ring today. Breeders and exhibitors would not breed or show dogs which judges refused to place.

—From Hilary Harmar, *Showing & Handling Dogs* (Arco, 1977)

Talking Dog

In a large class or group, the judge will often choose some dogs to pull out for further consideration, maybe from four or five to as many as a dozen. The rest of the dogs are no longer in the running. The ones pulled out have "made the cut" and may still end up in the ribbons.

Many exhibitors *want* an actual expressed opinion from the judge. This is sometimes possible—we'll talk about it later in the chapter. But a better plan is to take part in breed seminars, where you can learn more about the details of your breed, and fun matches, where you are freer to chat with the judge. Save your show ring conversations for those few occasions when you truly don't understand the placements made.

A good judge not only understands what to look for in the dogs, but because of this knowledge is also self-assured, at ease in the ring. He or she should be pleasant and relaxed, and gentle in going over the dogs. There is no need for rough handling of dogs or exhibitors. Breeder/judges will often have the added difficulty of passing judgment on dogs from their own lines. This calls for scrupulous honesty and a total disregard for the dog's background. No judge can afford to be accused of *kennel blindness.*

A good judge will judge the dogs brought before him or her on the day, ignoring everything but the qualities of the dog. He or she will give each dog equal time in the initial exam and judge the *whole* dog, not just a head or flashy movement. A good judge makes his or her choices with assurance and ignores ringside gossip and even the comments of "friends" about not having their dogs chosen.

Talking Dog

Kennel blindness is an affliction infecting some breeders. It makes them totally oblivious to any faults in their own dogs, usually while retaining a heightened ability to find fault with dogs of others' breeding. This can be ignored in a breeder/exhibitor, but it is unforgivable in a breeder/judge.

Because exhibitors are not always paragons of virtue themselves, judges must be quick-witted, patient, and tactful, but firm. Within the confines of the ring, the word of the judge is law—transgressors must be quietly and politely brought into line. Judges need good memories both to recall lengthy breed standards and to keep the good and bad points of a whole class of dogs in mind. Good observation is essential, as is decision-making ability.

THE BREED STANDARD AND JUDGING

Dogs are supposed to be judged against their breed standard rather than directly against each other, with the dog closest to the standard being awarded top place. In reality, the standard is words on paper, and the dog is a living, vibrant, three-dimensional being. The standard is the starting point and yardstick, but experience with the actual representatives of the breed is every bit as essential.

To demonstrate the potential shortcomings of relying on the standard only, have someone give you a copy of a standard to read, with all references to the actual breed deleted. Do you think you could identify the dog from the written standard? The conclusion you can draw from this exercise is that the standard is the blueprint, but it doesn't really show the substance and subtleties of the finished building. So while it's important to know and understand, it isn't the whole picture. Seeing the dogs in action, doing what they were supposedly designed to do, has to be part of the picture as well. Judges should be involved at least to some degree in whatever sports are fitting for the breeds they are approved to judge. To their credit, the AKC has been providing judges' seminars where the judges observe, for example, herding breeds actually herding stock.

Contrary to what most people seem to think, the AKC does not write the breed standards. The individual breed clubs both write and amend their breed standards and send them along to the AKC.

JUDICIOUS JUDICIAL CONVERSATIONS

Let's say you've gained a little experience. There's a judge you really respect, and you're showing under him or her for the first time. It's a medium-sized class. The judge takes a quick look at them all, then does individual exams, giving ample attention to each dog. After that, the judge sends the whole class around and points to the winner. It isn't you.

You don't mind not winning (well, maybe just a little), because the winner is a nice dog. But you wish you knew if you were in the running or not even under consideration. Is it all right to ask? Yes, it is. To truly learn something, however, don't ask, "What did you like about the winner?" or "What didn't you like about my dog?" Instead, ask if you can meet the judge, with your dog, at a convenient time for a critique. Don't do this unless you really want to hear what the judge thinks—it could be a pleasant surprise, but it could be something you really won't like.

Also, save the request for those occasions when you really want some input. Judges have a lot to do at a dog show and are often ready to quit and go sit down in the shade somewhere by the end of their last class. You are now asking them to spend additional time judging your dog. Most will try to accommodate handlers' requests. But don't become known as a pest.

Fancy That!

You may find that many judges disappear immediately after completion of their classes. In all likelihood, they have learned that they have few friends on the grounds. The ill-tempered behavior of a few exhibitors thus penalizes those who would enjoy an honest discussion.

Also don't go to a judge after a class to complain that another dog was over or under the height or weight limit. You have the right to question this during a class, and if you didn't have the nerve to do that, then you'll just have to keep quiet.

Don't whisper sweet nothings about your dog's impressive wins while the judge is going over your dog. If you're lucky, the judge will ignore you and concentrate on the dog. If you aren't so lucky, you will get one of the favorite responses of judges subjected to this:

"How nice that you have won so much you won't mind losing today."
or "I can't be responsible for the mistakes of other judges."

If you really want to carry on extended conversations with judges, there are several strategies. You can attend judging seminars. Don't interrupt the proceedings, but there are often question-and-answer periods, plus you

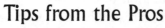

Tips from the Pros

It is extremely boring for the judge to hear from an exhibitor, after he has put his dog down, that such and such famous judges have previously put the dog up. If all judges placed the dogs in the identical order, there would be little point in having classes of more than three dogs, and even the constant winners would find life boring and somewhat monotonous.

—From Hilary Harmar, *Showing & Handling Dogs* (Arco, 1977)

could offer to take a judge to lunch. Or volunteer to steward at a show. There are breaks during the day, both planned and unplanned. Bring the judge the beverage of his or her choice, explain that you are a novice and want to learn more. Most judges will be more than happy to discuss the intricacies of the fancy with you. Or volunteer to pick up the judge at the airport, or to shepherd him or her to and from the hotel. It's best not to enter your dog if you are doing this, but the knowledge gained will be worth giving up a show.

JUDICIAL QUIRKS

It may be easy to forget this when you are trembling in the ring, but judges *are* human beings. They have likes and dislikes, strengths and weaknesses, the same as you and I.

The good judges are honest, knowledgeable about their breed(s), and work at keeping their knowledge up-to-date. They judge the dogs brought before them in the ring, without taking into account who is holding the other end of the leash. The best of these appreciate the efforts of every exhibitor and are kind to all. You will hear about these judges—they become living legends in the sport.

Some judges may lack in-depth knowledge of a breed, especially if they have been applying for a lot of additional breeds to fill out a group. Perhaps in the future, after further study, they will attain the heights of judgedom. For now, they may be influenced, either consciously or subconsciously, by seeing a dog or a handler that has done a lot of winning. The dog must be a good one if so many other judges rewarded it, after all.

There are, unfortunately, judges that are not quite honest. They can't resist giving the win to the show chairman of a club they'd really like to judge for, or a friend, or someone who stewarded for them at another show. They may even convince themselves that the dog *was* the best one in the ring.

There are judges who strive to be honest but simply lack confidence. They can be swayed by a heavy-duty advertising campaign or intimidated by the stare-down of a professional handler. They may improve with experience, or it may be a permanent character flaw.

Judges also have individual quirks about what they consider most important in judging dogs. This is where labels such as "head man," "coat specialist," "movement freak," and many others come from. You may not like it when an undersized dog with borderline markings but very flashy movement beats your beautifully proportioned and classically marked entry, but it's just part of the dog game.

PROTESTS

Most of the registries provide a prescribed method of bringing up questionable aspects of any other dog in the ring. Read your kennel club's rules and regulations for details.

We have already discussed asking that a dog be weighed or measured to determine if it meets the standard. Handlers can also question the markings or color of a dog and request an official opinion on whether they are disqualifying. Any of these protests must be made before each dog is individually examined and gaited. The judge must then fill out the appropriate paperwork to submit to the registry and announce the dog disqualified or excused or the protest as unfounded.

Similarly, any handler may question if another dog is blind, deaf, spayed, neutered, or changed in appearance by artificial means (other than as specified in the breed standard, such as by cropping, docking, or removal of dewclaws) (see chapter 11, section 8 of the AKC Rules Applying to Dog Shows). A judge finding such a charge to be valid must disqualify the dog.

Finally, the altering of a dog's coloring by artificial means is cause for withholding awards and reporting the handler and/or owner to the registry for disciplinary action.

Of course, accusing others of any of these things is not likely to make you a popular figure. Don't fling accusations around on the basis of ringside gossip. Gossip is just that, and some may even try to set up unsuspecting newcomers. Be very sure of your facts before lodging a protest.

Remember

○ Persons must have an extensive history in dogs to judge, but that doesn't ensure good judging.

○ Part of the judge's job is to give each dog a thorough examination.

○ The breed standard is useful information, but experience with the breed is necessary to actually judge dogs.

○ Only ask for a judge's opinion of your dog when you are truly unsure of what transpired in the ring, and when you want to hear the answer, whatever it is.

○ Go to breed seminars and judges' seminars and offer to steward to learn more about your breed and judging.

○ Judges are individuals—some are wonderful, some not so wonderful.

○ Protests can be brought against other dogs in the ring and must be adjudicated on the spot.

26

Beyond the Championship

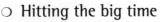

In This Chapter

- ○ Hitting the big time
- ○ Ratings systems
- ○ Advertising
- ○ Other options

By now, you've undoubtedly been to a few dog shows. Maybe you've collected some ribbons. Maybe, if you've stumbled onto a good dog, you have points toward a championship. If so, you're probably hooked on the sport of showing dogs and wondering what happens once you have that championship.

Well, there are a few answers to that question. You could get another dog and do the whole thing again. You could breed your dog (see the next chapter) and show the puppies. Or you can continue with the dog you already have. There are a couple of ways to do that.

You can work toward other championships on the same dog. We've included information on several U.S. registries, plus the CKC and FCI. So if you've shown under the AKC, now you can try the UKC for their championship or CKC for a Can. CH. There are also kennel clubs in Mexico and Bermuda. It could take you years to work your way through all of these.

Or you can keep showing with the registry that gave you your championship, as a "Special." In this chapter I explain what that is and how to go about it. There are also other dog sports you can try, and we'll take a quick look at those at the end of this chapter.

HITTING THE BIG TIME

If you've earned a championship, congratulations! If you're reading ahead to be prepared, also congratulations. You'll be ready to continue in your sport without a stumble.

AKC Specialing

Specialing is really nothing more, at its most basic, than regularly showing a dog in the Best of Breed competition. If you and your dog both enjoy showing, you may decide to continue just for the pleasure of it. That's terrific! But many people embark on a "Specials" career in the hopes of topping one of the various ratings systems and becoming Number 1 dog in their breed or group (more about ratings in a moment).

> ### Fancy That!
> Because Westminster is a champions-only show, every dog entered is, in effect, specialing. Champions-only shows are rare.

If your dog has scored some impressive wins or garnered praise from respected judges, you may be tempted toward specialing. Before you jump in, read all about it (and it wouldn't hurt to talk to someone who has been involved in Specials).

Specialing to compete in the ratings systems is expensive in terms of both time and money. Whether you show the dog yourself or hire a professional, there will be substantial travel expenses, plus many, many entry fees. You can't just enter shows within an hour or two of your home and expect to climb the ratings. (Well, there may be exceptions, as usual—if you have a really excellent example of a relatively rare breed and live in a very active dog show area, you might be able to live at home and conquer the ratings. But it's not the usual scenario.)

If you're continuing on because you enjoy the atmosphere and everything that goes on around a dog show, then sending your dog off with a professional is not going to keep you involved. Maybe you need to reconsider your goals. Is that Number 1 rating really important, or is continued time on the show grounds what you're after? It's crucial to consider everything while setting your goals.

Sending your dog off with a professional may get you that rating, but you might not see your dog for the next year or two. If you're content with only seeing your dog on television occasionally, maybe this will work for you. Yes, you can have the dog with you between show weekends, but with clusters running Thursday through Sunday or Saturday through Tuesday, plus travel time, there isn't much time between shows. And professionals often drive their RV rigs from cluster to cluster on a regular circuit and don't return home between events. Think seriously before signing a contract that will keep your dog away from you.

And of course it's not just yourself to consider. How is your dog going to handle being on the road in the hands of another? In fact, even if it's you at the other end of the leash, how is your dog going to handle being shown two or three or even four times a week, week after week? Can you both take it?

Some dogs are naturals, who turn on in front of a crowd. Obviously these are the easiest to show as a special. Less ring-motivated dogs keep handlers on their toes looking for ways to get the most out of the dog at each show. Dogs are generally easier than bitches—though at a recent Westminster, the group placements in two of the groups were all bitches. Dogs don't come into season and blow coat and get moody, as females do. Dogs are often flashier and more outgoing. And dogs don't have to interrupt a show career to sire litters. (See the next chapter for considerations in specialing or breeding a bitch.)

Competition gets more intense at this level. There are scathing comments about dogs, handlers, judges, kennel clubs, the food, the weather, the mats in the ring, even the flower arrangements! You may have supporters, but you will certainly have detractors. It's just one more source of stress.

Some will tell you that for the betterment of the breed, a good dog (meaning both sexes in this case) deserves to be campaigned so that everyone will know about him or her. Actually, it's probably much more important to a breed that the good, sound dogs be bred to other good, sound dogs. True, the whole country isn't likely to know about your champion if you don't campaign, but all the fanciers in your breed in your show area will if you're lucky enough to have a really good one.

Specialing is not an activity to be embarked upon lightly. Consider what it really is you want for you and your dog, don't be swayed by others telling you what you *should* do. Whatever is right for you and your dog is what you should do. Be sure to include things such as finances, family time, and fun times with your dog in your considerations, and take your time before making any big decisions. You can always continue going to local shows, or you can start over fresh in one of the many other dog sports (see the last section of this chapter). Your dog might really enjoy a new show-going routine, and so might you!

UKC Advanced Opportunities

The UKC has a few extra added attractions to keep dogs and handlers interested beyond the championship. They offer the UKC Grand Show Champion (GR CH) title. For this, a dog must win five Champion of Champions classes. Only dogs that are already champions may be entered in this class, and males and females compete directly against one another. The winner goes on to compete in Best of Breed. If there are at least three dogs entered and shown, the winner also gets the win credited toward the GR CH title. The necessary five wins must be at five shows under at least three different judges.

Grand Champions can compete in their own class, with the winner going on to compete in Best of Breed. But no further points are awarded because GR CH is the highest title available.

Tips from the Pros

You might want to consider enrolling in a therapy program visiting children, adults or the elderly regularly. These programs require some training, but those who become involved say they get far more than they give during these volunteer visits. Often there are reports of elderly people who haven't spoken in years who will suddenly begin to speak when a dog is brought into the room. Just the contact with that soft little body is so meaningful for so many people of all ages who are confined to a nursing home or a hospital bed.

—From Darlene Arden, *The Irrepressible Toy Dog*
(Howell Book House, 1998). Used with permission.

Talking Dog

An OTCH is as fervently pursued by obedience competitors as a championship is by those in conformation, and is as difficult to achieve if not more so. The dog must first earn a UD (Utility Dog) and then go on to place first time after time to earn points.

The UKC also offers a special Total Dog award to be given to any dog that performs in both conformation and either obedience or agility at a show. To earn this award, the dog must achieve a qualifying score in obedience or agility and win either Best Male/Female of Variety, Best Male/Female, Champion of Champions, Grand Champion, or Best of Breed in the show ring.

The AKC bases a similar idea on titles earned. A dog that earns the title Champion and specific titles in performance events such as field trials, lure coursing, and tracking may be designated as a Dual Champion. Add an OTCH (Obedience Trial Champion, the highest award in obedience competition) and you have a Triple Champion.

International Specialing

On the international scene, specialing isn't quite the same. Shows are fewer and often smaller in Canada, and the pace isn't quite so frenetic. Many top Canadian dogs come to the United States to do their specialing. In Europe, the pace may be even slower. The Kennel Club (of Great Britain) offers a total of only 25 all-breed championship shows per year and perhaps a dozen group championship shows (of which one or two might apply to the group your dog falls in). There are also individual breed championships, and these are more numerous, but even with everything combined, it's far more leisurely. A British dog being campaigned may be shown for five or six days a month at most, and in some months may scarcely be shown at all. A far cry from the AKC regimen of three- or four-day circuits weekend after weekend.

RATINGS SYSTEMS

The UKC makes this simple by having its own rating system, the Top Ten Show Dogs. Points are automatically calculated by the UKC when show

Watch Your Step

Some people do concentrate on climbing the ratings. This can require a great deal of showing, and, at the end, what have you really gained? Don't get carried away with the "We're number one" obsession common in all American sports. Do what works best for you and your dog.

results are tabulated, with the Best of Breed dog receiving one point for each dog defeated. Current standings are published in each issue of *Bloodlines*. The Top Ten Bench Show Dog Finals are held each year at the UKC's annual national show, the Premier.

Not all UKC-recognized breeds are included, however. The breeds tracked for their Top Ten are listed on page 241.

What is surprising to many is that the major ratings systems you tend to hear about and see advertised have no official connection to the AKC. They originate with and are tracked by magazines, newspapers, or companies dedicated to dogs and the fancy.

The parties involved change fairly frequently, so any specifics given here may be no longer true by the time you read this. So suffice it to say that ratings are now based on show results computerized by the American Kennel Club, and so they are all the same. They used to vary more, so that a dog would be number one in one system and lower down or not even in the top ten in another system. Now the only real difference is between all-breed ratings systems and single-breed systems. All-breed systems are based on Group Firsts and Best of Breeds. Currently, several dog food companies and a couple of magazines are involved.

A new wrinkle on the scene as this is being written is the Animal Planet National Championships. Animal Planet is a cable/satellite TV station devoted to pets and wild animals. They chose a number of shows to qualify for their ratings, televised some of them, and televised the finals among the top scorers. This provides more opportunities to see dog shows without leaving home, but the ratings themselves were criticized the first year for focusing on the West Coast. The second year showed more geographic diversity, and Animal Planet promises to do better at geographic dispersion in the future. Animal Planet is also now using *all* AKC shows to compute the ratings, with the top twenty dogs in each breed to be invited to a National Finals at the end of the season. The first National Finals is taking place in 2001.

ADVERTISING

Of course you can advertise your wins even if you aren't campaigning a dog, but advertising is a definite component of showing a Specials dog. It is one more, sometimes considerable, expense.

If you just want to tell the world about your biggest win yet or your first group placement, then choose a publication dedicated to your breed only or your area only. It will be much less costly and will reach those more interested in your news. In fact, breeders often file all issues of their breed magazine and flip back through them from time to time.

No matter where you are advertising, do not publish any photograph that does not show your dog to best advantage. Many people could form an opinion of your dog based solely on the published photograph, including judges, breeders you might want in a future breeding program, professional handlers you might want to hire sometime. So think carefully before selecting a photo.

Don't waste your money placing ads in the slick all-breed magazines unless you're seriously campaigning a dog. Advertising here is very expensive, used by owners of dogs out on the campaign trail. The magazines go to subscribers across the country and internationally, and most are sent free of charge to licensed judges. It would undoubtedly be a warm and fuzzy feeling to think of all these people admiring *your* dog's picture, but the truth is most people will flip past it with nary a glance. Their attention is reserved for those dogs whose names and reputations they already know.

If you *are* going to be specialing a dog, then the cost of advertising needs to be figured into your planning. Before beginning to place ads, study those already carried by the magazines. Being innovative is okay up to a point. Just keep in mind that your competitors are likely to be reading your ads, so don't say anything that might be construed as insulting. Most people simply publish a lovely photo of the dog, and note the latest wins.

Fancy That!

One place you can place ads for relatively little money is show catalogs. A "booster ad" wishing competitors luck in your local kennel club's catalog is a nice gesture, generally well received.

Some thank judges, but others advise against this, saying the judge was only doing the job hired for.

Why advertise at all? Well, to let other people know how wonderful your dog is, of course. That's a good enough reason on its own. Magazine advertising also helps to keep a record of the breed for posterity. If you've ever looked at old dog books, you were probably amazed at how a Pekingese or Bulldog or Collie or whatever looked 40 or 50 years ago. Books and magazines provide a record of how things changed.

And of course there are the judges. Does advertising have any effect on them? They will almost all say no, though some will make disparaging remarks about "paper judges" (those who are said to go by which dog they have seen pictured in magazine ads the most). Many judges are completely immune to influence of any kind. But there is that aspect of familiarity. Seeing a dog advertising big win after big win can have a subconscious impact. But that requires a long-term advertising campaign and a good deal of money. Be sure it's something you want to do.

OTHER OPTIONS

If you don't want to embark on a Specials career, but your dog is still young and eager to be out there, the world of dog sport offers plenty of other opportunities. These are also good options for dogs that you find don't enjoy the conformation ring. In fact, if you find a sport your dog really enjoys and can pursue that in conjunction with showing, it may perk your dog up in the ring and allow you to continue to show and get more out of your dog.

These are just quick, thumbnail sketches of other dog sports. If some appeal to you, contact your registry or local kennel club for more detailed information. Competing in other canine activities will *not* ruin your show dog for the ring.

Obedience

Obedience is a sport to demonstrate the training and teamwork of you and your dog. Basic-level classes use basic manners behaviors such as sit, down, come, and heel, while advanced classes include retrieving a scented dumbbell from among others and performing a series of exercises to signals only. Obedience classes are offered in almost every community, and most shows offer obedience along with conformation.

Agility

Agility is a newer sport, originally used for lunch break entertainment at large shows, now growing rapidly in popularity. Based on show ring jumping equine competitions, it has progressed far beyond that to include teeter-totters, tunnels, weave poles, and a host of other obstacles. The dogs run an obstacle course for the fastest time with the fewest faults. Most dogs love agility! You can often catch it televised on Animal Planet.

Field Trials

For the Sporting group dogs, there are a variety of hunting tests and trials. Instinct tests can be taken with some basic training. Trials are every bit as

Talking Dog

The titles in AKC obedience are CD (Companion Dog), CDX (Companion Dog Excellent), UD (Utility Dog), and OTCH (Obedience Trial Champion). The United Kennel Club puts a "U" in front of the abbreviations (U-CD, U-CDX, U-UD). Their UKC Obedience Champion (U-OCH) program is based on obtaining qualifying scores in Open and Utility classes, not winning the classes as the AKC requires. They put all obedience titles in front of the dog's name, the same as that CH for champion. The AKC puts anything but the designation CH after the dog's name.

intense and competitive as the big ring at Westminster or Crufts, and require dedicated training and practice. There are varying competitions for Retrievers, Pointers, Setters, Spaniels, Coonhounds, and Beagles.

Herding

For the Herding group, but also some from Working and Non-Sporting, there are instinct tests and trials. Some training is required even for instinct tests, and intensive training is required for the enormously difficult Border Collie trials. Some organizations are dedicated to herding, open to many breeds outside the Herding group, and even mixed breeds.

Tracking

Tracking is a sport open to all dogs, though some may be better at it than others. Dogs seem to enjoy this activity, which regularly gets them and their owners out into the fields and woods, and allows them to use their scenting abilities. This can be quite a strenuous sport for owners, who need to first lay a track for the dog to follow, then go along with the dog on the track.

Lure Coursing

For the sighthounds from the Hound group. Originally, this was simply "coursing," and the hounds were turned loose in a field to chase (and sometimes catch) wild rabbits. Although this sometimes still occurs, "lure" coursing is now more common, with the dogs chasing a lure pulled mechanically along a course.

Terrier Trials

Based on the instincts of the Terrier group, this event is also called a Go to Ground or a Terrier Dig or Earthdog. A rodent such as a rat is safely caged at the end of a tunnel. The dog is expected to go down the tunnel and "work" (bark and paw at) the rodent at the end.

Carting/Weight Pulling/Racing

All the draft sports rely on the draft heritage of the dogs. Carting is a test of control, reliability, and stamina, whereas weight pulling is a test of strength, and racing is a test of speed. Though unusual breeds have competed—there was an all-Poodle sled dog team at one time—the traditional draft breeds such as the Alaskan Malamute, Siberian Husky, Bernese Mountain Dog, and others excel.

Water Rescue

Originally a specialty of the Newfoundlands and Portuguese Water Dogs, the water rescue sport has expanded to include others. It involves activities such as towing a boat, taking a lifeline from shore to a boat, and towing a swimmer to shore. Owners must be willing to get wet because they have to be in the water with their dogs.

Flyball/Scent Hurdles

Flyball and scent hurdles are relay races for dogs. Both use low hurdles. The dog runs out and either triggers a launch box and catches a tennis ball, or chooses the owner's dumbbell from those of the entire team at the end before returning. The next dog then repeats the process. Teams are raced directly against one another side by side.

Freestyle

Probably the newest of the organized dog sports is freestyle. If you enjoy music and dancing, you'll probably love this sport, also known as dancing with dogs. You choreograph and practice a routine for you and your dog to perform to music. A routine generally uses exercises from obedience and trick training.

Fancy That!

Some sports have their own organizations devoted to the sport itself rather than to registering dogs. The International Weight Pulling Association has its own set of rules and its own events. The American Herding Breeds Association allows even mixed breeds to compete in its herding events.

Remember

○ It takes a great deal of time and money to "Special" a dog.

○ Consider if your dog is suited to the intensive showing, and if you either have the time to show the dog or want to be apart that much.

○ You can probably top the ratings systems only if you are willing to campaign the dog heavily.

○ Advertising should suit your goals—ads in breed magazines to show off your dog or a whole campaign of ads in all-breed magazines if you are campaigning.

○ There are many other dog sports that could keep you and your dog occupied and competing for years.

27

When Showing Leads to Breeding

> ## In This Chapter
>
> ○ Making the best match
> ○ Being ready for puppies
> ○ Considerations if you own the stud
> ○ Considerations if you own the bitch
> ○ Genetic disease and what fanciers can do about it

If I were to write only my most heartfelt sentiments on the issue of breeding, this would be a very short chapter indeed, consisting of the single sentence,

Don't do it!

But because that isn't likely to satisfy all of you who have read this far, I'll go into a little more detail. Just please keep that sentence in mind.

There was a time, not all that long ago, when the ultimate point of a dog show was to exhibit dogs so that local breeders could see each other's efforts and decide if someone else's line would be a good match for their breeding program. Now, shows—at least the big ones—aren't local any more, and the point seems to be to finish a champion as quickly as possible or to pile up the ratings points.

Everyone seems to want to breed to the current "hot" dog, whether or not he suits a particular line.

It would behoove exhibitors and breeders everywhere to take a deep breath, slow down, and consider what we're creating. In the wild, the healthiest, strongest, best able to survive male wolf breeds the females in the pack. Each generation receives the best chance of a long and healthy life. An undersized male, or one with bad hips or a malformed bite, isn't going to be top dog and won't be passing on his faults. And though all the bitches might be bred, the weakest probably won't have a successful delivery or will even die. Nature is not always kind, but it does tend to produce the strongest.

Breeding dogs, because we humans control the matches made, involves many, many responsibilities and is not to be entered into lightly. Responsible breed clubs are working hard to conquer such genetic disabilities as hip dysplasia, patellar luxation, epilepsy, and juvenile cataracts. You should be fully aware of all concerns and how to minimize them before even considering breeding.

MAKING THE BEST MATCH

Breeding is a whole lot more than introducing a pretty dog to a pretty bitch, standing back, and letting nature take its course. All dogs, no matter how many ratings points or Best of Breed wins they may possess, have faults or weaknesses. Mating two dogs with the same weaknesses is likely to accentuate those flaws. This will certainly not improve the breed, and improving the breed is one of the cornerstones of breeding.

Tips from the Pros

Wait at least two years before breeding your first litter. Have the dog checked out for defects. Study the other dogs out there. Don't rush to breed to the biggest winner. Pick a dog with a good pedigree and breed type that will go well with what you have. Check with your mentor.

—Sharon Irons Strempski, AKC exhibitor and breeder of Affenpinschers

Before even considering breeding a dog, you must understand your breed's standard completely; be fully aware of all health issues, genetic and otherwise; consider temperament; understand your own dog's strengths and weaknesses; achieve impartial objectivity. This is a lot to consider and can take years of experience to appreciate fully. Many dog owners *never* achieve objectivity. Finding fault in your beloved dog is difficult, indeed, but it is a skill that must be mastered before considering breeding. A breeding undertaken without acknowledging faults is likely to strengthen those faults.

Say you own a bitch. It's not likely to be your first show dog unless you've been extremely lucky because breeders will rarely let go of a worthy bitch. But maybe the breeder guessed wrong in deciding which puppy to sell and which to keep. Or you've purchased or leased or are co-owner of a very nice bitch who for one reason or another doesn't fit into the breeder's plans. How do you go about choosing a stud?

What you don't do is pick the dog whose picture you've been seeing in every magazine or who sits at the top of the ratings. While this could be a good match for your girl, it won't be simply because of the dog's lofty position in the fancy.

Before you even go out looking, you must know every good and bad point of the bitch and what you hope to accomplish with the breeding. In fact, your plans should extend far beyond this breeding to the goals you have for your "line." Vast improvements are seldom accomplished in a single generation, and you need a consistent, ongoing plan if you are to make a positive contribution to the breed. What does your dream ideal specimen of a (fill in the breed) look like, keeping in mind that you must comply with the standard? Do you know how to get there from here?

I hope I am discouraging you. This is not a path to be entered upon lightly. Few novice exhibitors have the expertise necessary to conceive and conduct a methodical beneficial breeding plan. But we press onward with our mythical bitch.

Suppose she is an Am. Can. CH, has done some group winning, and been admired by judges and breeders. You have gotten critiques from some important people in your breed, and the consensus has been that your bitch is very "typey." She has excellent shoulders, which contribute to her flashy movement in the ring, and a wonderful outgoing personality. Her ears are a little too small and set a little too low, but otherwise her head is good, though her bite is level rather than the scissors preferred by the standard. Her hips are rated fair to good, and there are no problems with her rear quarters other than a slightly gay tail that has displeased a judge or two along the way. Her color is at the light end of acceptable.

Now you have decided to breed this bitch rather than campaign her. She is healthy and has done enough winning that you should have the pick of studs. You've been impressed by a dog that's beaten you a couple of times, and you call his owner to talk about a breeding. When she hears your bitch's name, she turns you down. You're astonished and hurt. What happened here?

If you asked, you would likely hear that the dog's owner believes her dog mirrors the faults of your bitch. His gay tail has also caused him to miss being placed, and his bite is also level. But the deciding points for the dog's owner were the OFA rating—she's trying to work toward an "excellent" rating—and the bitch's personality. Her dog verges on being hyper, and she's afraid that a mating with such a self-assured bitch will result in truly hyper problematic puppies. She might be wrong, but the risk is real enough to avoid producing the litter.

After some serious soul-searching, you reconsider and try again. One dog you might use hasn't done quite as much winning, but he is a champion and his owners don't campaign him heavily, preferring to keep him at home. His ears and tail are absolutely correct for the standard, he has a scissors bite, and though he shows well, he is calm and laid back. His color may be a shade darker than your bitch, but just barely. A second dog has more wins to his credit, but he's on the road more. His tail set is perfect, but his ears are just a little big and high set. His color is on the darker side,

Tips from the Pros

Is your dog a good specimen of your breed? This answer should come from the opinions of several knowledgeable people, not just friends telling you that your dog is beautiful. Do you know enough about the pedigree to make an intelligent choice of sire? Are you aware of genetic problems in your breed? Has your bitch been checked for these problems? Has the potential sire been tested for them?

—Lilian S. Barber, AKC judge and exhibitor, author of *The New Complete Italian Greyhound*

and his bite is a scissors. He is a calm, pleasant dog. Which of these candidates is better for your bitch?

Well, a study of genetics is certainly beyond the scope of this book. But to choose wisely, you'll have to have some understanding of how traits are passed along. If a light color is recessive in your breed, then breeding to the light-colored stud is going to assure you light-colored puppies, perhaps light enough to be disqualified, because both the bitch and the stud are light and carry only the genes for light color. Moreover, combining the genes for large high-set ears with those for small low-set ears is *not* likely to blend to create the correct size of correctly set ears. Instead, you are likely to have puppies with large low-set ears, small high-set ears, or ears exactly like either parent.

So which is the better choice? Well, which is more important, color or ear set? Remember, you are in this for the long term. Maybe you can use the first dog and choose the darkest puppy to continue your program.

BEING READY FOR PUPPIES

No one is ever really ready for puppies the first time. Although the bitch may be perfectly fine on her own, the owner is a nervous wreck. You should certainly know in advance if yours is a breed likely to have problems in whelping. Even more preparations will be necessary, and a cesarean might even be scheduled.

But more breeders are presented with puppies without much fuss on their part. Problems occur after the puppies have entered the world.

Tips from the Pros

Are you prepared to raise a litter, which means socializing the puppies as well as taking care of their needs and the mother's? Can you be there when the mother needs you? Are you aware of possible complications and the cost of emergency veterinary care? Is there enough demand for puppies of this breed so you can be sure to screen potential buyers and sell only to those who will treasure your breed as much as you do?

—Lilian S. Barber, AKC judge and exhibitor, author of *The New Complete Italian Greyhound*

One problem no breeder should ever face is placing the puppies. You should not be breeding a bitch unless you have people clamoring for the pups in advance. Keep in mind that you will need both show homes and pet homes, and you won't know in advance how many of each, or indeed how many puppies, there will be. Any puppies not placed in good loving homes are *your* responsibility. Even those placed with other owners are your responsibility—any reputable breeder will take back dogs she has produced at any time.

Many novices rush into breeding, sure that there will be a ready market for their wonderful pups and hoping to make a little money on the deal. *Do not be one of them!* Puppies raised right are *not* a moneymaking venture. Breeders generally *lose* money on every litter. They are working toward betterment of the breed, not funding their retirement. You may also find that no one in the fancy wants your puppies. You'll end up either keeping them and being "overdogged," or resort to selling them through newspaper ads, or descend to the despicable depths of selling puppies in front of your local Safeway. With animal shelters already overflowing with unwanted dogs, what are you doing bringing more into existence?

I think Keeshonden are possibly the most wonderful form of life on the face of the earth, but I also own mixed breeds rescued from shelters. I have never bred a litter, never intend to, and have rather strong views on the subject. There are more than enough unwanted dogs on this earth—and *many* of them are purebreds. We don't need more people adding to the problem. Only those who have embarked on serious study of their chosen breed and can make an impact on lessening genetic problems and improving health and well being should be breeding dogs.

You must, of course, provide veterinary services for the bitch and her pups. The puppies will need checkups and their series of initial immunizations. Any unexpected problems that arise must be dealt with. There could be more pups than the bitch can provide with nutrition (which means you'll be playing surrogate mom), or one or more pups might have health problems. There might be removal of dewclaws. Or yours might be a breed that is usually docked or cropped. Some veterinarians will not perform these procedures, being opposed to such unnecessary surgery. Others may be willing to perform the surgery, but not well acquainted with show standards.

Before you have a puppy docked or cropped, consider what you are doing. Although docking is quick and less painful, you are removing one of the dog's primary communication tools and possibly interfering with a natural balancing mechanism. Cropping is much more serious and painful and takes much longer to perform and heal. Puppies in fine health and free of pain are put to sleep and wake up with their ears cut and taped and held in racks, first painful, then itchy. Elizabethan collars are often added to keep the pup from fussing at his aching ears. And if you have international aspirations, cropped ears will bar you from many countries. Dogs in natural ears are slowly starting to win here in the United States.

CONSIDERATIONS IF YOU OWN THE STUD

Odds are good that your first show dog will be a male. Owners are extremely reluctant to part with a good bitch, as I've noted previously. So how do you go about having puppies if you only own the stud?

If the dog has turned out nicely, and you have done your share of winning in the ring, and no health problems have cropped up, the breeder of your dog may be willing to do a test breeding with your stud and one of her bitches. This truly is a test to see what sort of progeny the stud produces. The greatest dog of a breed in the ring is not necessarily the greatest sire. What matters now is what sort of characteristics the stud passes along to his puppies.

The breeder will choose the bitch for the test breeding. He or she has much more experience than you, and probably understands what qualities in the bitch may fit best with the stud. Ask questions so you understand the choice, if you wish, but do not argue about it.

Before the breeding, agree on the conditions. Perhaps you can take the bitch of your choice and hope she will prove to be the foundation of your own breeding program at some future date. Maybe the breeder will only agree to co-ownership so that your future breeding choices will still be done under a more experienced eye. Whatever the conditions, get them in writing so that everyone knows exactly what is being agreed to.

> **Fancy That!**
>
> Some studs become famous in the breed for producing pups readily identifiable as their offspring. The Boxer CH Bang Away of Sirrah Crest is said to have changed the breed all by himself. Bichon Frise CH Chaminade Mr. Beau Monde created a recognizable line. Most breeds have one or two well-known names.

Watch Your Step

Because brucellosis (from *Brucella canis*, a bacterium) is contagious and causes infertility in bitches and sometimes studs, the infection of one dog can result in destruction of an entire kennel. Unfortunately, a dog in the first eight weeks of infection can test negative.

If the offspring from the test breeding turn out well and are a credit to the breed, others may want to use your stud. Legally your responsibility will end with the breeding; ethically you are responsible for much more.

For the health of your dog, every bitch must be tested for brucellosis, mycoplasma, and other sexually transmitted diseases. Such problems are rare, but infection can mean permanent sterility, so do not take the risk. Veterinary certificates showing negative results for these diseases are the norm, and owners should be prepared to produce them.

You do not have to agree to a breeding with every bitch that is proposed. In fact, it behooves you to check that the owner of the bitch is a responsible breeder, prepared to provide the best care for the puppies. You should not agree to any breeding where the owner will not agree to details in writing or discuss plans for the puppies. All the bitches bred by your dog should be ones you would be happy to have a pup from. Remember, your stud's name will be on all those pedigrees and will be held half responsible for the puppies brought into the world.

CONSIDERATIONS IF YOU OWN THE BITCH

Though science will tell you that the bitch contributes only half of the attributes to the puppies, she actually imparts more, because she is with the pups and the stud is not. Her stable temperament while with the puppies is essential to giving them a good start in life. A schizoid dam who snaps if anyone comes near her nest or flies off the handle if a car backfires outside will make her puppies nervous and flighty. They can generally be resocialized into reasonably stable dogs (and their early socialization is *your* responsibility), but it's better just to avoid the problem.

Most novices will not have a glorious bitch as their first or even second dog. If you have somehow happened to acquire one, you can do the breed a great service or disservice, depending on the choices you make. Get advice from your mentors, the breeder of your bitch, anyone you respect in the breed. You can only take full advantage of your bitch's wonderful qualities by choosing the correct stud. This will not necessarily be the dog with the Number 1 rating or the "hot" dog everyone wants to breed to. It will be the dog best suited to enhance your bitch's strengths and minimize her weaknesses.

You must have the necessary health certificates, and if your bitch must be shipped to the stud, you will pay for the shipping. (You will pay in both money and your own peace of mind as you agonize over the trips in both directions—and not without reason: Dogs have died during shipping. Just another item to consider.)

Terms of the agreement should be spelled out in writing. If the breeding doesn't "take," do you get a second try? Does the owner of the stud want a puppy, and if so, who gets first pick? Try to think of all the details that need to be addressed.

Before the breeding takes place, do you have both show homes and pet homes for the puppies? Are you prepared to handle an enormous litter? What if there's only a single puppy? Do you have the energy to advise your puppy owners through the years, perhaps in the middle of dinner or the dead of night? Could you raise and keep the entire litter if you had to? Even with a great bitch, there's no point in bringing puppies into the world if no one will want them.

Do not breed your bitch every time she comes into heat. You have a responsibility to her well being as well.

GENETIC DISEASE AND WHAT FANCIERS CAN DO ABOUT IT

A lot of finger pointing goes on in the world of purebred dogs. Proponents of raw food diets blame all the ills of dogdom on commercial dog foods. Some breeders blame everything bad in dogs on puppy mills. Now vaccinations are coming in for their share of blame.

The truth is that many problems are genetics, or at least genetically predisposed. Epilepsy, eye problems, blood problems, heart problems, joint

Talking Dog

The organizations that track a specific disease or condition can be opened or closed. With an open registry, everyone knows all the results, whether they're good or bad. This is the system that worked so well in Switzerland. Unfortunately, the two major registries in the United States—OFA and CERF—are closed. This means that the results are provided only to the owner of the dog, who can then choose to make them known or not. Because of this, if yours is a breed with problems in joints or eyes, you should ask for a dog's ratings or only consider dogs who advertise their excellent ratings.

problems are all being shown to have at least some genetic component. This sad truth must be faced by breeders.

Genetic disease must play a part in all breeding considerations. Switzerland's Bernese Mountain Dog club has come a long way toward eliminating hip dysplasia by adopting it as a major goal, using an open registry so that *all* dogs' hip ratings, both good and bad, are known to all, and choosing breeding stock carefully. Such a committed effort is necessary if problems are to be addressed.

If everyone concentrated as much on eradicating genetic disease as on producing the next top dog, our purebreds would be a lot healthier.

Remember

- ○ Breeding dogs is a very serious proposition, not to be taken lightly.
- ○ Before breeding, you must understand your breed, the standard, the genetic diseases, and your dog's strong and weak points.
- ○ Before breeding, you must have good, responsible homes for all the puppies that may result.
- ○ Breeding, done correctly, is not a moneymaking activity.
- ○ As a stud owner, you do not have to agree to breed all the bitches whose owners approach you—breed only those you think will result in improvement to the breed.
- ○ As a bitch owner, choose the stud carefully, based on a goal of accentuating your bitch's strong points and playing down any faults.
- ○ Always work toward eliminating genetic disease.

APPENDIX **A**

Additional Addresses

REGISTRIES

American Kennel Club (AKC)
5580 Centerview Drive
Raleigh, NC 27606
Phone: 919-233-9767
(for matters regarding registration)

American Kennel Club (AKC)
260 Madison Avenue
New York, NY 10016
Switchboard: 212-696-8200
Event records: 212-696-8281
(for matters regarding events)
www.akc.org

United Kennel Club (UKC)
100 East Kilgore Road
Kalamazoo, MI 49001-5597
Phone: 606-343-9020
www.ukcdogs.com

States Kennel Club (SKC)
P.O. Box 389
Hattiesburg, MS 39043-0389
Phone: 601-583-8345

ARBA
9921 Frank Tippett Road
Cheltenham, MD 20623
Phone: 301-868-5718
www.arba.org

Canadian Kennel Club (CKC)
89 Skyway Avenue
Etobicoke, Ontario M9W 6R4
Canada

Federation Cynologique Internationale
Place Albert 1er, 13
6530 Thuin
Belgium
www.fci.be

The Kennel Club
1-5 Clarges Street
Piccadilly, London, England

Federacion Canofila Mexicana
Apartado Postal 22-535
CP14000
Mexico

Bahamas Kennel Club
P.O. Box N-9870
Nassau, Bahamas

AKC Dog Show Superintendents

Antypas, Bill
Newport Dog Shows
P.O. Box 7131
Pasadena, CA 91109-7131
Phone: 626-796-3869
Fax: 626-577-2444

Bradshaw, Jack
Jack Bradshaw Dog Shows
P.O. Box 227303
Los Angeles, CA 90022-0718
Phone: 323-727-0136
Fax: 323-727-2949
www.jbradshaw.com

Brown, Margery
M. M. Brown Dog Shows
P.O. Box 494665
Redding, CA 96049
Phone: 916-243-0775

Woodward, Doris J.
Brown Dog Show Organization, Inc.
P.O. Box 2566
Spokane, WA 99220-2566
Phone: 509-924-1089
Fax: 509-924-1421

Campbell, James M.
Western Dog Shows Ltd.
P.O. Box 3070 MPP
Kamloops, B.C. 62C 6B7
Canada

Crowe, Thomas J.
MB-F, Inc.
P.O. Box 22107
Greensboro, NC 27420-2107
Phone: 336-379-9352
Fax: 336-272-0864
or

P.O. Box 9999
Madison Heights, MI 48071
Phone: 248-588-5000
Fax: 248-588-7380
www.infodog.com

Houser, M. Helen
P.O. Box 420
Quakertown, PA 18951-0420
Phone: 215-538-2032
Fax: 215-376-4939

Johnson, John R.
R & R Dog Shows
11012 Canyon Road, East #8-387
Puyallup, WA 98373
Phone: 253-531-3616
Fax: 253-531-3667

Matthews, Ace H.
Matthews Dog Shows
3840 NE 66th Ave.
Portland, OR 97213
Phone: 503-287-7740
Fax: 503-287-7937

McNulty, Eileen
McNulty Dog Shows
1745 Route 78
Java Center, NY 10482-9610
Phone: 716-457-3371
Fax: 716-457-9533

Onofrio, Jack
Onofrio Dog Shows
P.O. Box 25764
Oklahoma City, OK 73125-0764
Phone: 405-427-8181
Fax: 405-427-5241
www.onofrio.com

Peters, Bob
Peters Dog Shows, Ltd.
P.O. Box 579
Wake Forest, NC 27588-0579
Phone: 919-556-9516
Fax: 919-554-0519

Berkheimer, Kathleen
Jim Rau Dog Shows, Ltd.
P.O. Box 6898
Reading, PA 19610-0898
Phone: 610-376-1880
Fax: 215-376-4939
www.raudogshows.com/rau1.html/

Rogers, Kevin B.
Kevin Rogers Dog Shows
P.O. Box 230
Hattiesburg, MS 39403-0230
Phone: 601-583-1110
Fax: 601-582-9909

Salvidar, Elaine
4343 ½ Burns Ave.
Los Angeles, CA 90029
Phone: 323-663-5868
Fax: 323-644-1471

Sleeper, Kenneth A.
Roy Jones Dog Shows, Inc.
P.O. Box 828
Auburn, IN 46706-0828
Phone: 219-925-0525
Fax: 219-925-1146
www.royjonesdogshows.com/

Wilson, Nancy
8307 E. Camelback Road
Scottsdale, AZ 85251-1715
Phone: 602-949-5389

APPENDIX B

Varieties and Class Divisions

AKC VARIETIES

Cocker Spaniels	Black (to include black and tan), ASCOB (any solid color other than black), Parti-Color
Beagles	Under 13 in., 13 to 15 in.
Dachshunds	Longhaired, Smooth, Wirehaired
Bull Terriers	Colored, White
Manchester Terriers	Standard, Toy
Chihuahuas	Long Coat, Smooth Coat
English Toy Spaniels	Blenheim and Prince Charles, King Charles and Ruby
Poodles	Miniature (in Non-Sporting), Standard (in Non-Sporting), Toy (in Toys, not to exceed 10 in.)
Collies	Rough, Smooth

AKC CLASS DIVISIONS

By Color

Basenjis	Red, Black, Black & Tan, Brindle
Boxers	Brindle, Fawn
Chow Chows	Black, Red, Any other color
Collies	Sable & White, Tricolor, Blue Merle, White
Dachshunds (standard)	Red, Black & Tan, Any other color (Open class only)
Dachshunds (miniature)	Red, Black & Tan, Any other color (Open class at National Specialty only)
Dalmatians	Black Spotted, Liver Spotted
Doberman Pinschers	Black, Any other allowed color

English Cocker Spaniels	Solid color (to include any solid color except white with tan points), Parti-Color (including roans and ticks)
French Bulldogs	Brindle, Cream & Fawn, Pied & White
Giant Schnauzers	Black, Salt & Pepper
Great Danes	Brindle, Fawn, Blue, Black, Harlequin
Japanese Chins	Black & White, Red & White
Labrador Retrievers	Black, Yellow, Chocolate
Miniature Pinschers	Black & Rust, Chocolate, Rust & Red
Miniature Schnauzers	Salt & Pepper, Black & Silver, Black
Newfoundlands	Black, Other than Black
Pekingese	Fawn, Biscuit, Gray, Red & Sable, Parti-Color, Black, Any other allowed color
Pomeranians	Red, Orange, Cream & Sable, Black, Brown & Blue, Any other acceptable color
Pugs	Black, Fawn
Shetland Sheepdogs	Sable & White, Black (tricolor), Blue Merle, Any other acceptable color

By Weight

Boston Terriers	Open Classes-under 15 lb, 15 lb & under 20 lb, 20 lb & under 25 lb *OR* under 15 lb, 15 lb & over
Dachshunds (Miniature)	Open Class-under 10 lb & 12 mo or over
Dachshunds (Standard)	Open Class-10 lb & over & 12 mo or over
French Bulldogs	Open Class-under 22 lb, 22 lb & not over 28 lb
Italian Greyhounds	Open Class-8 lb & under, over 8 lb
Japanese Chin	Open Class-7 lb & under, over 7 lb
Manchester Terrier (Standard)	Open Class-over 12 lb & under 16 lb, over 16 lb & under 22 lb
Manchester Terrier (Toy)	Open Class-7 lb & under, over 7 lb & not over 12 lb
Pekingese	At All-Breed Shows: Open Dogs Class-under 8 lb & 12 mo or over, 8 lb & over (& under if less than 12 mo); At specialties: Open Dogs Class-under 6 lb & 12 mo or over, 6 lb & under 8 lb & 12 mo or over, 8 lb & over (& under if less than 12 mo)

By Coat

Brussels Griffons	Rough Coat, Smooth Coat
Chow Chows	Rough Coat, Smooth Coat
Chinese Crested	Hairless, Powderpuff
Saint Bernard	Longhaired, Shorthaired
Saluki	Smooth Coat, Feather Coat

By Ears

Papillon	Erect Ears, Drop Ears
Skye Terrier	Drop Ears, Prick Ears

UKC VARIETIES

Alaskan Klee Kai	Toy, Miniature, Standard
American Eskimo	Miniature, Standard
Belgian Shepherd Dog	Groenendael, Lakenois, Malinois, Tervuren
Berger de Pyrenees	Rough-Faced, Smooth-Faced
Collie	Rough, Smooth
Dachshund	Miniature, Standard
Fox Terrier	Smooth, Wirehaired
Jack Russell Terrier	10 in.–12 in., over 12 in.–15 in.
Manchester Terrier	Standard, Toy
Xoloitzcuintli	Toy, Miniature, Standard

FCI VARIETIES

Belgian Shepherd Dog	Groenendael, Laekenois, Malinois, Tervueren
Schipperke	3–5 kg, 5–8 kg
Majorca Shepherd Dog	Shorthaired, Longhaired
Catalan Sheepdog	Longhaired, Smooth-Haired
Beauceron	Black & Tan, Harlequin
Briard	Slate, Fawn, or Gray
Puli	White, Black or Gray, or Fawn
Dutch Shepherd Dog	Shorthaired, Longhaired, Rough-Haired
Doberman Pinscher	Black with Rust Red Markings, Brown with Rust Red Markings, Red-Brown to Stag Red, Black with Red-Brown Markings
Miniature Pinscher	Red-Brown to Stag Red, Black with Red-Brown Markings
Giant Schnauzer	Pepper & Salt, Black
Schnauzer	Pepper & Salt, Black
Miniature Schnauzer	Pepper & Salt, Black, Black & Silver, White
Boxer	Fawn, Brindle
Great Dane	Fawn, Brindle, Black, Harlequin, Blue
Newfoundland	Black, Brown, White with Black Markings
Serra da Estrela Mountain Dog	Smooth-Haired, Longhaired
Saint Bernard Dog	Shorthaired, Longhaired
Bull Terrier	Standard, Miniature

Dachshund	Standard, Miniature, Rabbit (each further broken down to smooth-haired, longhaired, wirehaired)
German Spitz	Keeshond, Giant Spitz (white, brown, or black), Medium-Sized Spitz (white, brown or black, orange and gray shaded and other colors), Miniature Spitz (white, brown or black, orange and gray shaded and other colors), Pomeranian
Mexican Hairless Dog	Standard, Miniature
Peruvian Hairless Dog	Large, Medium-Sized, Miniature
Ibizan Warren Hound	Rough-Haired, Smooth-Haired
Portuguese Warren Hound	Rough-Haired (large, medium-sized, miniature), Smooth-Haired (large, medium-sized, miniature)
Swiss Hounds	Bernese Hound, Jura Hound, Lucerne Hound, Schwyz Hound
Smaller Swiss Hounds	Smaller Bernese Hound (smooth-haired, coarse-haired), Smaller Jura Hound, Smaller Lucerne Hound, Smaller Schwyz Hound
Weimaraner	Shorthaired, Longhaired
Italian Pointing Dog	White-Orange, Chestnut Roan
Brittany	White & Orange, Other colors
Italian Wire-Haired Pointing Dog	White-Orange, Chestnut Roan
English Cocker Spaniel	Red, Black, Other colors
American Cocker Spaniel	Black, ASCOB, Parti-Color
Portuguese Water Dog	Curly, Wavy
Standard Poodle	White, Brown, Black, Gray, Apricot
Medium size Poodle	White, Brown, Black, Gray, Apricot
Miniature Poodle	White, Brown, Black, Gray, Apricot
Toy Poodle	White, Brown, Black, Gray, Apricot
Chinese Crested Dog	Hairless, Powderpuff
Chihuahua	Smooth-Haired, Long-Haired
Cavalier King Charles Spaniel	Black & Tan, Ruby, Blenheim, Tricolor
King Charles Spaniel	Black & Tan, Ruby, Blenheim, Prince Charles (tricolor)
Papillon	1.5–2.5 kg, 2.5–4.5 kg
Phalene	1.5–2.5 kg, 2.5–4.5 kg
French Bulldog	Fawn with Limited Patching, Fawn with Medium to Predominating Patching
Pug	Fawn, Black, Silver, Apricot
Saluki	Long-Haired or Fringed, Short-Haired

Alphabetic List of Breeds and Their Registries

Note: The designation "nc" in a UKC listing indicates that the breed does not currently have conformation privileges, but may be shown in other dog sports. Also note that kennel clubs recognize new breeds periodically, so check with the registries for the most up-to-date information.

A

Affenpinscher: AKC (Toys), UKC (Companion), CKC (Toys), FCI (Group 2)

Afghan Hound: AKC (Hounds), UKC (Sighthounds), CKC (Hounds), FCI (Group 10)

Aidi: ARBA (Working)

Ainu: UKC (nc)

Airedale Terrier: AKC (Terriers), UKC (nc), CKC (Terriers), FCI (Group 3)

Akbash Dog: UKC (Guarding), ARBA (Herding)

Akita: AKC (Working), UKC (nc), CKC (Working), FCI (Group 5)

Alapha Blue Blood Bulldog: ARBA (Working)

Alaskan Klee Kai: UKC (Northern Breeds), ARBA (Spitz)

Alaskan Malamute: AKC (Working), UKC (Northern Breeds), CKC (Working), FCI (Group 5)

Alpine Dachsbracke: UKC (nc), FCI (Group 6)

American Black & Tan Coonhound: UKC (Scenthounds)

American Bulldog: ARBA (Working)

American Eskimo Dog: AKC (Non-Sporting), UKC (Northern Breeds)

American Foxhound: AKC (Hounds), UKC (Scenthounds), CKC (Hounds), FCI (Group 6)

American Hairless Terrier: ARBA (Companion)

American Pit Bull Terrier: UKC (Terriers), ARBA (Terriers)

American Staffordshire Terrier: AKC (Terriers), CKC (Terriers), FCI (Group 3)

American Water Spaniel: AKC (Sporting), UKC (Gun Dogs), CKC (Sporting), FCI (Group 8)

Anatolian Shepherd: AKC (Working), UKC (Guardian Dogs), FCI (Group 2), ARBA (Working)

Anglo-Français de Moyen Venerie: UKC (nc)

Anglo-Français de Petite Venerie: UKC (nc), FCI (Group 6)

Anglo Français Tricolor: ARBA (Hounds)

Antique Perro: FCI (Group 1)

Appenzeller: UKC (Guarding Dogs), FCI (Group 2), ARBA (Herding)

Ariegeois: UKC (Scenthounds), FCI (Group 6)

Ariege Pointing Dog: FCI (Group 7)

Atlas Shepherd Dog: FCI (Group 2)

Australian Cattle Dog: AKC (Herding), UKC (nc), CKC (Herding), FCI (Group 1)

Australian Kelpie: UKC (Herding), CKC (Misc.), FCI (Group 1), ARBA (Herding)

Australian Shepherd: AKC (Herding), UKC (Herding), CKC (Herding)

Australian Terrier: AKC (Terriers), UKC (Terriers), CKC (Terriers), FCI (Group 3)

Austrian Black & Tan Hound: FCI (Group 6)

Austrian Short-haired Pinscher: FCI (Group 2), ARBA (Working)

Auvergne Pointing Dog: FCI (Group 7)

Azawakh: UKC (Sighthounds), FCI (Group 10), ARBA (Hounds)

B

Barbet: UKC (Gun Dogs), FCI (Group 8), ARBA (Sporting)

Basenji: AKC (Hounds), UKC (Sighthounds), CKC (Hounds), FCI (Group 5)

Basset Artesian Normand: UKC (Scenthounds), FCI (Group 6), ARBA (Hounds)

Basset Bleu de Gascogne: UKC (Scenthounds), ARBA (Hounds)

Basset Fauve de Bretagne: UKC (nc), ARBA (Hounds)

Basset Griffon Vendeen: ARBA (Hounds)

Basset Hound: AKC (Hounds), UKC (Scenthounds), CKC (Hounds), FCI (Group 6)

Batard: ARBA (Hounds)

Bavarian Mountain Scenthound: UKC (nc), FCI (Group 6)

Beagle: AKC (Hounds), UKC (Scenthounds), CKC (Hounds), FCI (Group 6)

Beagle Harrier: UKC (nc), FCI (Group 6)

Bearded Collie: AKC (Herding), UKC (Herding), CKC (Herding), FCI (Group 1)

Beauceron: UKC (Herding), FCI (Group 1), ARBA (Herding)

Bedlington Terrier: AKC (Terriers), UKC (Terriers), CKC (Terriers), FCI (Group 3)

Belgian Griffon: UKC (Scenthounds), FCI (Group 9)

Belgian Malinois: AKC (Herding)

Belgian Sheepdog: AKC (Herding), UKC (Herding), CKC (Herding), FCI (Group 1) [*Note:* UKC, CKC, and FCI group all three (or four, including the Laekenois) Belgian sheepdog breeds under this one heading]

Belgian Tervuren: AKC (Herding)

Bergamasco: UKC (Herding), FCI (Group 1), ARBA (Herding)

Berger de Picard: UKC (Herding), CKC (Herding), FCI (Group 1)

Berger de Pyrenees: UKC (Herding), CKC (Herding)

Bernese Hound: FCI (Group 6)

Bernese Mountain Dog: AKC (Working), UKC (Guarding Dogs), CKC (Working), FCI (Group 2)

Bichon Frise: AKC (Non-Sporting), UKC (Companion Dogs), CKC (Non-Sporting), FCI (Group 9)

Billy: UKC (nc), FCI (Group 6)

Black & Tan Coonhound: AKC (Hounds), CKC (Hounds), FCI (Group 6)

Black Forest Hound: UKC (Scenthounds), ARBA (Hounds)

Black Mouth Cur: UKC (nc)

Black Russian Terrier: UKC (Guarding Dogs), FCI (Group 2), ARBA (Working)

Bloodhound: AKC (Hounds), UKC (Scenthounds), CKC (Hounds), FCI (Group 6)

Blue de Gascogne: ARBA (Hounds)

Blue Gascony Basset: FCI (Group 6)

Blue Gascony Griffon: FCI (Group 6)

Blue Picardy Spaniel: CKC (Sporting), FCI (Group 7)

Bluetick Coonhound: UKC (Scenthounds)

Bohemian Terrier: CKC (Misc.)

Bohemian Wire-Haired Pointing Griffon: FCI (Group 7)

Bolognese: UKC (Companion Dogs), FCI (Group 9), ARBA (Companion)

Border Collie: AKC (Herding), UKC (nc), FCI (Group 1)

Border Terrier: AKC (Terriers), UKC (Terriers), CKC (Terriers), FCI (Group 3)

Borzoi: AKC (Hounds), UKC (Sighthounds), CKC (Hounds), FCI (Group 10)

Bosnian Coarse-Haired Hound: FCI (Group 6)

Boston Terrier: AKC (Non-Sporting), UKC (Companion Dogs), CKC (Non-Sporting), FCI (Group 9)

Bourbonnais Pointing Dog: FCI (Group 7)

Bouvier des Flandres: AKC (Herding), UKC (Herding), CKC (Herding), FCI (Group 1)

Boxer: AKC (Working), UKC (Guarding Dogs), CKC (Working), FCI (Group 2)

Boykin Spaniel: UKC (Gun Dogs)

Bracco Italiano: UKC (Gun Dogs), ARBA (Sporting)

Braque d'Auverge: UKC (Gun Dogs), ARBA (Sporting)

Braque du Bourbonnais: UKC (Gun Dogs), ARBA (Sporting)

Braque Dupy: ARBA (Sporting)

Braque Français, de Grand Talle: UKC (Gun Dogs), CKC (Sporting), ARBA (Sporting)

Braque Français, de Petite Talle: UKC (Gun Dogs), CKC (Sporting), ARBA (Sporting)

Braque Saint-Germain: UKC (Gun Dogs), ARBA (Sporting)

Briard: AKC (Herding), UKC (Herding), CKC (Herding), FCI (Group 1)

Briquet Griffon Vendeen: UKC (nc), ARBA (Hounds)

Brittany: AKC (Sporting), UKC (Gun Dogs), CKC (Sporting), FCI (Group 7)

Broholmer: FCI (Group 2)

Bruno de Jura: ARBA (Hounds)

Brussels Griffon: AKC (Toys), UKC (Companion Dogs), CKC (Toys), FCI (Group 9)

Bulldog: AKC (Non-Sporting), CKC (Non-Sporting), FCI (Group 2)

Bullmastiff: AKC (Working), UKC (Guarding Dogs), CKC (Working), FCI (Group 2)

Bull Terrier: AKC (Terriers), UKC (Terriers), CKC (Terriers), FCI (Group 3)

Burgos Pointing Dog: FCI (Group 7)

C

Cairn Terrier: AKC (Terriers), UKC (Terriers), CKC (Terriers), FCI (Group 3)

Canaan Dog: AKC (Herding), UKC (Sighthounds), CKC (Working), FCI (Group 5), ARBA (Spitz)

Canadian Cur: UKC (Scenthounds)

Canadian Eskimo Dog: UKC (nc), CKC (Working), ARBA (Spitz)

Canadian Warren Hound: FCI (Group 5)

Cane Corso: CKC (Misc.), ARBA (Working)

Cao da Castro Laboreiro: ARBA (Herding)

Cao da Serra Aire: ARBA (Herding)

Cao de Fila Miguel: ARBA (Herding

Cardigan Welsh Corgi: AKC (Herding), UKC (Herding), CKC (Herding), FCI (Group 1)

Carolina Dog: UKC (Sighthounds), ARBA (Spitz)

Castro Laboreiro Dog: FCI (Group 2), ARBA (Herding)

Catalan Sheepdog: FCI (Group 1), ARBA (Herding)

Caucasian Ovcharka: UKC (Guarding Dogs)

Caucasian Shepherd Dog: FCI (Group 2), ARBA (Working)

Cavalier King Charles Spaniel: AKC (Toys), UKC (Companion), CKC (Toys), FCI (Group 9), ARBA (Companion)

Central Asian Shepherd Dog: UKC (Guarding Dogs), FCI (Group 2), ARBA (Working)

Cesky Fousek: UKC (nc)

Cesky Terrier: UKC (Terriers), FCI (Group 3), ARBA (Terriers)

Chart Polski: UKC (nc), CKC (Misc.), ARBA (Hounds)

Chesapeake Bay Retriever: AKC (Sporting), UKC (Gun Dogs), CKC (Sporting), FCI (Group 8)

Chien D'Artois: UKC (Scenthounds), FCI (Group 6)

Chien Français Blanc et Noir: UKC (nc)

Chien Français Blanc et Orange: UKC (nc)

Chien Français Tricolor: UKC (nc)

Chihuahua: AKC (Toys), UKC (Companion), CKC (Toys), FCI (Group 9)

Chinese Crested: AKC (Toys), UKC (Companion), CKC (Toys), FCI (Group 9)

Chinese Foo Dog: ARBA (Spitz)

Chinese Shar-Pei: AKC (Non-Sporting), UKC (Northern Breeds), CKC (Non-Sporting), FCI (Group 2)

Chinook: UKC, ARBA (Spitz)

Chow Chow: AKC (Non-Sporting), UKC (Northern Breeds), CKC (Non-Sporting), FCI (Group 5)

Cirneco dell'Etna: FCI (Group 5), ARBA (Hounds)

Clumber Spaniel: AKC (Sporting), UKC (Gun Dogs), CKC (Sporting), FCI (Group 8)

Cocker Spaniel: AKC (Sporting), UKC (Gun Dogs), CKC (Sporting), FCI (Group 8)

Collie: AKC (Herding), UKC (Herding), CKC (Herding), FCI (Group 1)

Coton de Tulear: UKC (Companion), CKC (Misc.), FCI (Group 9), ARBA (Companion)

Croatian Sheepdog: CKC (Misc.), FCI (Group 1), ARBA (Companion)

Curly-Coated Retriever: AKC (Sporting), UKC (Gun Dogs), CKC (Sporting), FCI (Group 8)

D

Dachshund: AKC (Hounds), UKC (Scenthounds), CKC (Hounds), FCI (Group 4) *Note:* Dachshunds are the *entire* Group 4 of the FCI.

Dalmatian: AKC (Non-Sporting), UKC (Companion), CKC (Non-Sporting), FCI (Group 6)

Dandie Dinmont Terrier: AKC (Terriers), UKC (Terriers), CKC (Terriers), FCI (Group 3)

Danish Broholmer: UKC (nc)

Denmark Feist: UKC (nc)

Deutsche Bracke: UKC (nc)

Dingo: ARBA (Spitz)

Doberman Pinscher: AKC (Working), UKC (Guarding Dogs), CKC (Working), FCI (Group 2)

Dogo Argentino: FCI (Group 2), ARBA (Working)

Dogue de Bordeau: UKC (Guarding Dogs), FCI (Group 2), ARBA (Working)

Drentse Patrijshond: UKC (nc), FCI (Group 7)

Drever: UKC (nc), CKC (Hounds), ARBA (Hounds)

Dunker: UKC (nc)

Dupuy Pointing Dog: FCI (Group 7)

Dutch Shepherd: UKC (Herding), FCI (Group 1), ARBA (Herding)

E

East Siberian Laika: UKC (nc), FCI (Group 5)

English Bulldog: UKC (Companion)

English Cocker Spaniel: AKC (Sporting), UKC (Gun Dogs), CKC (Sporting), FCI (Group 8)

English Coonhound: UKC (Scenthounds)

English Foxhound: AKC (Hounds), UKC (Scenthounds), CKC (Hounds), FCI (Group 6)

English Pointer: UKC (Gun Dogs), FCI (Group 7)

English Setter: AKC (Sporting), UKC (Gun Dogs), CKC (Sporting), FCI (Group 7)

English Shepherd: UKC (nc), ARBA (Herding)

English Springer Spaniel: AKC (Sporting), UKC (Gun Dogs), CKC (Sporting)

English Toy Spaniel: AKC (Toys), UKC (Companion), CKC (Toys)

English Toy Terrier: FCI (Group 3), ARBA (Companion)

Entelbucher: UKC (Guarding Dogs), CKC (Working), FCI (Group 2), ARBA (Herding)

Epagneul Bleu de Picardie: UKC (nc)

Epagneul Picard: UKC (nc)

Epagneul Pont-Audemer: UKC (nc)

Estonian Hound: UKC (Scenthounds)

Estrela Mountain Dog: UKC (nc), ARBA (Herding)

Eurasier: UKC (nc), CKC (Working), FCI (Group 5), ARBA (Spitz)

F

Fauve de Bretagne: ARBA (Hounds)

Fawn Brittany Basset: FCI (Group 6)

Fawn Brittany Griffon: UKC (Scenthounds), FCI (Group 6)

Field Spaniel: AKC (Sporting), UKC (Gun Dogs), CKC (Sporting), FCI (Group 8)

Fila Brasileiro: CKC (Misc.), FCI (Group 2), ARBA (Working)

Finnish Hound: UKC (nc), FCI (Group 6)

Finnish Lapphund: UKC (Northern Breeds), CKC (Misc.), FCI (Group 5), ARBA (Spitz)

Finnish Reindeer Herder: FCI (Group 5)

Finnish Spitz: AKC (Non-Sporting), UKC (Northern Breeds), CKC (Hounds), FCI (Group 5)

Flat-Coated Retriever: AKC (Sporting), UKC (Gun Dogs), CKC (Sporting), FCI (Group 8)

Foxhound: AKC (Hounds), CKC (Hounds), FCI (Group 6)

Fox Terrier: AKC (Terriers), UKC (Terriers: breaks into Wire and Smooth), CKC (Terriers), FCI (Group 3)

French Bulldog: AKC (Non-Sporting), UKC (Companion), CKC (Non-Sporting), FCI (Group 9)

French Pointing Dog, Gascogne type: FCI (Group 7)

French Pointing Dog, Pyrenean type: RCI (Group 7)

French Spaniel: UKC (nc), CKC (Sporting), FCI (Group 7)

French Tricolor Hound: FCI (Group 6)

French White & Black Hound: FCI (Group 6)

French White & Orange Hound: FCI (Group 6)

French Wire-Haired Pointing Griffon: FCI (Group 7)

French Woolly-Haired Pointing Griffon: FCI (Group 7)

Frisian Pointing Dog: FCI (Group 7)

Frisian Water Dog: FCI (Group 8)

G

German Broken-Coated Pointing Dog: FCI (Group 7)

German Hound: FCI (Group 6)

German Hunting Terrier: FCI (Group 3)

German Long-Haired Pointer: UKC (Gun Dogs), CKC (Sporting), FCI (Group 7)

German Pinscher: UKC (Terriers), CKC (Misc.), ARBA (Working)

German Pointing Dog: FCI (Group 7)

German Shepherd Dog: AKC (Herding), UKC (Herding), CKC (Herding), FCI (Group 1)

German Short-Haired Pointer: AKC (Sporting), UKC (Gun Dogs), CKC (Sporting), FCI (Group 7)

German Spaniel: UKC (nc), FCI (Group 8)

German Spitz: ARBA (Spitz)

German Wire-Haired Pointer: AKC (Sporting), UKC (Gun Dogs), CKC (Sporting), FCI (Group 7)

Giant Schnauzer: AKC (Working), UKC (Herding), CKC (Working), FCI (Group 2)

Giant Spitz: FCI (Group 5)

Glen of Imaal Terrier: UKC (Terriers), CKC (Misc.), FCI (Group 3), ARBA (Terriers)

Golden Retriever: AKC (Sporting), UKC (Gun Dogs), CKC (Sporting), FCI (Group 7)

Gordon Setter: AKC (Sporting), UKC (Gun Dogs), CKC (Sporting), FCI (Group 7)

Grand Anglo-Français: UKC (nc), ARBA (Hounds)

Grand Basset Griffon Vendeen: UKC (nc), ARBA (Hounds)

Grand Bleu de Gascogne: UKC (Scenthounds), ARBA (Hounds)

Grand Gascon-Saintongeois: UKC (Scenthounds)

Grand Griffon Vendeen: UKC (nc)

Great Anglo-French Tricolor Hound: FCI (Group 6), ARBA (Hounds)

Great Anglo-French White & Black Hound: FCI (Group 6)

Great Anglo-French White & Orange Hound: FCI (Group 6)

Great Dane: AKC (Working), UKC (Guarding Dogs), CKC (Working), FCI (Group 2)

Greater Swiss Mountain Dog: AKC (Working), UKC (Guarding Dogs), CKC (Misc.), FCI (Group 2), ARBA (Working)

Great Gascon Saintongeois: FCI (Group 6)

Great Griffon Vendeen: FCI (Group 6)

Great Pyrenees: AKC (Working), UKC (Guarding Dogs), CKC (Working)

Greenland Dog: UKC (nc), CKC (Working), FCI (Group 5), ARBA (Spitz)

Greyhound: AKC (Hounds), UKC (Sighthounds), CKC (Hounds), FCI (Group 10)

Griffon Fauve de Bretagne: UKC (nc)

Griffon Nivernais: UKC (Scenthounds), FCI (Group 6), ARBA (Hounds)

H

Halden Hound: FCI (Group 6)

Hamilton Hound: UKC (Scenthounds), FCI (Group 6), ARBA (Hounds)

Hanoverian Hound: UKC (nc), FCI (Group 6), ARBA (Hounds)

Harrier: AKC (Hounds), UKC (Scenthounds), CKC (Hounds), FCI (Group 6)

Havanese: AKC (Toys), UKC (Companion), CKC (Misc.), FCI (Group 9), ARBA (Companion)

Hellenic Hound: FCI (Group 6), ARBA (Hounds)

Hokkaido: FCI (Group 5), ARBA (Spitz)

Hollandse Smoushond: FCI (Group 2), ARBA (Herding)

Hovawart: UKC (Guarding Dogs), FCI (Group 2), ARBA (Working)

Hrvatska: FCI (Group 6)

Hungarian Greyhound: FCI (Group 10)

Hungarian Short-Haired Pointing Dog: FCI (Group 7)

Hungarian Wire-Haired Pointing Dog: FCI (Group 7)

Hygen Hound: FCI (Group 6)

I

Ibizan Hound: AKC (Hounds), UKC (Sighthounds), CKC (Hounds)

Ibizan Warren Hound: FCI (Group 5)

Iceland Dog: UKC (nc), CKC (Misc.), FCI (Group 5), ARBA (Spitz)

Irish Red & White Setter: UKC (Gun Dogs), CKC (Misc.), FCI (Group 7), ARBA (Sporting)

Irish Setter: AKC (Sporting), UKC (Gun Dogs), CKC (Sporting), FCI (Group 7)

Irish Terrier: AKC (Terriers), UKC (Terriers), CKC (Terriers), FCI (Group 3)

Irish Water Spaniel: AKC (Sporting), UKC (Gun Dogs), CKC (Sporting), FCI (Group 8)

Irish Wolfhound: AKC (Hounds), UKC (Sighthounds), CKC (Hounds), FCI (Group 10)

Istrian Coarse-Haired Hound: FCI (Group 6)

Istrian Short-Haired Hound: FCI (Group 6)

Italian Greyhound: AKC (Toys), UKC (Sighthounds), CKC (Toys), FCI (Group 10)

Italian Pointing Dog: FCI (Group 7)

Italian Segugio: FCI (Group 6)

Italian Wire-Haired Pointing Dog: FCI (Group 7)

J

Jack Russell Terrier: AKC (Terriers), UKC (Terriers), CKC (Misc.), ARBA (Terriers)

Jagdhund: ARBA (Spitz)

Jagdterrier: UKC (Terriers), ARBA (Terriers)

Japanese Chin: AKC (Toys), UKC (Companion), FCI (Group 9)

Japanese Spaniel: CKC (Toys)

Japanese Spitz: CKC (Non-Sporting), FCI (Group 5), ARBA (Spitz)

Japanese Terrier: FCI (Group 3)

Jindo: UKC (Northern Breeds), ARBA (Spitz)

Jura Hound: FCI (Group 6)

K

Kai: UKC (Northern Breeds), FCI (Group 5), ARBA (Spitz)

Kangal Dog: UKC (Guarding Dogs)

Karelian Bear Dog: UKC (Northern Breeds), CKC (Working), FCI (Group 5), ARBA (Spitz)

Karst Shepherd Dog: FCI (Group 2)

Keeshond: AKC (Non-Sporting), UKC (Northern Breeds), CKC (Non-Sporting), FCI (Group 5)

Kelpie: FCI (Group 1) (known as Australian Kelpie by other registries)

Kemmer Stock Cur: UKC (nc)

Kerry Blue Terrier: AKC (Terriers), UKC (Terriers), CKC (Terriers), FCI (Group 3)

King Charles Spaniel: FCI (Group 9)

King Shepherd: ARBA (Herding)

Kirghiz: ARBA (Hounds)

Kishu: FCI (Group 5), ARBA (Spitz)

Kleiner Münsterlander Vorstehund: CKC (Misc.)

Komondor: AKC (Working), UKC (Guarding Dogs), CKC (Working), FCI (Group 1)

Kooikerhondje: UKC (Gun Dogs)

Krasky Ovcar: UKC (nc)

Kromfohrlander: UKC (, FCI (Group 9)

Kuvasz: AKC (Working), UKC (nc), CKC (Working), FCI (Group 1)

Kyi-Leo: ARBA (Companion)

L

Labrador Retriever: AKC (Sporting), UKC (Gun Dogs), CKC (Sporting), FCI (Group 8)

Laekenois: ARBA (Herding)

Lakeland Terrier: AKC (Terriers), UKC (Terriers), CKC (Terriers), FCI (Group 3)

Landseer: FCI (Group 2)

Large Basset Griffon Vendeen: FCI (Group 6)

Large Blue Gascony Hound: FCI (Group 6)

Large Munsterlander: UKC (Gun Dogs), FCI (Group 7), ARBA (Sporting)

Large Spanish Hound: UKC (nc)

Leonberger: UKC (Guarding Dogs), CKC (Working), FCI (Group 2), ARBA (Working)

Leopard Cur: UKC (nc)

Lhasa Apso: AKC (Non-Sporting), UKC (Companion), CKC (Non-Sporting), FCI (Group 9)

Little Lion Dog: FCI (Group 9)

Long-Haired Pyrenean Sheepdog: FCI (Group 1)

Louisiana Catahoula Leopard Dog: UKC (Herding), ARBA (Herding)

Lowchen: AKC (Non-Sporting), UKC (Companion), CKC (Non-Sporting), ARBA (Companion)

Lucerne Hound: FCI (Group 6)

Lundehund: UKC (Northern Breeds)

M

Magyar Agar: ARBA (Hounds)

Majorca Mastiff: FCI (Group 2)

Majorca Shepherd Dog: FCI (Group 1)

Maltese: AKC (Toys), UKC (Companion), CKC (Toys), FCI (Group 9)

Manchester Terrier: AKC (Terriers), UKC (Terriers), CKC (Terriers), FCI (Group 3)

Maremma Sheepdog: UKC (Guarding Dogs), FCI (Group 1), ARBA (Herding)

Mastiff: AKC (Working), UKC (Guarding Dogs), CKC (Working), FCI (Group 2)

Medium Griffon Vendeen: FCI (Group 6)

Medium-Sized Poodle: FCI (Group 9)

Medium-Sized Spitz: FCI (Group 5)

Mexican Hairless: CKC (Toys), FCI (Group 5)

Miniature Bull Terrier: AKC (Terriers), UKC (Terriers), CKC (Terriers)

Miniature Pinscher: AKC (Toys), UKC (Terriers), CKC (Toys), FCI (Group 2)

Miniature Poodle: AKC (Non-Sporting), UKC (Companion) CKC (Non-Sporting), FCI (Group 9)

Miniature Schnauzer: AKC (Terriers), UKC (Terriers), CKC (Terriers), FCI (Group 2)

Miniature Spitz: FCI (Group 5)

Mini-Pei: ARBA (Companion)

Mountain Cur: UKC (Scenthounds), ARBA (Hounds)

Mudi: UKC (Herding), FCI (Group 1), ARBA (Herding)

Mullins' Feist: UKC (nc)

N

Neapolitan Mastiff: UKC (Guarding Dogs), CKC (Misc.), FCI (Group 2), ARBA (Working)

Newfoundland: AKC (Working), UKC (Guarding Dogs), CKC (Working), FCI (Group 2)

New Guinea Singing Dog: UKC (Sighthounds), ARBA (Spitz)

Norbottenspet: UKC (nc), CKC (Hounds), FCI (Group 5), ARBA (Spitz)

Norfolk Terrier: AKC (Terriers), UKC (Terriers), CKC (Terriers), FCI (Group 3)

North American Shepherd: ARBA (Herding)

Norwegian Buhund: UKC (nc), CKC (Herding), FCI (Group 5), ARBA (Spitz)

Norwegian Elkhound: AKC (Hounds), UKC (Northern Breeds), CKC (Hounds), FCI (Group 5)

Norwegian Hound: FCI (Group 6)

Norwegian Lundehund: CKC (Hounds), FCI (Group 5), ARBA (Spitz)

Norwich Terrier: AKC (Terriers), UKC (Terriers), CKC (Terriers), FCI (Group 3)

Nova Scotia Duck Tolling Retriever: UKC (Gun Dogs), CKC (Sporting), FCI (Group 7), ARBA (Sporting)

O

Ogar Polski: ARBA (Hounds)

Old Danish Bird Dog: UKC (nc), FCI (Group 7), ARBA (Sporting)

Olde English Bulldog: ARBA (Working)

Old English Sheepdog: AKC (Herding), UKC (Herding), CKC (Herding), FCI (Group 1)

Otterhound: AKC (Hounds), UKC (Scenthounds), CKC (Hounds), FCI (Group 6)

Owczarek Podhalanski: UKC (Guarding Dogs), ARBA (Herding)

P

Papillon: AKC (Toys), UKC (Companion), CKC (Toys), FCI (Group 9)

Patterdale Terrier: UKC (Terriers), ARBA (Terriers)

Pekingese: AKC (Toys), UKC (Companion), CKC (Toys), FCI (Group 9)

Pembroke Welsh Corgi: AKC (Herding), UKC (Herding), CKC (Herding), FCI (Group 1)

Perdiguero de Burgos: UKC (nc)

Perdiguero Navarro: UKC (nc)

Perdiguero Portugues: ARBA (Sporting)

Peruvian Inca Orchid: UKC (nc), FCI (Group 5), ARBA (Hounds)

Petit Basset Griffon Vendeen: AKC (Hounds), UKC (Scenthounds), CKC (Hounds), FCI (Group 6)

Petit Blue de Gascogne: UKC (Scenthounds), ARBA (Hounds)

Petit Gascon-Saintongeois: UKC (Scenthounds)

Petit Griffon Bleu de Gascogne: UKC (Scenthounds)

Phalene: FCI (Group 9)

Pharaoh Hound: AKC (Hounds), UKC (Sighthounds), CKC (Hounds), FCI (Group 5)

Picardy Shepherd: ARBA (Herding)

Picardy Spaniel: FCI (Group 7)

Pinscher: FCI (Group 2)

Plott Hound: AKC (Hounds), UKC (Scenthounds), ARBA (Hounds)

Podengo Canario: ARBA (Hounds)

Podengo Pequeño: ARBA (Hounds)

Podengo Portugueso: UKC (Sighthounds)

Pointer: AKC (Sporting), UKC (Gun Dogs), CKC (Sporting)

Poitevin: UKC (nc), FCI (Group 6), ARBA (Hounds)

Polish Hound: UKC (nc), FCI (Group 6)

Polish Lowland Sheepdog: AKC (Misc.)

Polish Owczarek Nizinny: UKC (Herding), FCI (Group 1), ARBA (Herding)

Pomeranian: AKC (Toys), UKC (Companion), CKC (Toys), FCI (Group 5)

Pont-Audemer Spaniel: FCI (Group 7)

Porcelaine: UKC (nc), FCI (Group 6), ARBA (Hounds)

Portuguese Pointer: UKC (nc), FCI (Group 7)

Portuguese Sheepdog: FCI (Group 1)

Portuguese Warren Hound: FCI (Group 5)

Portuguese Water Dog: AKC (Working), UKC (Gun Dogs), CKC (Working), FCI (Group 8)

Posavaz Hound: FCI (Group 6), ARBA (Hounds)

Presa Canario: ARBA (Working)

Presa Mallorquin: ARBA (Working)

Pudelpointer: UKC (Gun Dogs), CKC (Sporting), FCI (Group 7)

Pug: AKC (Toys), UKC (Companion), CKC (Toys), FCI (Group 9)

Puli: AKC (Herding), UKC (Herding), CKC (Herding), FCI (Group 1)

Pumi: UKC (nc), FCI (Group 1), ARBA (Herding)

Pyrenean Mastiff: FCI (Group 2), ARBA (Working)

Pyrenean Mountain Dog: FCI (Group 2)

Pyrenean Shepherd: FCI (Group 1), ARBA (Herding)

R

Rabbit Dachshund: FCI (Group 4)

Rafeiro of Alentejo: FCI (Group 2)

Rastreador Brasileiro: ARBA (Hounds)

Rat Terrier: UKC (Terriers)

Redbone Coonhound: UKC (Scenthounds), ARBA (Hounds)

Redtick Coonhound: ARBA (Hounds)

Rhodesian Ridgeback: AKC (Hounds), UKC (Sighthounds), CKC (Hounds), FCI (Group 6)

Rottweiler: AKC (Working), UKC (Guarding Dogs), CKC (Working), FCI (Group 2)

Russell Terriers: UKC (Terriers)

Russo-European Laika: UKC (nc), FCI (Group 5), ARBA (Spitz)

S

Saarloos Wolfdog: FCI (Group 1)

Sabueso Hound: ARBA (Hounds)

St. Bernard: AKC (Working), UKC (Guarding Dogs), CKC (Working), FCI (Group 2)

Saluki: AKC (Hounds), UKC (Sighthounds), CKC (Hounds), FCI (Group 10)

Samoyed: AKC (Working), UKC (Northern Breeds), CKC (Working), FCI (Group 5)

Sanshu: ARBA (Spitz)

Sarplaninac: UKC (Guarding Dogs), ARBA (Herding)

Schaependoes: UKC (nc)

Schiller Hound: FCI (Group 6), ARBA (Hounds)

Schipperke: AKC (Non-Sporting), UKC (Companion), CKC (Non-Sporting), FCI (Group 1)

Schwyz Hound: FCI (Group 6)

Scottish Deerhound: AKC (Hounds), UKC (Sighthounds), CKC (Hounds), FCI (Group 10)

Scottish Terrier: AKC (Terriers), UKC (Terriers), CKC (Terriers), FCI (Group 3)

Sealyham Terrier: AKC (Terriers), UKC (Terriers), CKC (Terriers), FCI (Group 3)

Serbian Hound: FCI (Group 6)

Serra de Estrela Mountain Dog: FCI (Group 2)

Shapendoe: UKC (Herding)

Shetland Sheepdog: AKC (Herding), UKC (Herding), CKC (Herding), FCI (Group 1)

Shiba Inu: AKC (Non-Sporting), UKC (Northern Breeds), CKC (Non-Sporting), FCI (Group 5)

Shih Tzu: AKC (Toys), UKC (Companion), CKC (Non-Sporting), FCI (Group 9)

Shikoku: FCI (Group 5)

Shiloh Shepherd: ARBA (Herding)

Siberian Husky: AKC (Working), UKC (Northern Breeds), CKC (Working), FCI (Group 5)

Silky Terrier: AKC (Toys), UKC (Terriers), CKC (Toys), FCI (Group 3)

Skye Terrier: AKC (Terriers), UKC (Terriers), CKC (Terriers), FCI (Group 3)

Sloughi: UKC (Sighthounds), FCI (Group 10), ARBA (Hounds)

Slovak Cuvac: UKC (nc), FCI (Group 1), ARBA (Herding)

Slovakian Hound: FCI (Group 6), ARBA (Hounds)

Slovakian Wire-Haired Pointing Griffon: FCI (Group 7)

Smaland Hound: FCI (Group 6)

Small Blue Gascony Hound: FCI (Group 6)

Small Brabant Griffon: FCI (Group 9)

Small Dutch Waterfowl Dog: FCI (Group 8)

Smaller Bernese Hound: FCI (Group 6)

Smaller Jura Hound: FCI (Group 6)

Smaller Lucerne Hound: FCI (Group 6)

Smaller Schwyz Hound: FCI (Group 6)

Small Gascon Saintongeois: FCI (Group 6)

Small Münsterlander: UKC (Gun Dogs), FCI (Group 7), ARBA (Sporting)

Small Spanish Hound: UKC (nc)

Smooth Fox Terrier: UKC (Terriers)

Soft-Coated Wheaten Terrier: AKC (Terriers), UKC (Terriers), CKC (Terriers), FCI (Group 3)

Southern Blackmouth Cur: UKC (nc)

South Russian Ovcharka: UKC (nc), FCI (Group 1), ARBA (Herding)

South Russian Steppe: ARBA (Hounds)

Spanish Greyhound: FCI (Group 10)

Spanish Hound: FCI (Group 6)

Spanish Mastiff: UKC (nc), CKC (Misc.), FCI (Group 2), ARBA (Working)

Spanish Water Dog: UKC (Gun Dogs)

Spinone Italiano: AKC (Misc.), UKC (Gun Dogs), CKC (Misc.), ARBA (Sporting)

Stabyhoun: UKC (nc), ARBA (Sporting)

Staffordshire Bull Terrier: AKC (Terriers), UKC (Terriers), CKC (Terriers), FCI (Group 3)

Standard Poodle: AKC (Non-Sporting), UKC (Gun Dogs), CKC (Non-Sporting), FCI (Group 9)

Standard Schnauzer: AKC (Working), UKC (Terriers), CKC (Working), FCI (Group 2)

Stephens' Stock Cur: UKC (nc)

Stumpytail Cattle Dog: UKC (nc)

Styrian Coarse-Haired Hound: FCI (Group 6), ARBA (Hounds)

Sussex Spaniel: AKC (Sporting), UKC (Gun Dogs), CKC (Sporting), FCI (Group 8)

Swedish Dachsbracke: FCI (Group 6)

Swedish Elkhound: FCI (Group 5)

Swedish Lapphund: UKC (Northern Breeds), FCI (Group 5)

Swedish Valhund: UKC (Herding), CKC (Herding), FCI (Group 5), ARBA (Spitz)

T

Tatra Sheepdog: CKC (Misc.), FCI (Group 1)

Teddy Roosevelt Terrier: UKC (Terriers)

Telomai: ARBA (Hounds)

Thai Ridgeback: UKC (nc), ARBA (Spitz)

Tibetan Kyi-Apso: ARBA (Working)

Tibetan Mastiff: UKC (Guarding Dogs), CKC (Misc.), FCI (Group 2), ARBA (Working)

Tibetan Spaniel: AKC (Non-Sporting), UKC (Companion), CKC (Non-Sporting), FCI (Group 9)

Tibetan Terrier: AKC (Non-Sporting), UKC (Herding), CKC (Non-Sporting), FCI (Group 9)

Tosa Ken: UKC (Guarding Dogs), FCI (Group 2), ARBA (Working)

Toy Fox Terrier: UKC (Terriers), ARBA (Companion)

Toy Manchester Terrier: AKC (Toys), CKC (Toys)

Toy Poodle: AKC (Toys), UKC (Companion), CKC (Toys), FCI (Group 9)

Transylvanian Hound: FCI (Group 6), ARBA (Hounds)

Treeing Cur: UKC (nc)

Treeing Feist: UKC (nc)

Treeing Tennessee Brindle: UKC (nc), ARBA (Hounds)

Treeing Walker Coonhound: UKC (Scenthounds), ARBA (Hounds)

Trigg Hound: ARBA (Hounds)

Tyrolean Hound: FCI (Group 6), ARBA (Hounds)

V

Verelade: ARBA (Hounds)

Vizsla: AKC (Sporting), UKC (Gun Dogs), CKC (Sporting)

Volpino Italiano: FCI (Group 5)

W

Wachtelhund: FCI (Group 10), ARBA (Hounds)

Weimaraner: AKC (Sporting), UKC (Gun Dogs), CKC (Sporting), FCI (Group 7)

Welsh Springer Spaniel: AKC (Sporting), UKC (Gun Dogs), CKC (Sporting), FCI (Group 8)

Welsh Terrier: AKC (Terriers), UKC (Terriers), CKC (Terriers), FCI (Group 3)

West Highland White Terrier: AKC (Terriers), UKC (Terriers), CKC (Terriers), FCI (Group 3)

Westphalian Dachsbracke: FCI (Group 6)

West Siberian Laika: UKC (nc), FCI (Group 5)

Whippet: AKC (Hounds), UKC (Sighthounds), CKC (Hounds), FCI (Group 10)

White German Shepherd: UKC (Herding), ARBA (Herding)

Wire Fox Terrier: UKC (Terriers)

Wire-Haired Istrian Hound: FCI (Group 10)

Wire-Haired Pointing Griffon: AKC (Sporting), UKC (Gun Dogs), CKC (Sporting)

X

Xoloitzcuintli: UKC (Companion), ARBA (Spitz)

Y

Yorkshire Terrier: AKC (Toys), UKC (Companion), CKC (Toys), FCI (Group 3)

Yugoslavian Herder: FCI (Group 2)

Yugoslavian Mountain Hound: FCI (Group 6), ARBA (Hounds)

Yugoslavian Shepherd Dog: CKC (Misc.)

Yugoslavian Tricolor Hound: FCI (Group 6)

APPENDIX **D**

The Big Time

Though there are literally hundreds of dog shows across the United States and thousands worldwide every year, a select few stand out above all others. If you have the opportunity to attend any of these shows, even just as a spectator, go for the sheer experience of it. The shows included here are from my own experience and the recommendations of David Frei, Afghan enthusiast and announcer for USA Network's presentation of the Westminster Kennel Club and, for the first time in 1999, the World Show.

THE WORLD SHOW

This is the once-a-year spectacle of the FCI, hosted by one of the member nations. The 1998 show in Helsinki, Finland, hosted over 16,000 dogs from 44 different countries over four days. Each of these many competitors receives a written critique, in accord with FCI judging rules. Of course, there are dog shows every day, offering Aptitude Certificates from both the host country and the FCI. But there are also other events, before, during, and after the dog shows. In Finland, all the competitors and many of the townspeople marched through the streets to the show site in a grand parade. In Mexico City in 1999, the competitions included obedience, agility, and flyball, and Frisbee dogs did demonstrations. The FCI Congress of Veterinary Medicine in Small Animal Practice also met at the same location, presenting scientific studies to 2,000 veterinarians and students.

CRUFTS DOG SHOW

Charles Cruft was assistant to the first successful purveyor of prepared dog food in Britain before embarking on a career organizing dog-related events. He organized the first "Crufts" in 1891, including entries from Queen Victoria's kennels. After his death, the Kennel Club took over. Though quarantine regulations mean the dogs are nearly all British, Crufts is one of the biggest shows in the world, with 20,000 entries and over 100,000 visitors. The many competitions and displays other than conformation welcome mixed breeds, and the trade show associated with the event is enormous. Agility was popularized here as a lunchtime entertainment, and many dog events are demonstrated each year. With the new relaxing of quarantine regulations, Crufts will host dogs from other European nations for the first time in 2001.

ROYAL SYDNEY

Every year, each capital city of Australia's provinces holds an agricultural show. These shows, somewhat equivalent to the state fairs of the United States, go on for 10 days and include a plethora of events. The sheepherding competitions are the main dog draw, but the Sydney event in particular puts on magnificent dog shows. Few U.S. competitors put their dogs on the long flight, and the spectators aren't as numerous as at Crufts, but the Sydney show is one of the biggest and best in the southern hemisphere.

ROYAL CANADIAN INVITATIONAL

Dog shows were once a regular feature of Canada's Royal Agricultural Winter Fair, but in 1949 the dog show portion disappeared. In 1998, however, the event made a comeback, billed as the World's Richest Dog Show, with cash awards for everything from Best of Breed upward. Winners from the World Show, Crufts, and Westminster came together to compete with many others. Group judging was extensive, with a dozen judges in each ring assessing the dogs. The future of this show is unknown at this writing. No event was held in 1999.

WESTMINSTER KENNEL CLUB

The only fully nationally televised dog show in the United States, Westminster is the second oldest uninterrupted annual sporting event in the country, surpassed only by the Kentucky Derby. Westminster was made a "champions only" show in 1992, and its 2,500 available slots are typically filled an hour after entries open. It is unusual among the big shows in offering conformation only—no obedience or other performance events. It is preceded by two days of breed specialties. Though the rings and the benching area at the Garden (that's Madison Square Garden in New York City) are crowded, visitors flock to the show.

UKC PREMIER

The UKC focuses more on performance events, especially coonhound and beagle hunts, but they do offer conformation and once a year put on their national event, the Premier. This three-day show features conformation, obedience, and agility in equal measures. All-breed shows are rare under the auspices of the UKC, and they don't even put their registered breeds list into groups, but this is a full-blown all-breed show with group wins and a Best in Show.

THE LOUISVILLE CLUSTER

Also known as the Kentuckiana Cluster, this four-day event boasts the highest entry in the United States. Thursday is hosted by River City Kennel Club, Friday by Kennel Club of Columbus, Indiana, and Saturday by the Evansville Kennel Club. The Louisville Kennel Club runs the Sunday finale. Situated at the State Fairgrounds conveniently located directly across the street from the airport, the final day attracts about 4,500–5,000 dogs to its 35 rings.

WESTCHESTER WEEKEND

Another four-day cluster, the final day is renowned for its show grounds— the Lyndhurst Estate in Tarrytown overlooking the Hudson River. The

Thursday show is hosted by the Rockland County Kennel Club and has been held at Bear Mountain State Park. Friday's show is run by Tuxedo Park Kennel Club and Saturday's by Somerset Hills Kennel Club, both taking place in Tarrytown. The Westchester Kennel Club wraps it up with the Sunday show. Entries rise from roughly 1,000 to more than 2,000 over the course of the Labor Day weekend.

DETROIT KENNEL CLUB

This club hosts back-to-back all-breed benched shows, with many educational presentations, including search and rescue and field work, and an enormous vendor hall. If you can't manage to get to Crufts, British visitors have proclaimed Detroit as the U.S. show most like the British extravaganza.

DEL VALLE/GOLDEN GATE

Del Valle Dog Club of Livermore is growing rapidly in both entry numbers and prestige. It is preceded each year by a variety of specialties with enormous entries, on the same grounds.

Golden Gate Kennel Club has a two-day benched show in the Cow Palace in South San Francisco. Much like Detroit, there are exciting demonstrations of other dog sports and capabilities, and lots and lots of vendors.

APPENDIX E

For Further Reading

Dog Magazines

AKC Gazette and Events Calendar
260 Madison Avenue
New York, NY 10016

Bloodlines
United Kennel Club
100 E. Kilgore Road
Kalamazoo, MI 49001-5597

Dog World
260 Madison Avenue, 8th Floor
New York, NY 10016

Dog Fancy
P.O. Box 6050
Mission Viejo, CA 92690-6050

Front and Finish
H&S Publications
P.O. Box 333
Galesburg, IL 61402

Purebred Dogs in Review
P.O. Box 30430
Santa Barbara, CA 93130

Books

A good place to find and find out about dog books is *Dogwise,* the book catalog of Direct Book Service. Their Web site is at www.dogwise.com, and their phone number is 800-776-2665.

American Kennel Club. *The Complete Dog Book,* 19th ed. Official Publication of the American Kennel Club. New York: Howell Book House, 1997.

Arden, Darlene. *The Irrepressible Toy Dog.* New York: Howell Book House, 1998.

Cosme, Felix. *Junior Handling: The Complete Guide on How to Show Your Dog.* Seven Hills Book Distributors, 1993.

Donaldson, Jean. *Culture Clash.* Berkeley, CA: James & Kenneth Publishers, 1996.

Elliott, Rachel Page. *The New Dog Steps: A Better Understanding of Dog Gait Through Cineradiograph.* New York: Howell Book House, 1983. Also available as a video.

Freeman, Robert, and Toni Freeman. *The Road to Westminster: How to Select and Train a Purebred Dog and Prepare It for the Show Ring.* Betterway Publications, 1990.

Lewis, Janet R. *Smart Trainers, Brilliant Dogs.* Lutherville, MD: Canine Sports Productions, 1997.

Shojai, Amy. *The Purina Encyclopedia of Dog Care.* New York: Ballantine Books, 1999.

Walkowicz, Chris, et al. *Successful Dog Breeding: The Complete Handbook of Canine Midwifery.* New York: Howell Book House, 1994.

Weston, David. *Dog Training, The Gentle Modern Method.* New York: Howell Book House, 1990.

Wilcox, Bonnie, and Chris Walkowicz. *The Atlas of Dog Breeds of the World.* Neptune, NJ: TFH Publications, 1995.

Zink, Christine. *Peak Performance.* New York: Howell Book House, 1992.

And whatever breed book best covers your breed.

A grooming book for your breed or type (such as Terrier) of dog.

Glossary

Ageing out Becoming too old to compete in Junior Showmanship.

Agent A person other than the owner responsible for bringing the dog to a show—usually a professional handler.

All-breed club A kennel club not focusing on one breed, but on pure-bred dogs in general.

All-breed show A show at which every breed recognized by a kennel club is eligible to compete.

American-bred A class for dogs bred in the United States.

Angulation The angles formed by the bones at the joints of the legs.

Ankle Lower joint of the hind leg, often called the *hock*.

AOAC Any Other Allowed Color, a class division offered for some breeds (see Varieties in appendix B).

AOC Any Other Color, a class division.

Apple-headed A dog with a high, domed skull, appropriate for dogs such as a Chihuahua or some of the brachycephalic dogs, but a fault in others.

Apron The longer hair on a dog's chest, as a bib.

Armband An identifying number worn by the exhibitor, usually on the left arm.

ASCOB Any Solid Color Other than Black, used as a class division in Cocker Spaniels.

Baby gates Barriers, either folding or rigid, used to mark the boundaries of rings.

Back Generally, the topline of the dog, from the withers to the croup, although anatomically speaking the back only covers four vertebrae.

Bait An edible treat, such as cooked liver or steak, used to entice the dog and achieve an alert look. May also be a squeaky toy, fur rat, and so on.

Balance   Correct proportions, such as head to body and angles of front and rear quarters. Also, dog's control of its body and position.

Benched show   A show where the dogs not in the ring must be on exhibit on a bench for the public to view throughout the show's duration. Now a rare event.

Best in Show (BIS)   The top award at a multibreed or all-breed show.

Best in Specialty Show (BISS)   The top award at a specialty for a single breed.

Best of Breed   The top award in each breed, or overall top award at a specialty. In a multibreed or all-breed show, this dog goes on to compete in group.

Best of Opposite Sex   The best bitch if Best of Breed is a male, or the best male if Best of Breed is a bitch.

Best of Winners   The better of the Winners Dog or Winners Bitch.

Bitch   A female dog.

Bitchy   A male dog that is overly delicate or refined.

Bite   How the teeth meet when the mouth is closed.

Blind courtesy turn   An optional maneuver for making an about turn, sometimes used in Junior Showmanship to demonstrate handling skills.

Bloom   The shine of a dog's coat in top condition.

Blowing coat   Shedding heavily.

Brace   Two dogs owned by the same person and shown together, judged on their similarities and quality.

Brachycephalic   Dogs with shortened noses, "pushed-in" faces, such as the Boxer and Bulldog.

Bred by Exhibitor   An AKC class for dogs bred, owned, and handled by the same person.

Breed   A particular type of dog, with similar characteristics passed from one generation to the next.

Breeder   Officially, the owner of the bitch being bred. Hopefully, an experienced, knowledgeable, and careful fancier of the breed.

Breed standard   A written set of specifications describing the ideal type, structure, coat, and color of each breed of dog, compiled by the national "parent" club for each breed.

Broken coat A harsh, wiry short coat such as found on Airedales and Wire Fox Terriers.

CAC Certificate of Aptitude, Champion; a rating awarded at a specialty or all-breed show by an FCI member country's kennel club. Only two may be awarded per show, and three or four (depending on country) are required to achieve a national championship under FCI regulations.

CACIB Certificate of Aptitude, Championship International, Beauty; a rating awarded at an all-breed FCI show. Only two may be awarded at a show, and four must be earned to achieve the title of International Champion.

Campaigning Showing a dog on a fairly constant basis.

Catalog Booklet listing all entrants, judges, awards, judging times, etc.

Catalog order Determining the order of dog/handler teams entering the ring according to their order in the catalog.

Cat foot Compact, round foot resembling that of a cat.

CC Challenge Certificate, a British championship award.

CERF Canine Eye Registry Foundation, an organization certifying a dog's status regarding genetic eye problems.

Champion (CH) Title awarded when a dog has acquired the necessary points or certificates to become a champion. Details vary among registries. In the U.S., titles other than AKC are generally designated, such as Can. CH for a Canadian title, U-CH for a UKC championship, and so on.

Champion of Champions UKC class for Champions only, to choose the best among them, counting toward the title of Grand Champion.

Character The combination of appearance, behavior, and spirit that go into the "look" of a dog.

Circuit Several shows in the same general geographic area over one weekend.

CKC Canadian Kennel Club, the Canadian equivalent of the AKC.

Class A subgrouping for competition within a breed, such as Puppy or American-Bred. Also the quality all handlers should exhibit by congratulating the winner and making no excuses for their own performance.

Class division An optional breakdown of a class, such as into the three colors of Labrador Retrievers, usually seen at National Specialties.

Clip   A specific style for trimming a dog's coat.

Clipping   The back foot hitting the front foot when the dog is gaiting.

Close-coupled   A dog short in body between the hips and the withers.

Close of entries   Date after which no more entries for an event will be accepted.

Cluster   Several shows at the same location over a weekend.

COCA   Confederation Canina Americana, a central grouping of the various national registries in Central and South America.

Condition   The general muscle tone and/or coat quality of a dog.

Confirmation of entry   Notification from a show-giving club that your entry has been received.

Conformation   The "dog show," in which it is determined how well a dog's structure matches the official standard for the breed.

Coupling   The part of dog anatomy between the last rib and the front edge of the pelvis.

Courtesy turn   A small circle often made by handler and dog before beginning an individual gaiting pattern.

Covering ground   The distance each stride covers over the ground as a dog moves.

Cowhocked   Inward-turning hocks, usually with the feet turned out.

Crabbing   The dog moving forward with his body at an angle to the direction of travel rather than in a straight line, also called *side-winding*.

Crate   A portable kennel, wire or closed, for transporting and housing of a dog.

Cropped   Ears that have been surgically altered to force them to stand erect.

Croup   The upper back just forward of the tail, commonly known as the *rump*.

Dam   The female parent of a dog.

Dewclaws   Extra "toes" or claws above the paws, often surgically removed while the dog is young, but required for conformation in some breeds.

Disqualification   Some physical fault or transgression on the part of dog or handler that renders a dog ineligible to compete, banned from the ring for life.

Docking   Shortening or removing a dog's tail via surgery.

Dog   All members of the canine family, or males only, depending on usage.

Dolichocephalic   A long-headed dog, such as a Borzoi.

Dolly cart   A flat wire platform on wheels, used for hauling show equipment.

Double coat   A long, coarse outer coat over a soft, short undercoat.

Double handling   In the United States, unethical behavior of a person not exhibiting the dog by assisting the performance through signals, talking, or other means. Commonly seen and tolerated outside the United States.

Down and back   A gaiting pattern where the dog and handler move directly away from the judge, turn, and come back directly toward the judge.

Drive   Strong, solid thrust of the hindquarters in movement.

Dropping (the front or rear)   One method of setting the dog's front and/or rear legs for the stack, done by lifting the dog until the front or rear feet are off the ground, then letting them down gently.

Dual Champion (DC)   A title awarded to a dog that has earned a Championship and an OTCH in obedience or a field or coursing title.

Duck dryer   A small portable dryer, resembling a duck when sitting in its stand.

Excused   Dismissed from the ring for a single event, often for showing a limp when gaiting.

Exercise pen (ex-pen)   A portable enclosure that can be set up to contain a dog or dogs.

Faking   Illegal alteration of dogs to make them more suitable for the show ring, such as coat dyeing or surgical alteration.

Fancier   A person active in the breeding and/or showing of dogs.

Fancy   Another term for the world of conformation showing.

Faults   Attributes of the dog that do not conform to the standard.

Federation Cynologique Internationale (FCI)   An international registry with member countries in Europe, Asia, Latin America, and Australia/New Zealand.

Finger works   Small movements of the exhibitor's hands to call attention to a dog's good points, sometimes used in Junior Showmanship.

Finish   To earn enough points to receive the title Champion, thus "finishing" the title.

Flank   The outer area of muscle between the ribs and the hips.

Flyer   A dog who earns a championship very quickly.

Flying trot   A fast, long-reaching trot, in which the hind feet reach forward beyond the front feet, and all feet are off the ground in each half stride. Also called the *suspension trot.*

Forequarters   The front legs, shoulders, withers, and chest, taken together.

Foul color   A color permitted in the standard, but not desired.

Free stack   A pose taken by the dog, usually at the end of a gaiting pattern.

Front   How a dog looks head on, concentrating on the front legs, chest, and shoulders.

Fun match   An unsanctioned event, at which dogs and handlers can gain experience but not win any points toward a championship.

Gaiting   Moving the dog around the ring, in various patterns, at a trot.

Genotype   The genetic makeup of a single dog, capable of being passed along to progeny.

Grand Champion   UKC title awarded after a dog has won several Champion of Champions classes.

Groom   To care for the dog's coat, by brushing, combing, trimming.

Grooming table   Elevated platform for easier grooming of a dog.

Group First   The dog awarded Best in Group.

Groups   A division of dog breeds by type or function into groups used for judging purposes. Also, competition of all Best of Breeds within a group for placements at a multibreed or all-breed show.

Hackney gait   A showy, high-stepping trot, specified for Miniature Pinschers.

Hallmark   A distinguishing breed characteristic, such as the spectacles of the Keeshonden.

Handler   The person working the dog in the ring.

Hare foot   A long, narrow foot, like that of a rabbit or hare.

Hindquarters   The hind legs, buttocks, thighs, and hips, taken together.

Hocks   The joints of the dog's rear legs between the second thigh and the pastern.

Indefinite Listing Privilege (ILP)   A limited registration offered for purebred dogs without registration papers and, in the case of the UKC's LP, for mixed breeds as well; allows these dogs to compete in performance events (not conformation).

Intact   A dog retaining all of his or her reproductive structures.

Judge   The presiding official in the ring, who evaluates the dogs.

Judging schedule   A listing of each class, including the number of dogs entered and the estimated showing time.

Junior Showmanship   A class for younger handlers (exact ages vary depending on registry) in which judging is based on the ability of the handler rather than on the quality of the dog.

Kennel blind   A breeder blind to the faults of his or her own dogs.

"L"   A gaiting pattern where dog and handler move directly away from the judge, then across the back width of the ring, and back the way they came. The favored pattern of ARBA.

Layback   The angle of the shoulder blade from the vertical.

Level bite   A bite wherein the front teeth of the upper and lower jaws meet edge to edge when the mouth is closed.

Level gait   A trot with no rising or falling of the withers.

Loin   The vertical surfaces (sides) of the dog between the ribs and the hip bones.

Major   A class where there are sufficient entries for the Winners Dog or Winners Bitch to be awarded three or more points at an AKC show.

Make the cut   Remain in contention when the judge reduces a class to only those entries still being considered for awards.

Match (fun match, sanctioned match)   An event not counting toward a championship, used to prepare handlers, dogs, and judges for the more formal show.

Measured out When measured, found to be taller or shorter than specified by the standard.

Microchip Form of permanent identification implanted into the dog between the shoulder blades.

Miscellaneous class An AKC class for certain breeds in the process of being recognized by the AKC, but not yet fully recognized and placed in a group.

Mismarked A dog whose color pattern does not conform to the breed standard, such as a Boxer with white markings over more than a third of the body.

Multibreed show A show open to more than one breed but fewer than all the breeds recognized by a kennel club.

Non-Sporting One of the seven AKC groups; originally the only group other than Sporting, hence its name.

Novice An AKC class for dogs not having won two firsts in a novice or higher class.

Occiput The high point at the back of the skull, the peak of the dog's head.

OFA The Orthopedic Foundation of America, a registry begun to track the incidence of hip dysplasia in dogs, but now including other genetic defects.

Open An AKC class in which any eligible dog may compete; an FCI class for dogs more than 2 years old.

Overdogged Having too many dogs at one time.

Owner The person or persons named on the dog's registration papers.

Padding Lifting the front feet too high in compensation for overreaching.

Paddling Throwing the front feet out wide to the side.

Papers The form registering a dog with a kennel club.

Parent club The national organization representing a breed.

Parti-color A white coat with colored patches, with neither color dominant.

Pastern The forelegs from the wrist joint to the paw.

Patella luxation Dislocation of the knee cap.

Pattern   The configuration in which the dog is gaited, such as up and back, triangle, or around the ring.

Pedigree   The written record of a dog's lineage.

Pet quality   A dog not thought to be of quality necessary to do well in the ring.

Phenotype   The visible characteristics or physical appearance of an individual dog, not necessarily genetically capable of being passed to offspring.

Plucking   Removing dead hair by hand.

Point schedule   The number of points awarded by breed and by region, depending on the number of dogs competing (AKC) or simply by number of dogs competing (UKC).

Point show   A sanctioned show, where a dog may earn points toward a championship.

Posting   A bad habit a dog can develop of leaning back, reacting to constantly being pulled forward into the stacked position.

Pre-entry   An entry sent in before the actual day of the match or trial.

Premium list   A printed pamphlet with advance details of a show, match, or trial.

Prepotency   The ability to transmit one's own characteristics to offspring.

Professional handler   A person paid to handle a dog in the show ring, often including preparing the dog for the event.

Put down   Prepared and trimmed for show. Also, a dog unplaced in the show ring.

Put up   A dog chosen as winner.

Reach   Forward movement of the forelegs when gaiting.

Regular class   Classes included at all shows, from which the winner will be selected to receive championship points.

Ring mats   Runners put down in rings at indoor shows to provide better footing.

Roadwork   Exercise of a dog by jogging or biking along the road.

Schedule of points   The chart provided by a registry indicating how many points are earned by beating various numbers of other dogs.

Scissors bite A bite wherein the back of the front teeth in the upper jaw touch the front of the front teeth in the lower jaw when the mouth is closed.

Second (lower) thigh The middle portion of the rear leg, between the stifle and the hock, what would be the calf in a human.

Shoulder layback The angle of the shoulder blade from the vertical.

Show and go An unsanctioned event with no awards, where you enter the ring, do the routine, and leave.

Show lead Very slender lead used to show the dog in the ring.

Show quality A dog thought to have the conformation quality necessary to do well in the ring.

Sickle hocks Sharply angulated hock joint, which is not free to move readily.

Sire Male parent of a dog.

Slicker A wire pin brush.

Specialing Showing a dog, usually intensively, after the championship has been attained.

Specials Best of Breed class, open only to the Winners Dog, Winners Bitch, and any Champions entered.

Specialty club A club concerned with a single breed, working toward its improvement, and often running conformation, obedience, tracking, or field trials.

Specialty show A show limited to a single breed.

Sporting One of the original AKC groups of dogs originally bred for fieldwork.

Spring of ribs Rib curvature that provides good heart and lung capacity.

Stack To set up a dog in the best position by adjusting the placement of its feet and head to show off its good points and conceal its bad.

Standard Official written description of the characteristics that constitute the ideal specimen of a breed.

Standoff coat A long coat that stands out from the body, as seen in the Chow Chow.

Steward The judge's assistant in the ring.

Stifle   The "knee" of the rear legs, between the femur and the tibia and fibula.

Stringing them up   Keeping the lead so short that the dog's head is held up, sometimes even pulling the dog onto his toes in the front.

Stripping   Grooming of wirehaired breeds by pulling out excess dead hair.

Stud book   Breeding records kept by the various kennel clubs and registries.

Superintendent   Person hired as a professional to handle the many arrangements in connection with a dog show.

Sweepstakes   Classes offered by specialty clubs, often for puppies from 6 to 18 months old, sometimes for veteran dogs, in which the entry fees are divided among the winners.

"T"   The most complex gaiting pattern, seldom used.

Table   An elevated platform in the ring, used by the judge to examine smaller breeds of dogs.

Tack box   Container of some sort for holding grooming supplies.

Take them around   Command to gait the entire class counterclockwise around the ring.

Tail set   The relationship between a dog's body and tail, including position and angle of the tail attachment to the body.

Topline   The upper outline of the dog, viewed from the side, from the base of the head to the rump.

Total Dog   UKC award for a dog that wins at least Best Male or Female of Variety against competition and posts a qualifying score in Obedience or Agility at the same show.

Triangle   A pattern of movement directly away from the judge, across the back of the ring, then directly back to the judge across the diagonal of the ring.

Triple Champion (TC)   An AKC title awarded to a dog that has attained a championship, field or coursing championship, and obedience trial championship.

Typey   A dog that exhibits the characteristics of the breed.

Unbenched A show in which the handlers and dogs must only arrive in time to show and may leave when finished.

Undercoat The short, fine hairs generally concealed by the guard hairs, providing insulation.

Up and back Gaiting pattern moving straight away from and then straight toward the judge.

Variety A subgrouping within a breed, usually according to color, coat type, or size.

Winners Bitch/Dog The female/male chosen best among the winners of the regular breed classes and earning championship points.

Withers The highest point of the shoulders

Withholding awards Not handing out some ribbons or other prizes because the judge feels there are no dogs worthy of them.

Wire coat Hard and coarse coat, also known as "broken."

Working A class under FCI regulations for dogs that have already earned the working certificate required by their breed club.

Workshop Very informal event for practicing, usually without any awards offered.

A SELECTION OF COAT, COLOR, AND GROOMING TERMS

Coat

Blousy A soft, woolly coat.

Cuff Short hair on the pastern.

Open coat Coat that should be tight but is loose and parted.

Trousers Longer hair on the backs of the upper rear legs.

Veiled coat Coat overlaid with long, fine hairs.

Color

Badger Mixture of black, brown, gray, and white hairs.

Blenheim A white coat with markings of a rich chestnut color.

Ground The predominant color of a coat.

Pointed   Coat in which the muzzle, ears, and usually feet and tail are a darker color than the main color.

Snip   The part of a blaze around the nose.

Grooming

Hound glove   A glove with a roughened palm for grooming shorthaired dogs.

Rake   Brush with heavy, widely spaced teeth for breaking up mats.

Stripping   Thinning out a coat by hand, done with terriers.

Index

About the Author

Cheryl S. Smith writes in a variety of forms, from greeting cards to screenplays, but always enjoys projects dealing with dogs. She has written books about walking with dogs, camping with dogs, feeding dogs, natural health for dogs, and teaching dogs tricks. She hopes this will be the first of several books to take a look at the various dog sports. Her work is seen often in the pages of *Dog World* and the *AKC Gazette*, and her own Web site at www.writedog.com. *The Absolute Beginner's Guide to Showing Your Dog* is her seventh dog book.

Cheryl has worked on the newsletter for the Dog Writers Association of America (DWAA), served on the board of the Cat Writers' Association (CWA), and is a long-time member of the Association of Pet Dog Trainers. Her books and articles have been nominated for DWAA's Maxwell medallion and won the CWA's Muse medallion. She regularly attends veterinary and dog training conferences, and is honored to wander ringside at Westminster wearing a press ribbon. In the fall of 2000, she started hosting "PetSmith," a local pet talk show on KONP radio (which can be heard over the Web—listen for the show the third Tuesday of the month at 1 p.m.). In the spring of 2001, she began instructing dog training classes with renowned behaviorist/trainer Terry Ryan.

Cheryl currently lives on the beautiful Olympic Peninsula in Washington State with her Kelpie mix Nestle and six sheep (three of which were bought specifically for better herding practice with Nestle). She is mentoring a Standard Schnauzer in Scotland toward an appearance at Crufts 2001.